Monograph 57

THE AMERICAN ETHNOLOGICAL SOCIETY

Robert F. Spencer, *Editor*

*

SOCIAL IMAGES
AND PROCESS IN
URBAN NEW GUINEA
A Study
of Port Moresby

by
ALAN REW

WEST PUBLISHING CO.
St. Paul • New York • Boston
Los Angeles • San Francisco

Library of Congress Cataloging in Publication Data
Rew, Alan, 1942–

    Social images and process in urban New Guinea.
    Bibliography: p.
    1. Port Moresby, Papua New Guinea—Social
conditions. 2. Urbanization—Port Moresby, Papua New Guinea. I. Title.
HN936.P36R48 1975   309.1'95'3   74–17389
ISBN 0–8299–0024–1

Rew, Port Moresby Study—CTB

PREFACE

What's wrong with Port Moresby? A shipload of Americans came here last week but they only looked at the wharves and then returned to their ship—yet before they came here they had been to Lae and stayed all day. So what's wrong with this place? What is Port Moresby—is it a passenger ship or a cargo vessel?

I think *I* know. The New Guinea side is like a cargo vessel. We are well endowed there; we have good food, good soil and grow many things. But here it's only a passenger ship; it's a rubbish place, there's always trouble and too much drinking and fighting.

These complaints—translated from a fixture of English and Pidgin— were made to me early in 1967 by a native policeman in a Port Moresby bar. Originally from the Madang District in the Trust Territory of New Guinea, he had been stationed at Lae—that Territory's largest town—for eight years. Posted at Port Moresby—the capital of Papua– New Guinea, an administrative union of the Trust Territory and the Australian Territory of Papua—he had been there just seven months. Like all newcomers from afar he had disliked the town on sight; seven months of residence had only confirmed his initial reaction.

His statements evidence more subtle issues, however, than just the experience of being an alien in a strange, and in this case often barren, town. They are of course open to varying interpretations. One can read in them, together with those who find "cargo-cult" thinking under every unturned stone within the Melanesian cultural fabric, a confirmation of the continuing role of chiliastic thought and activity in even this the least "traditional" of all Papua–New Guinea environments. I look on them, however, as principally a statement of the complex, and often contradictory, character of the town's functions and social relations.

"Passenger" in the local idiom refers to all those Papua–New Guinean migrants who daily flock into town without visible means of support and are liable to be picked up by the Police Vagrancy Squad formed to deal with them. Between 1961 and 1970 the annual growth rate of the indigenous population has varied between 7.7 and 9.8 percent, in large part a result of immigration. (Langmore 1969:32; Bureau of

Statistics 1970.) These newcomers are thought of, at least by the local Europeans, as parasites, sponging on their urban kinsmen and *wantok(s)* (speakers of the same language, or simply, compatriots), and as a cause of much of the town's crime and social malaise. By extension, the bulk of indigents may appear as an unstable *lumpen*: "living on the bread-line in shanties erected in increasing numbers on the bare brown hills of that disagreeable town, is a polyglot force of men without jobs, women or land—the dispossessed of the new dispensation" (Hastings 1969:103).

Additionally, the town can be presented as a parasite in its relations to the nation. Cut off from the more populous and richer parts of the Territory by massive mountain ranges and serving as home to a highly centralized public administration it is seen as "a distant hungry capital" taking much but giving little (Hastings 1969:202) and reliant for its continuance on its administrative role and imports from Australia.

By extension too, the whole population, both European and indigenous, can appear as a motley of tourists who, however long their sojourn, remain wedded to their former commitments. In this view it is not that individual town dwellers are parasitic but rather that the town's constituent groups are related primarily to conditions elsewhere, not to Port Moresby but to their ports of embarkation. Thus the town's social forms are seen as simply urban-nesting cuckoos, replicating village modes of association and ways of life current in metropolitan Australia. And the town itself then appears as a set of spatially, but not socially, related groups, as "not so much an urban area as a conglomeration of geographically and ethnically distinct settlements" (Oram, quoted in Bettison et al. 1965:343) and in which there is little social cohesion (see also Oram 1964 and 1967).

Some commentators have argued, however, that in recent years its form has been changing. With its growth they have seen the town develop more positive functions—as a metropolis for the rest of the Territory (Groves 1964) or as a magnet for migrant labor and a dynamo for social change. Thus Rowley (1965:201, 202) has argued that here "the new order is being born" and that "an educated elite of [Papuans and] New Guineans has now a way of life which cuts them off from the village". Appropriate here is the metaphor of the cargo vessel, its members and task groups bound to each other by a web of interdependent activities and, although divided by their other commitments, by family obligation and loyalty to class and nation for example, are nevertheless united in their common purpose and their common identity as sailors. In this view the town, moreover, is no longer seen as merely a replication of patterns established elsewhere but is in itself a source of social change.

Both these views have merit: Port Moresby is at once a limited and temporary association of birds of passage, and yet is also evolving a more organic form. Nonetheless, this development is a slow and halting one. And, having once asked whether the town is merely a limited association or a more vital society, many residents (and perhaps some observers) will, like our policeman, quell their intellectual disquiet by opting for one polar state or the other.

Yet the town's complexities and contrasts are not so easily dismissed. I argue that the present town is hung in a state of endless becoming, caught midway between its earlier role as a small, European center with a surrounding and ragged galaxy of native villages and labor compounds, and the more integrated role its apologists would wish for it in the future. To use the terms employed by Geertz (1965) in a study of Modjukuto, a Javanese town, Port Moresby has developed from a "hollow" composite of disconnected societies or estates and is now striving to become a more "solid" urban unit. In Modjukuto the more solid form emerged with the growth of nationwide social movements contending in the local arena. The more solid form of Port Moresby is the subject of this monograph—to what degree is indigenous social organization akin to the passenger ship, to what degree the cargo vessel?

During eighteen months of field work focused on the town, between January 1967 and March 1969, I talked to and observed people of varied background in many of its labor compounds, suburbs, and traditional and nontraditional villages and settlements. This account, however, relies mainly on material gathered from one small part of Port Moresby —an industrial plant and its labor compound. The plant is unique in many ways: it is probably the most capital intensive of all the town's secondary industry, is among its largest employers, and has an extensive network of international connections. Moreover Port Moresby itself is not an industrial town but a composite administrative, educational, commercial, and garrison center with a fringe of service industry. The plant is therefore in no way a microcosm of the urban society. But I do claim that its social organization, although particular, is nonetheless an eloquent concretization of the town's social form.

Thus, after sketching, in Chapter 1, Port Moresby's development and the methodological and theoretical considerations which led me to select the plant for intensive study and presentation, I turn to an examination of the social concomitants of its technical organization. Basic to my approach is the notion that a Port Moresby industrial concern is both an organization and an urban sample. So in Chapter 2, I examine how the organization selects workers for its technical roles and how this in turn sets up a system of rewards, both of cash and housing, which further constrain the choice of its employees. In Chapter 3 I turn to a small group of workers living in the plant's compound and analyze in detail how, as an urban sample, their behavior is at once constrained by their place in the industrial system, by the web of dependence flowing from their common employment and coresidence, and by their social commitments to other town dwellers and to kinsmen and friends still living in their natal villages. In Chapters 4 and 5 I discuss the adjustment of other individuals and show how, under different circumstances, different symbols and social forms are generated while yet others remain constant.

The technique of exposition I use in these three chapters, especially Chapter 3, is similar to that employed for urban studies by Epstein (1961), building upon the extended case study methods of Gluckman (1940–42) and Turner (1957). I assume, with the extended case study theorists, that the broad accounts of structure and process toward which the anthropologist aims can best be essayed from the detailed examination of specific events and behavioral sequences. The regularities which arise from this examination are then tested against other qualitative and quantitative material. If the incipient generalization is found wanting, it can be referred back to the case material for more critical scrutiny to see if additional factors impinge on the variables of immediate issue. The stammer and circumlocution of the research process will need to be discarded in the final account, but sufficient material should remain to enable the reader to test generalizations by relating them to individual behavior.

Armed with social and symbolic forms generated from the analysis of individual adjustment and strategy toward urban residence, in the first part of Chapter 6 I show how these forms affect the workers' perceptions of, and strategies towards, their situation as migrants caught in a web of urban and rural involvements. This assessment of the dynamic of involvement leads directly, in the chapter's second section, to an analysis of how the workers respond to their position in the industrial authority system and in the system of racial relations which helps support it.

PREFACE

In Chapter 7 I examine the workers' urban situation as a whole. Based on this case study of the plant's workers and on generalizations from my other studies in the town, I place Port Moresby social forms within a wider comparative framework, suggesting how the ongoing choices and adjustments of its indigenous residents fall within broader patterns of social compatibility. The idiom of those compatibilities is, largely, "ethnicity" or compatriotism.

My conclusions refer to the years immediately preceding 1970. Since then, in December 1973, Papua–New Guinea has achieved self-government, though not complete independence from Australia. In March 1972 the town was incorporated as the city of Port Moresby and is administered by a separate municipal government headed by a lord mayor. I doubt that these events have unduly disturbed the social forms of that earlier period. Regional and local compatriotism will continue to steer urban diversity within manageable bounds and the force of inherited colonial institutions and authority continue to constrain, and perhaps predicate, Port Moresby's future administrative and economic institutions for some while.

A. R.

Minneapolis, Minnesota
August, 1974

*

ACKNOWLEDGMENTS

This account is based on fieldwork carried out during 1967–69 under the terms of a research scholarship at the Australian National University. I thank this body for its generous facilities and financial support.

In particular I am grateful to many members of both the Department of Anthropology and Sociology and the New Guinea Research Unit for their encouragement and criticisms. I single out for especial appreciation both Professor W. E. H. Stanner, who suggested the solution to a major problem of construction, and Professor A. L. Epstein. As my first teacher in social anthropology, it was Professor Epstein who first stimulated my interest in comparative urban studies. He also supervised my Port Moresby research, offering advice and incisive comment throughout. To Nigel Oram I owe a special debt of gratitude for sharing his perspectives on Port Moresby and for allowing me to read unpublished material. Professors Brookfield and Groves also kindly allowed me to consult unpublished material. Professor R. J. Frankenberg made many helpful comments on the doctoral thesis on which this book is based. The failings of the study are mine alone.

My greatest debt is to the many urban workers and families who gave me their friendship and introduced me to the town's social scene, and to the employers and organizations who allowed me to pry into their routines and their attempts to respond to a complex social and political situation. I hope they will accept this monograph as a balanced account of their dilemmas and adjustments.

Finally, I owe Meg her unstinting time, help, and tolerance of my distraction.

*

Contents

                                                              Page

CHAPTER 1.   INTRODUCTION   3
   The Setting   3
      Port Moresby in 1966 10
   An Industrial Organization and an Urban Sample 17
      Selecting an Urban Sample 17
      Fieldwork 19
   The Plant as Port Moresby: Structure and Process 21
      Urban Anonymity and Kinship 25
      Ethnicity and Race 26

CHAPTER 2.   WORKERS, WORK ROLES AND ROLE REWARDS:
             THE PLANT AND ITS SPATIAL PATTERN ...   29
   Selection, Propinquity, and Reciprocity 29
      The Organization of Work 31
      Managerial Selection, Work Roles, and Role Rewards .. 34
      Housing and Accommodation 40

CHAPTER 3.   SPATIAL PATTERN, SYMBIOSIS AND CULTURAL
             ADAPTATIONS: AN EXTENDED CASE STUDY   45
   The Old Office Residents 47
      Domestic Squalor and Strife 52
      James and Gabriel: Fellow Villagers, Fellow Residents   59
      Urban and Racial Styles 70
      Ethnogenesis, Leadership, and the Lack of Common
      Purpose 77
      Social Adjustment to the Fact of Community   87

CHAPTER 4.   WORKERS AS NEIGHBORS: THE OLD BOY-
             HOUSE   91
   The Barracks 92
   Sets and Groups 98
   "Popondetta Boys": The Background 102
   "Popondetta Boys": The Bases of Dyadic Relations 104
   Dyadic Relationships in the Barracks 116
   A System of Categories and Oppositions 124
   In Summary 133

Contents

Page

CHAPTER 5. WORKERS AS NEIGHBORS: THE MARRIED
    QUARTERS 137
  A Visit to the "Babalau" 137
  Discussion and Background 142
  Social Characteristics of Other Married Tenants 144
  A Dual Engagement 147
  Developments 150
  The P.M.D. Quarters as Social Systems and Cultural Seg-
    ments 153
  Migrant Statuses and Cultural Distance 168

CHAPTER 6. WORKERS AS MIGRANTS AND EMPLOYEES 171
  Workers as Migrants 173
    Sampling 173
    Commitments and Occupational Prestige 174
    Plans and Aspirations 181
    Measures of Involvement 185
    Dual Involvement and Individual Adaptations 191
    Workers as Migrants: Conclusions 195
  Workers as Employees 196

CHAPTER 7. WORKERS AS TOWN DWELLERS 213

Appendix
  A Visual Test of Attitudes to Occupational Prestige 231
Bibliography 245
Index 259

MAP I: PAPUA NEW GUINEA - Political

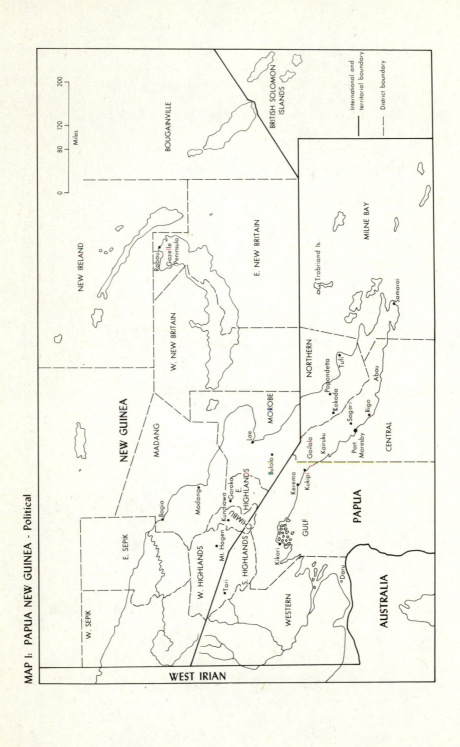

SOCIAL IMAGES
AND PROCESS IN
URBAN NEW GUINEA

A Study
of Port Moresby

*

1

Introduction

THE SETTING

> So long as the town's work force comprised contract labourers,
> repatriated at the end of their contract period, and local villagers
> for whom wage labour merely supplemented subsistence farming,
> the town belonged to Europeans only. Now it belongs to Papuans
> too: it has an important place in their lives, and they intend to
> use it for their own ends. [Groves 1964:2]

Modern Port Moresby is a town of contrasts. Set in a rain shadow
and brown and baked for most of the year, for three months or so it is
luxuriantly green, scented with frangipani and tinged with scarlet
poincianas like some fabled tropical island. The contrasts of season,
in turn, point to the contrasts of its urban society. In population predominantly Papuan and New Guinean, its more visible institutions and
architecture are European or Australian. Dispersed, fragmented, and
cut off from the more populous parts of the mainland by massive
mountain ranges, it is at the same time an emerging metropolis for its
indigenous population.

The first recorded discovery of its harbor was by Captain John
Moresby of HMS Basilisk in 1873. The following year the Reverend
Lawes, of the London Missionary Society, settled there with his wife

and young son and founded a mission station overlooking Hanuabada, the "great village." At that time the indigenous people of the area were Motu and Koita villagers: respectively, speakers of an Austronesian and a non-Austronesian language. The coastal villages belonged to the Motu, those in the surrounding hills to the Koita. Hanuabada itself, although situated on the coast, was a cluster of five separate villages; three were Motu and the other two Koita. Village traditions state that several generations before the arrival of the Europeans the Koita villagers had moved from their hill sites to the coast, although other traditions also imply that they were the autochthones while the seafaring Motu were the newcomers (Belshaw 1957:11). In 1887, Hanuabada was said to have "about 400 inhabitants" (Pitcairn 1892).

By 1884 when a British Protectorate was declared over "British New Guinea" and Port Moresby was proclaimed its capital, the town also boasted a "spacious store" owned by Andrew Goldie, a Scot (Bevan 1890). After the formation of the Australian Commonwealth, the possession became an Australian Territory and, in 1907, was renamed Papua. Port Moresby remained its capital and by 1910 had two stores, a hotel, and a "score of iron-roofed shacks striving in the sanctifying guise of white paint to conceal their architectural crimes and general decrepitude" (Lett 1944:5).

Between the wars, Port Moresby was a wholly European town with a fringe of satellite villages and compounds from which it drew its labor force. In the early 1930s a visitor recorded this division, and the racial attitude which maintained it, when he wrote, of the training of native medical assistants in Sydney, that "while there they live in the quarantine station, and several people in Papua rather criticise this practice of pushing the natives too much and making them more or less the equals of whites" (Teeling 1936:166). In 1940 one journalist described the town as "an Australian township set on a detached piece of the continent, in this equatorial land" (O'Neill 1940:4).

The natural resources of Papua were, and still are, limited, and those of the area around Port Moresby are even more so. Today, plantations on the Sogeri Plateau, some twenty miles from the town itself, produce much of the Territory's rubber, its major income-earning export. Between the wars, however, copra (none of which is grown in the immediate hinterland of the town), a little gold, and some copper (mined from near the town) were the only important exports. Some indication of the low level of development in the Territory in these earlier years is given by the fact that in 1940–41, just before the Japanese invasion of New Guinea, the total public revenue for Papua from *all* sources was under $380,000 (Papuan Annual Report).

Thus, with a very low level of development, the town's population grew only slowly. Oram has estimated that in 1935 its total population was 2,800, of whom 300 were nonindigenous, and the remainder were native villagers and migrant Papuan laborers on short-term contracts. Included in the nonindigenous population were "mixed-race" people tracing their descent to "European-indigenous" unions or, for example, to Pacific Islanders who had worked as missionaries or policemen in the early days of the colony (Oram 1964).

The first major development in the town's history came with World War II. Following the Japanese invasion of New Guinea in 1942, those people not required for military service, both indigenous and European, were evacuated, and Port Moresby became the headquarters of the allied forces in the southwestern Pacific. With the end of the war, it became the capital of the joint Territory of Papua and New Guinea. The capital of New Guinea itself—administered by Australia under a League of Nations mandate—had been at Rabaul but was being transferred to the New Guinea mainland when the Japanese invasion began. Port Moresby became the new capital for several reasons: it had an excellent harbor; it alone had any buildings left standing; it was already the headquarters for the temporary civil administration; and it was a Crown Possession, while New Guinea became a United Nations Trust Territory. The administrative headquarters of the new capital were located located at Konedobu, one mile from the commercial center of the town and near Hanuabada.

With the growth of local administration, the process of change quickened, but not so rapidly that it challenged the existing pattern. For at least a decade after the war Port Moresby retained its hollow character. Belshaw (1965) describes the town's effect on its hinterland in 1950 as "parasitic," or at best neutral. Even in the commercial sector of life, relationships between the European town and surrounding Papuan communities were distant. The large commercial houses sold directly to Europeans in their town stores, but distributed goods to the indigenous population by providing wholesale supplies to the largely European middlemen who were operating small trade stores along the length of the coast. Foodstuffs for Europeans and migrants in the labor compounds were primarily of overseas origin. Belshaw writes: "The European sector of Port Moresby had more contact with the small port of Samarai, 200 miles to the east, than it did with Papuan communities 10 or 20 miles away" (Belshaw 1965:93).

Economic separation was matched by social separation. Belshaw (1957:240–42) describes how there was a color bar but that it was variable in its application: in some instances there was the greatest liberality, in others the extreme of prejudice. His examples indicate, however, that the variation reflected greater or lesser degrees of overt rudeness rather than any fundamental variation in interests and activities. The Papuan population was still largely a menial labor force for a European town.

This period did, however, witness the substantial growth of the urban area. In 1951 the European suburb of Boroko was established on a plateau to the north of the original town. It largely replicated the pattern of the old although the wooden bungalows of the old township gave way, in the new development, to constructions of fibrocement boarding. At the same time there was a rapid growth of shanty settlements in the gullies between the hills and in other areas away from the main roads. After the war, the Administration had directed migrants from certain areas of the Gulf District towards huts left over from the wartime military installations and located behind the administrative headquarters at Konedobu. In those same years, people from areas to the east of Port Moresby coming to work in the town but lacking housing began to beach their canoes near Koke (Oram 1967). By 1956 there were fourteen settlements housing an increasingly urbanized population of Papuan workers and their families.

In that year, as a result of its growth as an administrative center and port, and through subsidiary developments in the building and other service industries, Port Moresby's indigenous population had grown to between 13,000 and 14,000 (Foster 1956). Of these, approximately 44 percent lived in native villages, 30 percent in labor compounds, and the remainder in the growing settlements and in domestic servant's quarters on their employer's property. But with this growth came problems not previously experienced by the District Office. These problems were thought to have arisen because of the "Foreign Native problem." At least one officer, however, was confident that with time, staff, and money the "Foreign Native problem" would be overcome! (Foster 1956).

Inevitably, however, the town continued to grow as the Administration and the service industries expanded, bringing migrants from all over the Territory as well as Australians and other Europeans. The causes of this expansion await a detailed historical analysis. It seems, however, to have owed something to the growing realization on the part of the Federal Government in Australia that the Territory must be prepared for eventual self-determination—however distant, in those halcyon days of paternalistic administration, that event may have appeared. Thus, between 1953–54 and 1957–58 the Federal Government's annual, nonrepayable grant to Papua itself doubled—from $4.6 million to $9.2 million (P.A.R.). As the principal port and center in Papua, Port Moresby must have benefited substantially from the increased employment and flow of goods and services arising from the increase in the annual grant. In the late 1950s and early 1960s, this realization grew as the majority of African nations advanced toward self-determination, as the United Nations became increasingly critical of Australia's administration in New Guinea, and as Indonesia's confrontation with the Dutch in West New Guinea (now West Irian and part of Indonesia) intensified. The annual grant grew with it, although not matching the rate of growth in the late 1950s. Between 1958–59 and 1962–63 the grant increased to $15.8 million—a growth rate of 70 percent over the five years. During this period internal revenue nearly doubled, and the grant towards the costs and administration of commonwealth agencies and departments based in the Territory increased substantially (P.A.R.).

Whatever the dynamics of this growth, the effect was clear. By 1961, when censuses of the European and indigenous population was taken, the total population had grown to 29,000, of whom 22,600 were indigenes. Of these latter residents, only 2,409 were from New Guinea (Bettison 1961). See Table 1.

TABLE 1

POPULATION OF PORT MORESBY

Source	Year	Indigenous	Nonindigenous	Total
Oram 1964	1935	2,500	300	2,800
Oram 1964	1954	12,000	3,700	15,700
Bettison 1961	1961	22,000	6,400	29,000
Bureau of Statistics 1966	1966	32,222	9,911	42,133
Bureau of Statistics 1970	1970	42,616	13,590	56,206

With the growth in population, other developments took place—some of them radical, all of them perhaps inevitable. In 1955, for example, the first block of houses for Papua–New Guineans was built on a small residential estate at Kaugere. A year later the Administration had worked out the details of a housing estate at Hohola for the better paid town dwellers—thus recognizing its obligations to house at least some of the many indigenes who had become increasingly dependent on urban wage employment. In 1961 the first tenants moved into the new estate at Hohola (Oeser 1969:2–3).

Perhaps one of the first events to augur radical change in the structure of urban relationships was in the industrial field. In 1957, twenty indigenes employed by the lines section of the Department of Posts and Telegraphs went on strike in protest at having to work on Saturday mornings: they pointed out that European employees in the section had a five-day week but that they did not. The strike was probably the first in the history of the Administration in Papua although indigenous Administration workers in Rabaul, New Guinea, had struck as early as 1929. In the same year, soldiers of the Pacific Island Regiment "ran riot," attacking Keremas and members of other ethnic groups. In January 1961 another seventy-four soldiers again rebelled against established authority, striking for better pay. They were thought to be making invidious comparisons with the Minimum Urban Wage Agreement. This agreement had only recently been negotiated by the newly emergent Papua and New Guinea Workers' Association, the first wholly indigenous trade union in the Territory. The agreement gave Port Moresby workers a minimum wage of $6 per week.

The Workers' Association—later the Port Moresby Workers' Association—grew out of attempts by Papuan town dwellers to establish voluntary organizations aimed at improving their welfare and conditions. In the discussions which led to its formation, the Kerema Welfare Association had played a key part. The first president of this group was Albert Maori Kiki, a public servant, first vice president of the Workers' Association and later fulltime secretary of the Pangu Pati, the first nationalist political party to escape being merely a paper organization. Perhaps because Kiki was transferred to Bougainville, the Kerema Welfare Association ran into financial difficulties and by 1964, was penniless (Kiki 1968:101).

The first, and most permanent of the welfare associations, the Methodist Welfare Society, was founded in 1955. It brought together migrants from the islands of Milne Bay; Lepani Watson, a Trobriand islander employed as a welfare assistant by the Administration, became its leader. According to him: "The main purpose of the society was—we look to the people who left their homes and came to work in Port Moresby. The Methodist group, they have no place to meet together to learn each other" (quoted in Fink 1965:291). The members later built a meeting hall at Badili and, with the incorporation of Methodists from the New Guinea Islands, renamed the groups the "Lord of the Isles Society." Regular weekly church meetings and the use of the hall for social events undoubtedly were prime factors in its success. Other welfare societies withered away within a year or two of their birth.

Of all voluntary associations in the town, the sports associations have proved the strongest. The town supports four types of football, together with basketball, cricket, and baseball leagues—with many teams in each league or association—as well as many minor sports. Thus the town is akin to Bamako, in French West Africa, during the colonial period: Meillassoux reports that some 30 percent of all voluntary associations at that time were sports organizations (Meillassoux 1968; see also Epstein 1958:12).

But even though the welfare associations often fell into disuse, the sense of regional or ethnic identity among groups in the town has remained strong, and animosity has often resulted. Thus in 1961 a large-scale fight between Morobe District natives and Goilalas from the Central District took place at Koke market and one man was killed (Hughes 1965:19). Perhaps something of the animosity of that occasion lingered because in late 1966 another battle broke out between Goilala men and Morobes from Buang (South Pacific Post, 11 February 1966).

There were also developments in the field of racial relations. In April 1957, for example, an 11 P. M. curfew on the movement of indigenes within the town was abolished. The most momentous events, however, occurred in 1962 and 1964. The first of these, on 2 November 1962, raised indigenous hopes of the eventual abolition of all discrimination: on that day all adult males, irrespective of race, became legally entitled to drink alcohol. For many years legal beer-drinking had been a European prerogative, and the most resented of all racial discriminations. The second event, the introduction of a dual wages and privileges structure within the public service, dashed indigenous hopes of racial equality to the ground and left a legacy of bitterness which will continue to color politics and industrial relations for some-time to come. Realizing that the principle of equal pay for equal work at mainland rates would eventually prove an impossible burden for the local economy, the Administration fixed indigenous public servants' salaries at about 40 percent of those of their European counterparts. This in turn set the standard for wage rates throughout the Territory.

Many Papuans and New Guineans acknowledge that salaries must be geared to the local economy and that expatriates with skills which cannot be supplied by the indigenous work force must be enticed with inducement allowances if Papua–New Guinea is to develop at the rate they would like it to. But they also point out that the dual wage structure does not just reflect skill since there are many Europeans receiving expatriate pay who have no educational qualifications and little skill. Moreover, whereas indigenes must pay economic rents for small, inadequate housing, the Europeans, they argue, have superior housing which is also subsidized. Finally, the resentment of many Papuans and New Guineans is a result of their frustrated hopes for a better way of life and, as Crocombe (1966) has argued, their emotional distaste for the European's power, privilege, and possessions.

Port Moresby in 1966

With this brief survey of Port Moresby's development in mind, let me turn now to the broader features I encountered when I began field-work in the town in late 1966. All population statistics for 1966 are taken from the census of that year (Bureau of Statistics 1966).

One of the first aspects of the town which strikes a newcomer is its diversity. Almost one-quarter of the total population is European, of whom 95 percent are British; some 60 percent of the total nonindigenous residents were born in Australia. The indigenous population is drawn from every sub-district in the joint Territories. Although the bulk of the indigenous population (74 percent) was born in one or the other of only two administrative districts—the Central and the Gulf—it is further divided into various language groups and differs greatly in physical type, culture, and occupational position within the town. The 15 percent from the various parts of New Guinea—with their sense of being strangers in an alien town and their allegiance to Pidgin English as a *lingua franca* as distinct from Police Motu and English used by the bulk of the Papuan population—add to the diversity. Particularly distinctive are the people from the Highlands. Although forming only

Plate 1   Port Moresby—the commercial centre

Plate 2   Settlements—Kogeva (inhabited mainly by migrants from Kerema Bay)

4 percent of the total indigenous population, their physical type, culture, and their role as an urban "proletariat," or perhaps "lumpenproletariat," distinguishes them from other urban residents. They began coming to the town in about 1961, and their numbers are growing every year. They come from by far the most populous, but also most recently contacted, part of the Territory.

Wandering through the streets of the town the newcomer will also discover that young, indigenous males predominate. It is not just that the women are tied to the house by domestic chores; the town is demographically selective because of its role as a magnet for migrant labor. It selects from those in the Territory who are most able to sell their labor. Thus the sex ratio among indigenous town dwellers is two males to one female. The sex imbalance is even more striking if only marriageable persons are considered: the ratio of unmarried men over twelve years of age to unmarried women in the same age category is eight males to one female. Youth is marked; if indigenous male resi-

TABLE 2

PERCENTAGE DISTRIBUTION BY INDUSTRY OF PORT MORESBY'S
WORK FORCE: CENSUS 1966

	Indigenous work force only		Total work force	
	No.	%	No.	%
Primary and Mining etc.	273	2	339	2
Manufacturing	1,155	8	1,471	7
Building and Construction	3,500	25	4,506	22
Public Authorities and Defense Services	1,605	11	3,330	17
Commerce and Finance	1,607	11	2,606	13
Transport and Storage	1,335	10	1,885	9
Community and Business Services (including professional)	1,211	9	2,036	13
Amusements, Hotels, Personal Service etc.	2,010	14	2,514	13
Other	666	5	1,082	5
Total	13,748	100	19,769	100

[A9826]

dents are grouped into five-year age cohorts the modal category is 20–24 years. The estimated median age for all adult males is 24 years of age. In contrast the sex ratio among Europeans is only 4–3 in favor of males. The modal age category among European males is 25–29 years.

As we have seen, Port Moresby's expansion has been based largely on the expansion of one of its major industries—administration. However, although undoubtedly still highly responsive to changes in the size and rate of expansion of the various agencies of public administration, a number of service and other industries have grown up and made Port Moresby far from a one-industry town. In 1966 building and construction employed the greatest number of workers—some 22 percent of a total labor force of 19,769. By comparison, only 17 percent of the town's labor force—and only 11 percent of indigenous workers—worked for public authorities of all kinds, including defense services. Manufacturing, although small, was growing. In 1966, 7 percent of the total labor force was employed in secondary industry. In 1968 the number of manufacturing enterprises was forty-five. Included in this figure were two breweries (one of which had only been formed in that year), a tobacco factory, and plants for the manufacture of aerated waters, batteries, paints, cement goods, and other products—mainly those produced directly for the consumer market or for the building industry.

From a small European township clustered around the harbor in the 1930s, Port Moresby has grown to a large and dispersed urban area. And with the growth of the town there has been a dispersal of its various functions (see Map 2). The dispersal created by the hilly terrain has been reinforced by the environment of racial relations, which has divided the population into racial groups, and the lack of municipal administration and policy, which has encouraged piecemeal development. Surprisingly, given its size, in 1966 there was no municipal authority nor an overall plan for its development.

Three major areas of the town are highly specialized: the administration complex of Konedobu, the industrial area and airport at Six Mile, and the educational complex, including the new University of

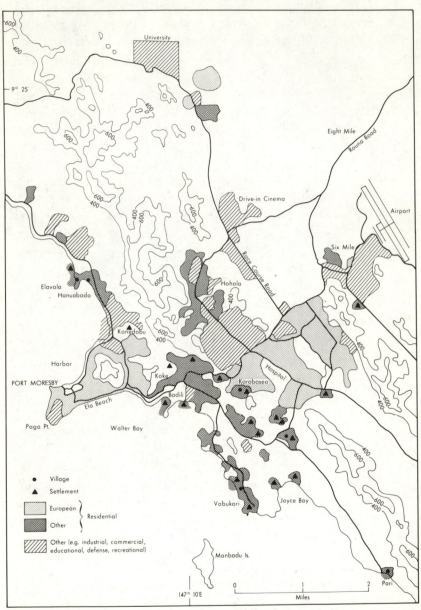

MAP 2: PORT MORESBY - Residential and Other Land Use

Papua and New Guinea, at Waigani. The four other major "natural areas" are less specialized, combining commercial, shopping, industrial, and residential functions. The first of these is the original township and commercial center on the peninsula at Ela. This is still the financial and commercial center and the area around it houses a major part of the town's European population. On the plateau, behind the hills which separate the coastal areas from those inland, is the European suburb and shopping area of Boroko. The shopping area includes a large supermarket, a number of Chinese-owned stores, and a few more specialized shops—for example, a bookstore. This center also serves the third major natural area, the Papua–New Guinean suburb of Hohola, which has only limited facilities. Finally, there are Koke-Badili and Koke market itself. These serve the weekday needs of the dense concentration of Papuan settlement from Koke to Vabukori village in the east. It is the Papuan heart of the town, and on weekends serves as a focus for all other indigenes. In 1966 the total area from Koke to Vabukori held over 35 percent of the town's indigenous residents and 6 percent of the nonindigenous, almost all of whom would be residents of the "mixed-race" residential area at Gabutu.

Koke itself was for many years a residential area for mixed-race people and "advanced Papuans." Increasingly, however, its marketplace function began to take precedence as traders came, selling their produce from canoes drawn up at Koke Beach (Belshaw 1952). Until the mid-1950s the only western commercial activity in the area was a store at Koke owned by one of the two Chinese men living in Papua (Oram: personal communication). Modern Koke, however, has scores of Chinese trade stores strung out along the main road from the old town to Boroko. It has also developed as a center for religious activity. Four major denominations have built churches there and the Salvation Army has built a hostel (used by both indigenes and Europeans), and a school.

In Badili the Roman Catholic Mission has established both a school and a maternity hospital. In general, however, Badili has developed as an industrial area. A brewery, twist-tobacco factory, joinery, aerated water plant, a bakery, and other, smaller concerns are established there, together with their labor compounds and those of the town's large com-

Plate 3   Koke-Badili—industrial establishments

Plate 4   Badili—a street scene

mercial enterprises. The plant and labor compound with which this book is principally concerned is located in the Koke-Badili area.

AN INDUSTRIAL ORGANIZATION AND AN URBAN SAMPLE

> The factory . . . constitutes both a social group and an institution. . . . and provides material for the observation of the type of the social relations existing between administrators and executives, rich and poor, manual and intellectual workers; and is of interest for the study not only of labour relations but also of the nature of urban society. [DeLauwe 1965:145]

Selecting an Urban Sample

As we have seen, a problem which suggested itself for study was an assessment of the two seemingly contradictory views of the town's social character. One of these views saw the town as a focus for sociocultural change. The other implied that its subunits owed their survival and continuity to nonurban imperatives; the town itself was not seen as a significant source of change. In the previous section, these somewhat divergent views were located historically. I suggested that Port Moresby is in the process of evolution from a largely Australian country town—with a fringe of independent native settlements and villages —to a town organized along more organic lines—although still with many fundamental oppositions between the constituent communities.

Common to both views, however, is a recognition of the town's heterogeneity. Many of Port Moresby's inhabitants are migrants and come from many different parts of the Territory. Yet others—the Motu and the Koiari peoples—are at home there. Some of the migrants are long-term residents, while others are little more than tourists. Some are in skilled, technical, and white-collar occupations while yet others are unskilled. Overriding all other factors of heterogeneity is the division between black and white, indigene and expatriate.

It is clearly not feasible to study every individual in a population of over 40,000 in order to cope with this diversity. Sampling procedures must be used. Yet at the same time, the very diversity creates difficulties in sampling procedure. While assumptions about sampling and representativeness must be examined critically even in rural areas (Colson 1954), the greater scale and diversity of a town such as Port Moresby requires that they be treated still more warily.

Rew, Port Moresby Study—CTB—3

A random sample of individuals or households drawn from a known population of town dwellers according to established procedures would allow inferences to be drawn about the universe. But while representativeness of basic social characteristics could be assured, the reliability of information gained on more general aspects of social behavior would be much harder to assess since its context would be lost.

"Cluster sampling," by which large units of study are randomly selected from a list of known units and the whole unit studied, would seem to be one solution to the difficulty. This procedure would allow statistical inference and yet also allow the observation of face-to-face behavior (Mitchell 1967:34). The more obvious "units" in a heterogeneous town, however, are rarely immediately comparable. Given the tendency of individuals and groups to sort themselves out into "natural areas," units which might conceivably be isolated for study as "communities" are likely to be dissimilar in content and function. Although cluster sampling of neighborhoods, organizations or associations might be feasible at some stage in an inquiry, the compilation of a meaningful, stratified sampling frame would require considerable prior ethnographic research.

In view of these general considerations, and the impressions I could gain of the town before arriving, I decided that "purposive" sampling must suffice. This method may range from the purely *ad hoc* selection of informants to sampling on a more purposive basis, whereby the anthropologist selects a unit for study either because he believes it typical of the universe or because it satisfies some condition he argues is important on theoretical grounds (Mitchell 1967:31). While ruling out the possibility of statistical inference, the procedure allows the selection of a sample where informants are in sufficiently close contact to make observational techniques worthwhile. Accordingly, I sought to isolate units which would evidence something of the diversity of basic social characteristics which other writers had noted, and yet would allow a close observation of interactions between participants, preferably through recurring and contrasted situations. Large, complex work situations met these requirements. These were presumably the situations where members of the supposedly discrete settlements and villages came together. Moreover, the necessity of daily, or near-daily, task performance in a restricted geographical area would make the participants continually available to me for observation. It would also give me ample contact to arrange to meet people informally, to interview them, and to follow their social networks out into the wider town.

Voluntary associations, which might have been selected for study, were rejected as unsatisfactory: I assumed they would not be sufficiently diverse. As Epstein has argued, in a review of urban studies in Africa, not all urban dwellers are joiners and those that are usually belong to higher socioeconomic levels (1967b:281). Polansky lends strength to this argument for Papua–New Guinea when he writes that voluntary associations play a major role only for the educated government servants and the younger generation (1966).

Although accessible to participant observation, neighborhoods were rejected for study because I assumed they also were not sufficiently diverse. Available evidence suggested that they were largely homogeneous in terms of ethnic factors, with Europeans, local villagers, and groups of migrants sorting themselves out into "natural" areas. However, I considered large, complex work situations as not being subject to quite the same pressures toward homogeneity.

Moreover, I could anticipate a bonus from drawing such a sample. Many employers in the town provide housing for their indigenous employees in labor compounds. I hoped that contacts established initially through the workplace would lead to my invitation to these quarters. As the labor compounds were thought to house a substantial proportion of the town population, and as they had not been studied previously, I hoped that my survey would help fill in the town's ethnographic map.

Finally, there was some indication that the employment and work situations of indigenous townsmen were in themselves a source of social change. In October and November of 1965 a wave of strikes had hit the town involving some hundreds of indigenous employees, suggesting that common employment led to common interests. Of Papuans and New Guineans in Rabaul, moreover, Polansky (1966) had written that "new social relations outside the home group were first and foremost established amongst people who met each other at their place of employment . . . ."

Fieldwork

I spent a total of eighteen months in Papua–New Guinea, divided into two periods of eleven and seven months. An initial six weeks were spent at Goroka in the New Guinea Highlands, the rest in Port

Moresby and surrounding areas. The languages of investigation were the three urban *linguae francae*: New Guinea Pidgin (Neo-Melanesian), Police Motu (a Papuan trade language), and English. I used a medley of research techniques: observation in compounds and work situations; participation in employee's work, residential, and leisure activities; and more formal interviewing—involving census forms, the analysis of photographs, projective tests, and structured questionnaires.

For seven months of the fieldwork period, I lived in quarters for young and more educated employees within a labor compound set aside for employees of Papuan Manufacturing and Distributing Proprietary Limited. During that time, and throughout the rest of my stay in Port Moresby, I was able to move freely within the company's labor compounds and plant, and also to participate in the social life of Koke-Badili, the Papuan heart of the town. My richest data are drawn from this study and so, in the interests of length and coherence, I have omitted discussion of the other studies I undertook in the town. But I will note that although I generate my analysis of urban social forms from the social relations of Papuan Manufacturing and Distributing employees, the other studies have also shaped my perspectives and underlie parts of my analysis in the final chapter.

Intrigued that a European should be living in a "boy-house," many employees came to inspect or talk to me and soon I had developed a wide range of contacts not only among employees but often among their kin and compatriots living and working outside company accommodation.

The company's management gave me permission to come and go and conduct my inquiries as I saw fit. And so, from the first, I worked in the plant in order to observe its routines and establish contacts. For the first month I worked in the plant almost every day, either on the day, morning, or night shift. Starting from a section employing almost a third of the total labor force, I afterward moved to other sections. As fieldwork progressed, I came to spend less and less time actually working at the plant, preferring instead to circulate within the compound itself and to pick up the day's gossip when workers finished a shift. Occasionally, however, I would return to a section for the day or night to keep pace with developments.

Initially there were some misgivings, particularly on the night shifts where, as one man admitted, workers feared I was a spy sent to report on industrial malpractice. Nonetheless, I believe that most employees came to accept my presence: the public consensus was that I was a teacher who had come to write a book on their customs and conditions. Certain of the more recent recruits to the company, however, appeared to assume that I was down on my luck and on several occasions urged me to return to their home area and start a business. While others seemed to accept the public definition of my presence, I sensed that their suspicions were never completely allayed. No one was overtly hostile, although some were restrained.

THE PLANT AS PORT MORESBY: STRUCTURE AND PROCESS

I have justified my decision to study Port Moresby through its larger industrial concerns on the grounds of sampling and the insight which could be gained if the units selected for study were heterogenous social arenas and not just isolated individuals or groups. I justify the decision to document my findings with material drawn from employees of only one plant on the grounds of context and coherence. These decisions, however, raise issues of wider theoretical importance concerning the appropriateness of the attempt to treat Port Moresby as a unit and the relationship between a worm's-eye, or "egocentric," view and a bird's-eye, or "sociocentric," view of that same entity.

Treating Port Moresby as a unit raises the question of whether or not anthropologists are entitled, for reasons of manageability, to bound their field of study by postulating an urban social system. Bruner (1967:285), objecting to the attempt to isolate an urban social system argues that "the rural and the urban are never completely independent and autonomous; they are invariably related in many diverse and subtle ways . . . Culture patterns are not so dependent upon locality or place of residence, nor does the city influence all aspects of life to the same extent." Salisbury and Salisbury (1972), writing of Siane migrants in Port Moresby, have argued that studies of Port Moresby urban migrants which focus on the urban end of the migration process can only be "descriptive:" the causes of urban-located behaviour are to be found in strategies oriented to village statuses and village resources.

If we accept these strictures on procedure we necessarily rule out one important question, namely, the degree of discontinuity or non-comparability between a particular urban social system and other urban social systems.   Thus Mitchell (1966:45f) has argued that we must proceed to study a town or city by thinking of it as an analytically distinct unit. While certain individuals in that study might also appear in a study of rural-urban migration *per se* the two inquiries must not be confused. Indeed broaching a study of the city with largely rural problems in mind necessarily prejudges the urban in favour of the rural.

Lévi-Strauss recognizes the issue when he writes :

> "What is called a 'culture' is a fragment of humanity which, from the point of view of the research at hand and of the scale on which the latter is carried out, presents significant discontinuities in relation to the rest of humanity. . . . should we become concerned with significant discontinuities between New York and Chicago, we would be allowed to speak of these two groups as different cultural 'units.' Since these discontinuities can be reduced to *invariants*, which is the goal of structural analysis, we see that culture may, at the same time, correspond to an objective reality and be a function of the kind of research undertaken.   Accordingly, the same set of individuals may be considered to be parts of many different cultural contexts . . ." (1963:295).

Abstracting the town as a cultural unit, then, is logically comparable to abstracting cultural units reflecting language or political discontinuity. In studying *any* population, however large or small, one must face two problems simultaneously: What is the system of social relations between members of the population? and how is it affected by being part of a larger social field? Thus all social arenas or cultures studied by anthropologists are only semi-autonomous and, as units of analysis, are dependent on the purposes and scope of the research.   Once this is understood the utility of abstracting Port Moresby as a unit is largely empirical and can be settled in the attempt to abstract, within a comparative framework, generalized patterns of social relationship from the detailed examination of urban-located events.

In view of these general considerations I focus, in the following five chapters, on the detail of social and sub-social interactions occurring within a single industrial plant and its compounds and in doing so abstract more generalised social forms which are also applicable to broader areas of Port Moresby social life.   From time to time, and particularly in the final chapter, I discuss the interrelationship of these abstracted patterns in the light of urban studies elsewhere in the Pacific and in parts of Africa.

Thus while the account aims at statements about Port Moresby urban structure it arrives there via a detailed discussion of social processes involving a small sample of urban workers. I see no other way to proceed. Residents lack a single elaborated theory of the town's social relations, and the town cannot be easily described as a set of social segments or corporations. The initial focus, therefore, has to be on individual residents and the networks of social relations in which they are involved. This is the minimum level at which social relations can be investigated (Epstein 1961 and Gutkind 1967:285–86). The Papuan Manufacturing and Distribution Company's employees simply provide a convenient and appropriate sample for this purpose.

Yet the account of individual workers is more than a chronicle. I have followed Barth (1966 and 1968) in taking *institutionalisation* as the key problem in the analysis of individual adjustments; that is "how a multiplicity of individual decisions under the influence of canalizing factors can have the cumulative effect of producing clear patterns and conventions" (1966:3). Thus the company's system of productive positions, and management's allocation of the concern's resources, act as a set of material constraints. These shape and canalize the way in which individual workers are able to allocate their time and resources to given social ends. The technical system sets a need for different types of labor and, in selecting this labor, management creates a set of spatial arrangements, which effectively constrain a worker's time and whom he associates with, and a set of rewards, which constrain the level and character of the worker's major resources—namely, wages, and housing.

The power of management is such that its disposition of people and resources is not effectively opposed, except in times of crisis. Moreover, the impersonal controls built into the technology, and amplified by close supervision, severely curtail the worker's attempts to restrict output or otherwise redefine his productive role. Given the worker's decision to seek employment at the company, the plant's industrial system is so compelling that his scope for decision-making within it is limited to the choice of whether or not to report for work—that is whether to produce, strike, become an absentee, or quit. Thus, once the system of productive roles has been understood, the worker's adaptation to his work situation is no longer problematic except in times of crisis. The worker's allocation of time to his technical role (and a major portion of his resources) arises directly from his status in the labor contract with minimal interference from other variables (cf. Mayer 1961:xv).

Management's need to reward labor differentially also creates spatial arrangements in the compounds. Moreover, given the nature of the colonial society, these arrangements bring about a situation of heterogeneity. Both the spatial pattern and the heterogeneity in turn constrain and direct worker's ongoing allocations. But whereas the constraints of the work place are compelling, those set by managerial allocations in the compound allow the observer to see how, day-by-day, workers adapt to these complex pressures and alter their behavior as circumstances change.

Because the labor compound operates as an arena for changing allocations and choice, rather than a structure of determinative statuses, I have chosen to document workers' overall adaptation from the vantage point of their offduty hours. In Chapters 3, 4, and 5 I show how the constraints of the industrial system, together with the constraints and enthusiasms set by the worker's other participations, shape the relationships arising from common employment and co-residence. Having documented worker's other involvements, and the processes by which they are related to the worker's status as employee, I show, in Chapter 6, how his overall adaptation to his offduty situation in turn affects his choice and allocations within the work place.

Whereas it is possible to derive technical and other industrial *roles* from the worker's *status* as employee, the division between role and status is less obvious in the complex social processes operating within the compound. There the division is rather between ecology and cultural involvements. But the ecological arrangements I have in mind are not simply a static environment for behavior. The ecology of compound life produces a complex process of subsocial dependence and competition, modifying and being modified by, the ongoing social and spatial relationships. Following the urban sociologist Park I have called this process *symbiosis* (Park 1939).

The notion of process is central to Park's conception of the social organization of the city and is at the root of his distinction between the biotic and cultural orders of communal life. Rather than viewing the city as a stable structure, he depicts its organisation as the product of two or more orders which are governed by different principles yet are constantly interacting. At successive stages in his writings, Park refers to these orders as "the ecological and social," "the biotic and cultural," "community and society," and (a related distinction) "the spatial pattern and the moral order"; he also writes of the processes of symbiosis and communication. Underlying all these contracts is the distinction between society as a collection of individual yet related units, and society based on consensus and communication. This distinction between the sub-social and fully social or cultural aspects of compound life is necessary because compound life was largely the result of strangers who, bound together by the impersonal division of labor, had to adjust to their common dependence.

Urban Anonymity and Kinship

Heterogeneity and anonymity was less pervasive for some compound residents than for others. The plant's arrangements sifted P.M.D. workers into small milieux with differing possibilities of heterogeneity and anonymity and, at the same time, some workers tried and were able to transfer "rural" ties of kinship and locality to the new setting while others could not or would not do so. Thus certain residential and industrial milieux within the plant were marked by the interaction of small *cliques* composed of kinsmen and compatriots. Many of these ties antedated the worker's urban residence. Other milieux within the plant were marked by the interaction and mutual adjustment of *individuals*. Lacking ties which antedated urban residence, these more socially isolated workers were forced to take greater account of the plant's heterogeneity in their everyday routines. The force of spatial juxtaposition and sub-social interdependence is most discernible in those milieux composed of isolated individuals.

The balance within the town between those milieux composed of discrete individuals and those milieux composed of small cliques of kinsmen and fellow villagers is an important element in the nature of Port Moresby social organization. The "passenger-ship" or "cargo-vessel" theme in indigenous social thought captures the contrast between a city of individuals and a city of people more organically related to their surroundings. A similar contrast underlies a great deal of urban social theory. Classic writings in urban sociology (for example, Wirth 1938) have stressed the ability of the city to break down on-going social structures and commitments and to replace them with more anonymous, individualized social arrangements. Other social scientists, particularly anthropologists, have responded by showing continuities between urban and rural social forms (for example, Lewis 1952, Bruner 1963 and Pocock 1960) or by showing that there are many village-like communities in even the largest cities (for example, Gans 1962). Establishing the precise balance between rural-to-urban continuity and the adjustment to impersonal interdependence for Port Moresby casts further light on this broader theoretical issue.

Ethnicity and Race

The simple contrast between urban milieux based on limited association and urban milieux based on rural community, however, ignores the developmental aspect of social relations in the town. Ties of community based on kinship and locality and ties based on urban association were bridged by ties based on other factors. These interstitial ties depended on urban style, on orientations towards the structure of racial relationships and on a vague, but socially effective, idiom of compatriotism or "ethnicity."

Brown Glick (1970) has treated the urban area of Vila, New Hebrides as a plural social structure showing that Vila residents meet but do not mix and that social relations within the town reflect conditions elsewhere. Port Moresby also had many "plural" features, reflecting the differential incorporation of the two major racial groups within the legal-administrative sphere. Pluralism and the effects of the indigenous town-dweller's orientations towards the structure of racial relations were very apparent in the detail of individual adjustments. A sense of racial injustice was also apparent in the field of industrial relations.

In many urban contexts, ethnic or cultural diversity within the indigenous population is even more important than racial and colonial cleavage. The history of incorporation of the various regions into the colonial economy and, after 1946, into a single colonial polity has produced marked differences in educational levels, and in wage-earning opportunities. It has also allocated individuals and groups to administrative divisions, each of which has a somewhat different colonial history. These differences in colonial incorporation have, in turn, effected the process of "ethnic" differentiation in Port Moresby. "Papuans" were distinguished from "New Guineans," "Chimbu" from "Tolai," "Kerema" from "Popondetta," and so on. Ethnic differentiation, however, did not give rise to cohesive groups or social segments with contrasted, core, cultural institutions, as it did in the case of racial cleavage. Thus, ethnic differentiation cannot be explained as only a reflection of "the plural society."

In Papua New Guinea there are few, if any, tribes in the usual, largely African, sense of large, closed societies holding to an inclusive idea of political, social, or territorial unity. Indeed, Hogbin and Wedgwood (1953), in a review of the Melanesian literature, state that there are no tribes, only groups of people who speak the same language and have a similar culture. These groups, or "phylai," often number only a few hundred persons (as in many areas along the coast of the New Guinea mainland) sometimes a few thousand and occasionally tens of thousands (as in parts of the Highlands, on the Gazelle Peninsula of New Britain, and in northern Papua). And although there are often important dialectical differences within each phyle, they tend to have the same social organization, similar traditions, and a similar patterning of economic and ritual activities. In no sense, however, are they politically united. In the majority of cases they do not even have a name to express their uniqueness as a group.

Thus there are rarely very sharp boundaries between peoples. The Motu, for example, share a common language and culture, and live in adjacent coastal villages around Port Moresby. Nonetheless, they are only one element of what Seligman has described as a "congeries" of people extending along the whole coastal area of the Central district (Seligman 1910). Lines can be drawn between the peoples who form the congeries—for example, the division between speakers of Austronesian and non-Austronesian languages—but in many other respects there is perhaps as wide a measure of continuity as there is of discontinuity (Groves 1963).

Although stable, military and ceremonial alliances of several thousand people are reported for many parts of the Highlands—and for one area of coastal Papua (Maher 1967)—the largest group which can be regarded as having any *permanent* political unity is what is often known as the village, the clan, or clan parish. These small locality groups are estimated to range from seventy to some four hundred persons and above, but very rarely are there more than a thousand. Their small size seems to be related to the type of country, to the efficient division of labor within subsistence agricultural systems, to the exploitation of land, and to the needs of defence.

Stable, military and ceremonial alliances do act as a buffer between the small, locality groups and surrounding populations in certain areas. But, with these exceptions, social ties beyond the clan or village take the form of a network of trading and affinal relationships centered, for the most part, upon the activities of prominent individuals. Mead (1967:5–8) has suggested that these trading networks may be utilized to aid the indigenous townsman's adaptation to the urban centers and that trading networks have more importance for the migrant than "ethnic" stereotypes.

Those few migrants, however, who cited rural trading links as the basis of certain Port Moresby social relationships were mostly from coastal Papua and the trading links they cited were between past generations. Those social ties which did not refer to common membership of a small locality tended to refer to encounters arising from urban associations and not from trading networks. As we shall see in Chapters 3, 4, and 5, "ethnic" stereotypes and the network of kinship and *wantok* (compatriot) ties arising from both rural and urban associations were interrelated in a complex social process. This process reflected residents' recruitment for work in the town, differences in the incorporation of their home regions into the colonial economy, the detail of urban-located events, and the importance given to relationships based upon *ples* (place or local region) within Papuan and New Guinean social thought. The urban migrant's "place" can refer to a small village or locality. Similarly *wantok* can refer to members of that village or locality or to people in ever larger vicinities. By bringing together people from many areas, the urban economy and administrative and residential structure increase the scale of urban associations and thus generalize the idioms of *ples* and *wantok*, enabling residents to deal with urban-located events within a framework of compatriotism. This appeal to a compatriotism based on identification with large socio-geographic regions is socially important even though the idioms of *ples* and *wantok* which express this appeal are broad and diffuse in their application. Indeed, much of the detail of urban compatriotism is provided by the details of urban spatial juxtaposition and sub-social interdependence and by urban micro-history. The account of P.M.D. employees is thus not only a sampling of "egocentric" relationships and individual adjustments. It is also an examination of the complex articulation and interdependence of urban social forms.

2

Workers, Work Roles and Role Rewards: The Plant and Its Spatial Pattern

It is because geography, occupation, and all the other factors which determine the distribution of population determine so irresistibly and fatally the place, the group, and the associates with whom each one of us is bound to live that spatial relations come to have for the study of society and human nature, the importance which they do. [Park 1926:17–18]

SELECTION, PROPINQUITY, AND RECIPROCITY

Spatial relations are immediately quantifiable, and can thus serve as readily available indices to more fundamental sociocultural phenomena. But the spatial order at Papuan Manufacturing and Distribution (P.M.D.) was not merely an index: spatial arrangements also acted as incentives and barriers to the formation of new relationships. Thus, although they were by no means the most important of the factors determining relations of either intimacy or distance, a consideration of the factors which helped to structure the spatial pattern is a very necessary background to the total analysis.

The assumption which underlies my argument in this chapter is that the close physical proximity of individuals with similar social charac-

29

teristics increases the chances of their association for purposes over and above those which produced the original proximity. Following the example of Barth and other anthropologists who have stressed the role of the individual in social process, I assume that interactions in the plant compounds and workplaces take place within a framework of individual decisions. These decisions are determined by each participant's desire to strike a balance between the benefits of the interaction so that he always makes a "profit" or at least minimizes the "costs."

Thus in examining the recruitment of an individual worker we might start with the profits and costs bearing on the decision of the worker to present himself for employment (i. e. self-selection), or we might start with those bearing on the decisions of either management or his fellow workers to influence him to make his application. Finally, we might consider management's power to veto or accept the application. Which of these factors is to be given the greatest weight depends upon the particular circumstances of the situation, and upon the strategies of the research process.

In this chapter I have deliberately chosen to concentrate on *management's* part in the selection processes. The three possibilities of selection by management, selection by fellow workers, and "selection" by the worker himself are all equally important. However, since we must relate what goes on "inside" the factory to what goes on "outside" in the wider town, it seems a sound tactic to deal first with the general situation which management faces and show how management's power and its interpretation of its own position set constraints on the individual migrant's choice of associates.

Management is clearly able to influence the nature of the costs involved for a worker by altering the range of choices available to him. One possibility would be to allocate him to a compound where his fellow residents are so alien that he would never seek to go beyond the attempt to get something for nothing, or where he is so afraid of their sorcery that he would seek to have as little to do with them as possible. Avoidance of neighbors, as we shall see, is very likely. Another possibility would involve placing workers with similar backgrounds together, thus greatly reducing the costs involved in initiating the first and subsequent interactions. Yet another possibility would be to "collapse" the range of choices available to our worker by making his kinsman his neighbor.

Each worker will, perhaps, phrase his choice in terms of a set of preferences which may be quite at variance with the goals and ends of managerial policy. But, at this stage of the presentation, I will leave these preferences and values as implicit elements in the account.

The spatial distribution of workers, both at work and in their housing arrangements, will be approached through an examination of the technical exigencies of the plant and the way in which management interprets, and seeks to satisfy, those needs. Thus, the examination of the technical system and the functional arrangement of tasks leads to an examination of the criteria used in recruitment and its practice. It also involves a consideration of management's use of its command over housing facilities to reward work roles.

The Organization of Work

The total number of indigenous workers employed by the company and based in Port Moresby varied from between 145 and 165 during the time I was concerned with the company's operations. The plant also employed some twenty-five expatriate staff; this figure included the senior officers of the company, technical staff, fitters and tradesmen, sales representatives, and female clerical assistants. The ratio of expatriate to indigenous employees was just under 1 to 6. Each of the main factory sections was supervised by Europeans, who were in turn responsible to the general manager or one of his senior officers. No European came under the control of a Papuan or New Guinean.

The total labor force was distributed through a number of buildings and work sections: fourteen in all. The sections' labor forces ranged in size from one of fifty-seven workers—deployed in two shifts—to four sections of two or three workers only. Production Section Four worked two shifts a day—from six to three o'clock and from three to midnight—its shifts rotating on a week-to-week basis. Its employees worked regularly on Saturday mornings together with all other employees at the plant but, if production was in full swing, might also work throughout the Saturday. Production Sections One and Two each had four shifts. On any one day three groups would be working (changing shifts at eight-hour intervals), and one shift would be resting. The sections were producing each day of the week; if a shift worked on a weekend, however, it was given time off instead during the ensuing week. Table 3 gives a breakdown of the labor force by work section and by racial status.

TABLE 3

P.M.D. Labor Force According to Work Section and Race[1]

	Indigenous	European
Production Section 1	12	
2	11	
3	3	4
4	52	
Fitters and Assistants	5	2
Distribution	22	1
Laboratory	8	2
Workshops 1	14	4
2	3	1
3	4	1
Office Workers	11	10
Miscellaneous Sections	15	
Total	160	25
	185	

[1] Unless otherwise stated, all statistics on the P.M.D. labor force apply to the end of August 1967.
[A9852]

The work of Production Sections One and Two was shaped by a more or less continuous-process technology. Once the raw materials had been added (manually), the process was largely continuous, requiring section employees to monitor it and make adjustments, institute controls, and channel and redirect quantities of the evolving product at appropriate points. There was overall supervision by trained expatriates. However, the routine work of the section (particularly on the night shift when the expatriate supervisor was only intermittently present) was supervised by indigenous shift supervisors. The responsibility involved in this task was considerable. Failure to monitor and control the process correctly could result in the loss of a complete production batch and thus six hours production for the whole plant. A typical shift labor force in each of these sections would involve a shift supervisor, an assistant, and perhaps a third worker, either a trainee supervisor or an additional laborer.

The product evolving from Production Two was then directed to either Production Three or Four. Section Three's work station was adjacent to that for Section Two. The three workers there were engaged in filling steel containers with units of the finished product. A minor degree of skill was required, but failure to fill the containers properly would be only minimally disruptive of the plant's process.

The work of the fourth production section was organized in terms of a conventional conveyor-belt technology. A normal shift would involve twenty-seven or twenty-eight workers: each shift had an indigenous supervisor and a "boss-boy." An indigenous trainee foreman helped an expatriate to superintend the whole section. Apart from three operators manning the three main machines (and in each shift supposedly tied to that position, although they might, on occasion, hand over the monitoring of the machine to an assistant), the other workers were all more or less interchangeable. There was some tendency for the newest recruits to be assigned tasks at the beginning of the process—opening boxes and loading the conveyors, etc.—and a tendency for some of the more senior shift workers to regard a particular position in the process as "theirs." Despite these tendencies, however, there was considerable movement between positions, both from hour to hour and from week to week. Supervisors and managers rarely, if ever, gave instructions about an individual's work station.

Each of the machine operators was expected to make both routine adjustments to his machine, and also to be able to take short-term measures if there was a breakdown in production. Major repairs, adjustments, and servicing of the machines and conveyors were carried out by a team of fitters and fitter's mates. This task group numbered between two to four workers per shift. Major work was planned for the day shift leaving one or two fitters working on the night shift to deal with contingencies. A senior expatriate tradesman was in charge of the group. Some managerial control of the process was exercised through regular tours of the departments during day shifts, and through occasional visits at night. For the most part, the managers were content to rely on shift supervisors and the trainee foreman to regulate the smooth running of the system. They assessed the performance of these employees the next day or on succeeding days through automatically registered records of product flow and by quality control in the laboratory. The laboratory carried out routine chemical testing of the product at all stages of its route through the plant.

Thus, routine control of the production worker's performance in his technical role was, in large measure, impersonal; it flowed from the arrangement of tasks and their need for constant attention. Expatriate managers would, on occasion, interrupt the normal supervision of a section. If they did so workers recognized that the managers' powers were considerable and the exercise of those powers usually emphatic. Control, however, was largely the province of the impersonal process and the personal but muted control of the indigenous supervisors and the trainee foreman. The ancillary sections, employing some 48 percent of the total indigenous labor force were more closely and personally supervised. This supervision was continuous but kindly for the office workers (who were equalled in their numbers by the expatriate desk workers), and intermittent but less kindly for the truck drivers and "truck-boys" employed in the Distribution Section. With the exception of that section and Workshop One, the ancillary sections employed very small labor forces in physically discrete work stations. They, too, were under close supervision by management.

Managerial Selection, Work Roles, and Role Rewards

In introducing the technical system, I have considered the arrangement of work tasks independent of the way in which individual native workers are recruited and allocated to them. It remains to specify how people were directed to available work roles.

An important variable affecting industrial recruitment is the supply of labor. If labor is in short supply, management may be forced to accept every applicant and thus be unable materially to influence selection. But where there is an abundant labor supply, and assuming that the workers are not organized to oppose management's control of the recruitment procedures, the part that management plays in the selection process is critical because of its power of veto.

My observations, admittedly impressionistic, of workers lining up outside the plant, and my conversations with managers, would suggest that there was never any serious shortage of unskilled and semiskilled applicants. Prospective members of the labor force seemed to be flooding each day into the town from the other districts, judging from the reactions of government departments and the local press (South Pacific Post 14:4.1967; 21.1.1969). Workers with good educational qualifications were somewhat scarcer, but even though the P.M.D. was sometimes unable to recruit people with the optimally desired educational standard there was almost invariably more than one applicant for any job. Management's role in the selection process was thus substantial.

This was the case despite the considerable attribution rate within the labor force. My analysis of employment figures for the year July 1967 thru June 1968 showed that the total annual indigenous employment was 337, and the total of workers who left their employment during that year was 259. Thus the mean monthly departure rate was approximately 21.6. Table 4 shows the total annual employment of indigenes for the period according to the number of months spent in the plant's employment. The majority of workers who left the plant during any period left of their own accord, either preparatory to leaving Port Moresby or, far more likely, to go to other work in the town. At the same time, however, recent arrivals to the town, and workers changing their employment, were also seeking work at the plant. Thus managers were able to dismiss workers without fear of being understaffed.

TABLE 4

LENGTH OF SERVICE (IN MONTHS) OF MEMBERS OF P.M.D.
INDIGENOUS LABOR FORCE
DURING 1967–68 (JULY–JUNE)

months employed	less than 1	1	2	3	4	5	6	7	8	9	10	11	12	Totals
no. of persons	43	48	40	28	23	21	11	12	8	11	8	6	78	337
percent	38.9%			21.4%			9.2%			7.3%			23.2%	100

[A9850]

In a large and technically complex factory like P.M.D., the labor exigencies of the technical system are not completely uniform. The complex technology and size of the unit sets demands on management for varied skills. In a large colonial policy, moreover, there will usually be quite marked cultural heterogeneity which, because of the varied impact of colonization, will result in an unequal distribution of education and manual skills between the regional or geographical sectors of the total population. Thus management, in seeking to serve the needs of the firm, is drawn into recruiting members of each of a number of these sectors.

Table 5 summarizes the range of skills required and gives the occupational distribution of the work force by "region" of origin. The "regions" were formed by grouping administrative districts into broader categories. It shows, for example, that almost one-half of the "white-collar" workers were drawn from the Central District (Central District workers constituted slightly less than 30 percent of the total work force), and that the senior and intermediary grades in the production departments were drawn almost exclusively from three Papuan districts—of these the vast majority were from the Gulf and Central Districts. All but one of the Highlanders were unskilled laborers. I will add that two-thirds of the drivers were from the Central District.

TABLE 5

REGION OF ORIGIN OF P.M.D. INDIGENOUS LABOR FORCE
ACCORDING TO OCCUPATIONAL CLASSIFICATION

	% White Collar	% Skilled and Semiskilled Production	Ancillary	% Unskilled	Total
Gulf	3.8	8.1	2.5	16.9	31.3
Central	6.3	5.0	10.0	8.1	29.4
Northern	–	1.2	3.2	7.5	11.9
Other coastal Papua	0.6	–	–	–	0.6
N.G. coastal	1.2	–	3.2	1.2	5.6
N.G. islands	1.2	–	–	–	1.2
Highlands	–	0.6	–	11.9	12.5
Unknown	–	–	–	7.5	7.5
Total	13.1	33.8		53.1	100.0

[A9853]

It should be emphasized that management does not regard each section as equally vital to the running of the enterprise. Furthermore, within each section some workers are highly valued and some are regarded as completely interchangeable with any unskilled laborer just arrived in town. This differential evaluation by management can be seen in its use of the chief rewards: namely, pay and housing. Managers were all in agreement that the workers in Production Section Four were at the bottom of the hierarchies of valuation and rewards. One manager pointed out that "when we take them off the streets we put them in Production Four." During his employment such a worker would be required merely as an unskilled laborer. Because of this low valuation the manager in charge of the section was not concerned to vet very many of the applicants for work. If he wanted extra "hands" his policy was to take almost anyone who turned up at the factory gates looking fit to work, and those "spoken for" by others already employed. The overwhelming tendency seemed to be for a worker to present the applicant to his superior; few employees were asked to help in finding replacements. As might be expected, Production Four workers were drawn from many regions. The resulting social pattern was complex: groups of kinsmen and relatively "isolated" workers rubbed shoulders.

The machine operators and the two "boss-boys" were unskilled laborers who had "risen from the ranks". One former machine operator had become a trainee shift supervisor in the section. The other shift supervisor and the trainee foreman had been promoted from outside the section. They had caught the eye of management, in part because in their leisure hours they were members of a sporting organization under the patronage of a senior manager. Apart from such cases as this, management usually had no detailed knowledge of a migrant prior to his recruitment. The case just noted, or one where the redundant domestic servant of a European employee was taken into the section, were the exception rather than the rule. For most of the Production Four workers, management would consider such prior knowledge irrelevant: it was not overly concerned with influencing the way in which workers were recruited to the section.

However, with Production One and Two and the task group of Production Four fitters, for example, management would not consider such knowledge at all irrelevant. Whereas most of Production Four workers were engaged in routine manual tasks, workers in other production sections were involved in nonroutine tasks which required them to understand and to carry out instructions given them daily by their European supervisors. And here, management was far more dependent on the quality of its employees.

One of the ways in which management felt it could control the quality of such workers was by requiring formal educational qualifications and perhaps a reference from a recognized organization. Apprentices —those working as Production Four fitters and fitters' mates and those in the workshop—clerks, some storemen, and laboratory workers were all recruited mainly in terms of these criteria. The minimum requirement for a young man straight from school applying for these jobs seemed to be Form I or II. His allocation to a given section was determined by the need to meet the current labor exigencies of the technical process and by management's estimation of the degree to which the applicant would be accepted by his coworkers. Managers were not so much concerned with the welfare of the new recruit as with the willingness of his coworkers to teach him the necessary skills.

Thus apprentices were allocated to either Workshop One or Two or the team of fitters in Production Four. They came from the Northern, Morobe, Central, and Gulf Districts. They were not, however, distributed at random through the sections. Thus Northern District apprentices, together with the one Gulf District apprentice and a Northern District trainee fitter, were allocated to the team of fitters in Production Four led by a Northern District tradesman. The other apprentices were assigned to the workshop. The rationale behind this clustering of Northern District workers was that it would facilitate the emergence of a self-managing task group in which experienced members would teach the less experienced.

We have now dealt with three managerial "decisions" affecting the recruitment process. The first, management's unconcern, is demonstrated by the way in which most of the Production Four workers were recruited. The second, shown in the method of recruitment of clerks, was management's concern with specifying certain minimum educational requirements. The third, shown in the placement of apprentices in Production Four, was management's concern with placing a worker within the social fabric of the plant in such a way that he would assimilate the skills which were particular and often unique to P.M.D. The attempt to reconcile the last two factors, which we might term *educational placement* and *social context placement,* posed a very real problem for P.M.D. management. It is in terms of attempts at such reconciliation that I shall look at the selection process operating in Production One and Two.

From the time of the establishment of the company until just prior to my research all of the nonroutine production work was assigned to European employees. They were assisted by a number of workers having a rudimentary primary education who were mostly from the Gulf District. In the previous two years, however, with the growth of the plant, a changing political climate, and with the example of the worth of one secondary school graduate—who had mastered many of the production skills and had then taught a number of other workers—management had delegated many of the supervisory tasks to indigenes. The firm's policy was to phase out all European employees and staff the plant wholly with indigenes, aside from a few senior European officers. To this end it had tried to involve only Papuans and New Guineans in shift supervision and was making strenuous efforts to recruit qualified indigenous tradesmen rather than European tradesmen. Such efforts ensure not only a lower wages bill for the present but probably also enhance the durability of the enterprise in a changing political climate.

It was in Production One that management had had the greatest success in placing and retaining a number of recruits with superior primary and lower secondary school qualifications. The past and present recruitment policy of the company has meant that Production One workers are socially heterogenous and have shown little section solidarity. Thus management has met with no organized resistance to its attempts to restyle the composition of the section, and this, in turn, has reinforced the heterogeneity. The range of educational achievement was wide: from "no standard reached" to Form II. Only two out of the eleven workers shared a common dialect, and the areas from which they were recruited were distributed along the Papuan coast and its immediate hinterland from Kikori in the Gulf District to Mailu Island in the Central District. At the end of August 1967, six had spent less than a year at the plant, four had spent between one and five years there, and one had spent over ten years.

Management has drawn a different lesson from its experiences with Production Two workers. An attempt there to introduce a young New Guinean was met with a stubborn refusal to teach him anything. Managers explained to me that the section workers were all "Keremas" and had banded together under the oldest worker there, the "line-boss." The great advantage of the "line" was that the older workers taught the younger workers the necessary skills; its great disadvantage was that it closed ranks to protect its members and refused to cooperate with non-"Kerema" workers.

Such a picture greatly oversimplifies the nature of ties between members of the "line," and ignores the fundamental divisions within its ranks, but it does succeed in portraying the quite considerable solidarity in the section. The workers were drawn from a number of areas in the Gulf District from Goaribari, in the Kikori delta, to Seboe, east of the Toaripi peoples, and near the boundary of the Central District. Five of the section workers were from the "Toaripi-speaking" villages in the Moveave and Kukipi areas. With the exception of one man from Goaribari, the others all spoke closely related dialects and were from the same cultural group—Elema. The *lingua franca* of the section was "Toaripi." The educational range was more restricted than that in Production One—from Standard 2 to Standard 6 of primary school. Two of the section's workers had spent less than one year at P.M.D., six had spent from one to five years there, and three had spent eight years or more. The longest serving worker, the so-called "line-boss," had been an employee since 1953.

Management's desire to increase the level of training and education was matched by a desire not to further jeopardize its control of the production process which was clearly threatened by a "line" system. Thus management's attempt to move away from "on the job training" by older workers may have been, in part, because it realized that success in such training would limit its own hegemony. One way in which management had tried to curtail the competing power of Production Two workers was to establish Production Three as a separate task group—its part in the process had previously been carried out by Production Two workers—and man it with "Kairukus." One other way in which management has sought to establish its control of training has been to require many Production Two workers, along with workers from other sections, to attend formal courses of instruction held in the plant. At the same time "Keremas" have been recruited to work in the section independent of the workers already there.

So far I have tried to show how the particular selection process arrived at for any category of indigenous workers will take one of three forms. Two of these forms I have termed educational placement and social context placement. The third "form" is the absence of any sustained interest in selection, or the making of occasional *ad hoc* decisions.

Whether or not management evinces interest in the quality of a section's work force depends on the degree to which it is vital to the total process. Moreover, within any section some workers are regarded as more valuable than others. Thus, I argue that management selects and places recruits for the factory in terms of a set of goals arrived at independent of the recruits. The result can often be that the recruit is engaged in a task with a stranger; on the other hand, he can find himself being allowed to work beside a close kinsman.

Housing and Accommodation

One way in which management rewards skill and formal educational attainment, and sets up further relationships of propinquity, is through the allocation of housing. Some of the plant workers have their own houses, and some, although not owning housing, have access to accommodation other than the plant's. Many, however, are dependent on the company to supply them with basic accommodation. But its housing is in short supply and management is careful to accommodate only those it thinks valuable enough to merit accommodating—both in terms of occupational and racial criteria—or those who have strong claims because of long service.

Three senior officers of the company lived within a half mile radius of the plant. The rest of the married, male, European employees lived side-by-side at Boroko in a set of company-owned flats; the single European men were accommodated within the factory complex; and the female expatriate employees were living with their husbands in other parts of the town. Apart from the European bachelors living within the factory complex (their quarters were within a stone's throw of a small house accommodating four native employees), and a senior officer living near the plant, the expatriate workers and managers lived in residential areas socially separated from those of the indigenous workers. The standard of accommodation was also markedly different.

Two indigenous employees—a fully qualified and experienced tradesman and a trainee sales representative—were doing work similar to that of Europeans and were at essentially the same occupational level. Yet they were housed in very different areas and circumstances than those of their European counterparts. Thus, although occupational differences between expatriate and indigenous employees were important determinants of the company's housing arrangements, in the last analysis these arrangements reflected the prevailing *racial* division of people, resources, and facilities in the town. Within the ranks of the indigenous labor force, however, occupational level, and marital and familial status were all important.

Roughly 62 percent of the plant's indigenous employees were housed in accommodation provided by the company. Each unit of accommodation was within easy walking distance of the factory. Two other long-service, indigenous employees occupied housing commission houses at Hohola and were given help in arranging their purchase by the company.

Sixteen married men, highly valued by the management as senior and key workers, together with their dependents and various lodgers, were housed in recently erected prefabricated houses about five minutes walk from the factory and ten minutes walk from its main housing area. I refer to this housing area as the "New Married Quarters." These houses were small double units with a common parting wall and are constructed from sheet metal. Each single unit, measuring approximately 18 feet by 9 feet, has one partitioned area for eating and general living purposes. The furniture included a table and two chairs, a stretcher and bag mattress, and at one end a wood stove and sink. There were also showering facilities in a small cubicle at this end of the room. A small bedroom led off the main living area and was supplied with stretchers and bag mattresses. Ventilation could be obtained through metal louvers in the wall. The whole area on which the sixteen units were sited was surrounded by a high wire fence.

The main housing area for indigenous employees, however, was near the plant. One unit was an office building which had been vacated and turned into accommodation for relatively valued single workers— clerks and apprentices. These quarters will be referred to as the "Old Office" or "Apprentices' House." Four valued single workers were housed in a small house within the plant complex itself.

Behind the Old Office was a bulk-store. This hid from public gaze the three-storey building known as the "Old Boy-House" which housed most of the employees the plant accommodates. On the ground floor of this large building were six units for married workers and their families. Four of these units were somewhat smaller than the New Married units and were divided by a central partition to provide a sleeping area and a living area. The other two were minute, half the size of the newer units. Floor mats and stretchers were provided, but other than these there was no supply of furniture on a systematic basis.

Facing these six units across a common courtyard was another row of four single-storey units even shabbier and smaller than the six they faced. In the open courtyard between the two rows of units was situated a bank of open, wood-burning hearths for the use of the residents; some, however, purchased their own kerosene stoves and used these inside their houses. I shall refer to the two rows as the "Old Married Quarters." The fourth side of the square formed by the courtyard marked the limit of the plant's property: the third side was occupied by a bank of toilets and showers.

The first and second floor of the large, three-storey building houses single laborers and married laborers unaccompanied by their wives (hereafter referred to simply as "bachelors"). For convenience I will restrict my use of "Old Boy-House" to these quarters. On the second floor, part of one of these lines of beds had been partitioned off into small cubicles. At the end of the first floor was another partitioned area which created a separate room accommodating, officially, six workers. Unskilled workers were at the bottom of the company's scale of priorities. After a few months in P.M.D. employment, they might merit accommodation in the Old Boy-House, but until they had acquired some skill of value to management they had no chance of obtaining married quarters. If they were accompanied by their wives and families (as were some from the Gulf District), they had to find their own housing in the settlements, villages, and suburbs of the town. Several workers already owned family accommodation before joining the plant. Some workers built, or inherited, houses in urban villages such as Tatana and Pari. Others have found accommodation, or built their own, in the settlements of Moresby; for example, Taikone, Gorobe, and the Badili canoe settlement. Yet others have found accommodation in the "boy-houses" of the town or in other companies' compounds.

But it was not just a case of other employers supplementing the plant's accommodation. The plant reciprocated, although in part unknowingly, by housing other companies' employees as well as a partially stable and partially highly transient group of "passengers." In some residential units, particularly at weekends, the number of unofficial residents could be as much as 100 percent over and above the number of official residents.

Table 6 gives a breakdown of the labor force by housing arrangements.

TABLE 6

HOUSING ARRANGEMENTS OF INDIGENOUS MEMBERS OF P.M.D.
LABOR FORCE

P.M.D. quarters and compounds	100
Other organizations and individual's quarters and compounds	13
Domestic servants' quarters in European areas	9
Settlements	17
Villages	5
Papuan Suburbs	8
Unknown	8
	160

[A9855]

I have now shown how management recruited its employees independent of many of their own goals and aspirations. By interpreting the short-term and long-term needs of the firm, management recruited and allocated workers to tasks and rewarded them by the allocation of contrasted housing. Together, work section membership and compound residence entailed a series of spatial arrangements which an analysis of social relationships between employees must take into account. This is because relationships of propinquity on the job and in the compounds could structure many of the costs and benefits involved in interactions between employees.

Operating, then, within the broader constraints of the racial structure of the town (and within terms of marital and familial criteria), the technical system and its division of labor gave rise to a spatial pattern. But the social organization of the plant and its compounds was not solely a product of human geography. At times the spatial distribution of the work force determined the context within which social behavior took place and thus acted as a catalyst for new friendships and enmities. At other times it acted not as a determinant but solely as an index to ongoing patterns of social behavior which were largely independent of the field of relationships set up by the industrial organization. Whereas the *spatial* pattern of plant and compound life served as a context or as an index to social action, the *symbiotic* and the fully *cultural* aspects of that behavior were determined by underlying relationships of competition and cooperation, and by the workers shared perceptions and evaluations of the relationships in which they were individually involved.

The effect of the spatial pattern on the social life of neighbors and the manner in which the spatial arrangements are modified by the feedback of the symbiotic aspects of living and the residents' continuing rural commitments are major themes of the following chapter. There I will consider a set of young workers as neighbors, migrants, employees, and residents of a racially divided town, referring their behavior continually to the developing domestic organization of their quarters. The events are offered as "a limited area of transparency on the otherwise opaque surface of regular, uneventful social life" (Turner 1957:93) and to show the force of sub-social interdependence.

3

Spatial Pattern, Symbiosis and Cultural Adaptations: An Extended Case Study

The French custom is to ignore people whose names, occupations and rank are unknown. But in the little restaurant, such people find themselves in a quite close relationship for one to one-and-a-half hours, and temporarily united by a similar pre-occupation. A conflict exists, not very keen to be sure, but real enough and sufficient to create a state of tension between the norm of privacy and the fact of community. They feel both alone and together, compelled to the usual reserve between strangers, while their respective spatial positions, and their relationships to the objects and utensils of the meal, suggest, and to a certain extent call for, intimacy.   [Lévi-Strauss 1969:59]

The spatial pattern which we examined in the last chapter served as an index of ongoing social relationships. Thus the segregation of the racial groups at the plant into two housing classes reflected the segregation of housing facilities in the town. Again, and within the broader limits set by the racial division, the spatial distribution of native employees within the plant and within the compounds was related to the

45

technical system and to the prevailing division of labor. Moreover, the spatial arrangement of the native labor force set up relationships of propinquity which may act as catalysts for new relationships of intimacy and distance.

But a division of labor also gives rise to relationships of competition and dependence. In a factory, individuals work together and, in doing so, frequently have to cooperate with others to complete the tasks set by their work roles. Failure to do so could lead to dismissal and to the loss of pay and housing. But absolute cooperation is almost impossible: the resources of the concern are likely to lead to competition. Workers may both compete with each other, for promotion, housing, space, and privacy, and with management, the final arbiter of the material rewards paid for the completion of technical tasks. Thus, to use Park's term (1939), the division of labor sets up relationships of subsocial *symbiosis* between workers and between individual workers and managers. The interests of members of the work force are opposed and they are therefore in competition. This competition, however, takes place within a framework of dependence flowing from the fact that their very diversity has been linked by the functional specialization of tasks and is mutually supporting.

Durkheim has argued, however, that the division of labor is a truly *social* phenomenon. Chastising Spencer, he pointed out that it should not be regarded as merely an impersonal process between individuals who regard each other as utilities, but that it involves elements of prior agreement and custom. This is so even for the contract, perhaps the urban-industrial society's most impersonal aspect (Durkheim 1933: Chap. 7).

To opt for either of these two theorists' standpoints on purely *a priori* grounds would be ill-advised and would obscure the developmental aspect of consensus and custom. The issue between them is largely empirical and one of degree. The attempt to use both perspectives and to relate the ecological to the truly cultural is a wiser procedure.

This account will consider a set of associations in a company compound which had, initially, a distinctly subsocial character. The young men who figure in the discussion were, with a single exception, strangers to each other before starting work at the plant and taking up residence in its quarters. These young men were all residents of the Old Office, a set of quarters set aside for apprentices and other unmarried, but valued, employees. At least initially, they were involved with each other in a purely spatial sense and through the sharing of facilities. The focus of my analysis is the way in which instances of social conflict and fellow-feeling arose from this impersonal base. For the seven months of my closest contact with this plant's work force, the Old Office served as my home. This chapter, then, is also devoted to my immediate neighbors.

THE OLD OFFICE RESIDENTS

Bounded on its southern, eastern, and western sides by a yard—used by occupants of the Boy-House and Old Married units on their way to their quarters, and by forklift trucks and lorries on their way to and from the bulk store at the rear—the Old Office faced, on its northern side, one of the town's major, arterial roads. The Old Office was a low, single-story building divided into seven sections: four independent bedrooms, a bathroom, kitchen, and residential area used both as a dining area and a bedroom. Originally an office, it had been converted into quarters for bachelors who merited accommodation superior to that in the Old Boy-House. The layout of the Old Office is given in Figure 1.

The "senior" inhabitant was Vincent, who had come from a village in the Tufi area of the Northern District of Papua. Educated at schools in the Northern District and at Idubada Technical College, just outside the official Port Moresby boundary, Vincent had joined the plant at the beginning of 1963 as an apprentice. He had been encouraged to do so by Humphrey, another Idubada Technical graduate who, at the time of my study, was P.M.D.'s only qualified indigenous tradesman, and second in command of the group of Production Four fitters. While still apprentices, these two young men lived together in the Old Office, and were firm friends. When his friend married and moved into other company accommodations, however, Vincent retained their joint room for his own use. He did so throughout the events I recount in this chapter.

Opposite him, in Room B, was John, a clerk from a Roro-speaking village in the Central District. Highly valued by management, and initially an assistant to the European wages clerk, John eventually became wages clerk on the termination of his supervisor's contract. He had joined the Territory's Public Service after leaving school and had trained to be an agricultural officer at the Popondetta Agricultural College. He left before completing his course and joined the Department of Public Works as a clerk at their head office in Port Moresby. Tiring of that, he joined P.M.D. (after working for another manufacturing company in Badili for a week) where he had been since October 1966. He was the only one of the Old Office residents who had mar-

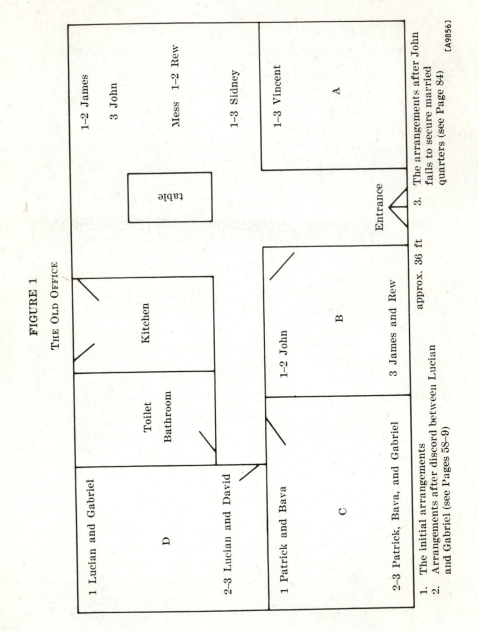

FIGURE 1

THE OLD OFFICE

1. The initial arrangements
2. Arrangements after discord between Lucian and Gabriel (see Pages 58–9)
3. The arrangements after John fails to secure married quarters (see Page 84)

approx. 36 ft

[A9856]

D — 1 Lucian and Gabriel

2–3 Lucian and David

Toilet Bathroom

Kitchen

1–2 James

3 John

Mess 1–2 Rew

table

1–3 Sidney

1–3 Vincent

A

Entrance

C — 1 Patrick and Bava / 2–3 Patrick, Bava, and Gabriel

B — 1–2 John / 3 James and Rew

ried: his wife, from the same village as himself, was living with his parents in their home village.

On my arrival at the beginning of May 1967, the occupants of Room C were Patrick and Bava, two young Papuan production workers, the first a supervisor in Production One, the second a supervisor in Production Two. Patrick was from a Roro-speaking village in the Central District of Papua, like John, but they spoke slightly different dialects. On leaving a local mission school he worked as an assistant in a trade store at Bereina, the administrative headquarters of his home sub-district. Tiring of rural life and a rural level of wages—$4 per week—he had, in his own words, "run away" from the storekeeper with another young man from his village and came to Moresby on a canoe bringing produce to sell at Koke. He had come straight to P.M.D. to find work. That was in June 1965. He had moved into the Old Office with Bava, his roommate, in the few months immediately prior to my arrival. Both young men were vital to the production process and management wanted them near at hand. Management's wish was made evident when on several occasions one or the other of these two young men failed to report for work after heavy drinking the night before. When they did not appear, a European manager would walk over to the Old Office and pound on the door until someone let him in and until the absentee assured him that he was on his way.

Bava was from a village at the far eastern end of the Gulf District; east that is, of Kukipu. He arrived in Port Moresby almost immediately after leaving school and completing Standard Six, and had been recommended to P.M.D. by his mother's brother, a senior clerk and nontechnical assistant to the European in charge of Production Two. That was in March 1966, and Bava had since risen to the position of shift supervisor.

Five weeks after my arrival, Gabriel, a junior apprentice attached to Workshop One, joined Patrick and Bava in Room C. Gabriel's home village is one of the Mekeo group of villages which are adjacent to the Roro-speaking group to which John and Patrick's villages belong. Both the Mekeo-speaking and the Roro-speaking villages are administratively part of the Kairuku subdistrict. A resident of the Old Office since the commencement of his employment with P.M.D. in January of that year, Gabriel had originally shared Room D with Lucian, another junior apprentice, also employed in Workshop One and a resident of the Old Office since joining P.M.D. in March 1966.

Lucian, who remained in Room D, was from the Morobe District of New Guinea. He had joined the plant after attending Lae Technical College, his last school. He had spent all his life in his home district, either in his natal village in the Mumeng area, at Bulolo where his father worked as a gold miner, or at boarding schools in Finschhafen and Lae. On Gabriel's departure, Lucian was joined in Room D by David, a fellow-Morobe, but from a village in the Markham Valley area. David, the son of a policeman, had spent a number of his school years at Goroka in the Eastern Highlands District of New Guinea and had been educated at Goroka High School and Idubada Technical College. He had joined P.M.D. in January 1967. Before moving to Room D with Lucian in the middle of June, he had lived with relatives in the town.

Other than myself, there were initially two residents sleeping in the messing area. These were James, also a Mekeo-speaker and from the same village as Gabriel, and Sidney, a Tolai, from the Gazelle Peninsula of New Britain. Both had joined the plant as clerks at the beginning of February. On joining the company, they were jointly allocated a small unit in the Old Married Quarters, whereupon they both threatened to resign, stating that as clerks and "educated people" they deserved more than the dingy box they were offered. Management then decided to ignore its own previous restriction on the use of the messing area, moved in two stretchers, and allotted them to Sidney and James. Both James and Sidney were high school graduates with Form III education: James had finished his schooling at Sogeri High School, some twenty-five miles from Port Moresby, while Sidney had completed his at Keravat High School on the Gazelle Peninsula. Initially, James worked in the main office, and Sidney in the dispatch office where he was under John's supervision. Later, Sidney was moved to the Main Office, where he worked beside James.

All of these young men were in their late teens or early twenties John was perhaps the eldest at nearly twenty-four years of age. Information on age and certain other characteristics is given in Table 7.

These nine, plus myself and two more ephemeral employees, were the official residents of the Old Office. But the quarters also supported a supplementary population which, although unstable and shifting, occasionally outnumbered those officially resident. Despite the instability of their residence, and in part because of it, these additional occupants had an important part to play in the social organization of the quarters

TABLE 7

RESIDENTS OF THE OLD OFFICE

Room	Name	Month Joined Company	Work Section	Occupation	Sub-District of Origin	District	Education	Age and Marital Status	Weekly Wage*
A	Vincent	Jan 1963	Prod. 4	Apprentice	Tufi	Northern	FII	22(S)	12.00
B	John	Oct 1966	Dispatch Office	Clerk	Kairuku	Central	FII	23(M)	14.00
C	Patrick	June 1965	Prod. 1	Prod. Super.	Kairuku	Central	Std 5	22(S)	13.00
C	Bava	Mar 1966	Prod. 2	Prod. Super.	Kukipi	Gulf	Std 6	20(S)	12.00
D & C	Gabriel	Jan 1967	Workshop 1	Apprentice	Kairuku	Central	FII	17(S)	6.50
D	Lucian	Mar 1966	Workshop 1	Apprentice	Mumeng	Morobe	FII	18(S)	8.00
D	David	Jan 1967	Workshop 1	Apprentice	Kaiapit	Morobe	FIII	18(S)	6.50
MESS	Sidney	Feb 1967	Dispatch & Main Office	Clerk	Rabaul	N. Britain	FIII	19(S)	8.00
MESS & B	James	Feb 1967	Main Office	Clerk	Kairuku	Central	FIII	22(S)	11.00

* These figures show standard levels of earnings at the start of research. Apprentices' earnings were stipulated by the Apprenticeship Ordinance and rose in limited yearly increments. The wages of the other workers rose steadily throughout the research; moreover, they could earn, on occasion, as much as 25 percent above their basic wage through overtime.

[A9796]

and in the adjustments and adaptations to the fact of community engendered by proximity and the sharing of facilities. But because they served as a supporting cast, their roles will be discussed in terms of the relationships of the official residents, who were the principal actors of the piece, rather than in their own right.

Since these young men were my neighbors something of my own position and introduction must be sketched in.

Between my first approach to the company and my arrival to take up residence in the compound, members of management had decided that the Old Office would be the most appropriate location for me. It involved no obvious intrusion into an established conjugal household and was much cleaner and "safer" than the barracks. It had also been decided to facilitate my introduction by recruiting a resident to act as a sponsor. This was James; of all the residents he had the easiest manner with Europeans. James' sponsorship was invaluable: he was able to prepare the other occupants for my arrival and quiet many of their anxieties about my motives and activities. But, although my introduction to the quarters was accomplished apparently without any major misgivings (the major concession to my arrival was the provision of a plastic tablecloth), I found the character of relationships I observed extremely unsettling.

Domestic Squalor and Strife

After the excitement and initial curiosity which greeted my appearance I was struck by the marked reserve and anonymity which characterized most of the encounters between the residents. I feared that my presence had dampened spirits and heightened anxieties. No doubt the personal reserve and timidity of certain of the younger residents was responsible in part, but after a few weeks I was left with the distinct impression that the key factor was a carefully maintained lack of interest in the other residents and their activities. Well-maintained distance and reserve overlaid with a veneer of muted companionship described my overall sense of the situation until the beginning of June. At that stage I became aware of an undercurrent of tension between certain of the residents which quickly flared into public grievance and hostility. A major part of that tension centered around the occupants of Room D.

It will be remembered that at the time of my arrival Gabriel and Lucian shared Room D. To the management it seemed an obvious match: two lads in their teens, both apprentices in the metal trades, employed on similar tasks in Workshop One and graduates of secondary technical institutions. Neither of them, however, perceived these shared characteristics as an important aspect of their association: their differences were much too apparent. A small and dumpy youth, Lucian was rather timid but had a capacity for warmth and friendliness once his fears were allayed. By contrast, Gabriel was tall and well-built for his age and disposed both to boisterousness and to a taciturn and challenging withdrawal. In addition to the differences in personality were differences in cultural loyalty and identity. The Papua/New Guinea distinction has a very real emotional significance for most Port Moresby residents. Gabriel and Lucian (Papuan and New Guinean, respectively) were able to express and to maintain their differences through their separate identifications with this opposition.

The immediate issue which led to open hostility was the introduction to Room D of three young men from Gabriel's home village. One of them was working in the town but was currently without accommodation, another was unemployed. Both of these had asked Gabriel and James to give them lodgings. The other unofficial resident was a young boy who was attending school at Hanuabada and who, as well as being Gabriel's fellow villager, was James' patrilateral parallel cousin. This young boy, whose name was Aite, was in town to complete his education in an urban school and was living in the Old Office as James' dependent. But as James was sleeping in the messing area, which was open to even the most casual visitor to the quarters, and as Aite was there unofficially, James arranged with Gabriel that Aite should sleep on the floor in Room D. The other two lodgers were much less dependent on James' sponsorship but similar considerations applied in their case as well.

Whatever form Lucian's initial misgivings took, the chatter, extra noise, and untidiness of the three new Mekeo occupants did nothing to assuage them. After some weeks of mild complaint, silent suffering, and irritation Lucian reported the incursion to a senior manager complaining that he could not study and could not sleep because of their presence. During this interview management learned that the other rooms also harbored unofficial guests, and there followed a general purge of "passengers." (This was not at all effective, apart from

Room D itself.) Later in the same week David moved into Room D and Gabriel into Room C.

This realignment ameliorated Lucian's problems. It also short-circuited any problems David may have faced had the residential pattern remained unchanged and had he been put into the same room as Patrick and Bava. It failed, however, to resolve the points of contention: the fact of community jarred with the desire of the residents to prevent excessive intrusions and violations of their personal space and property.

The periodic disappearance of unused portions of food from the refrigerator and provisions from the residents' private cupboards in the kitchen was a frequent source of resentment and tension. Vincent and the three New Guinean residents—Lucian, David, and Sidney—were the most frequently aggrieved on this score. They grumbled to each other and to me but felt they could do little to stop the thefts or find and punish the miscreants. Not even the purchase and fitting of padlocks was able to stop the thieving completely. On one occasion Vincent's padlock and staple were unscrewed, a tin of bully beef taken and the fixture replaced.

Another source of dispute was the squalor of the public areas: particularly, the kitchen and the bathroom toilet. Coagulated rice water flooding the gas stove and its burners, unwashed pans littering the sink, and betel nut husks and filth in the bathroom toilet were the specific items most frequently discussed. But the general litter and the stained and dirty floors served as an equally convenient and most easily articulated source of discontent.

Each of the residents played a slightly different part in the household strife and differed in their reactions to the underlying tension. Certain residents tended to foster it by growls and half-heard grumbling, and others just shrugged their shoulders. John did not hesitate to take people to task in a schoolmasterly fashion. Moreover, residents differed in the way they allocated blame. Vincent seemed to accept the situation philosophically and tended to blame no one; the three New Guineans muttered that the Papuans, and in particular the "Mekeos," were responsible, often singling out James' flood of visitors and his dependents as a prime cause of noise and disturbance; James grumbled half-heartedly at the New Guineans for not taking part in cleaning up, something which he occasionally goaded the younger Mekeo boys into undertaking with his help; Gabriel remained mute in the face of James' and John's criticism; and John himself tended to point his finger publicly at all untutored youth. Only Patrick and Bava seemed unaware of the disarray and unconcerned by requests for their help in cleaning up.

John also posted written notices in the messing area and on the bathroom door drawing residents' attention to their duty. Typical were: "This is a dirty house. Don't throw down your rubbish. YES, YOU", and "I have just washed the toilet and shower. Why don't you?" Signed John A". He used the same technique to try to keep the noise level down, posting notices up on his own door asking for quiet, consideration, no interruptions.

These tensions continued unabated throughout the period of my research, taking the form of occasional bickering, calls from John and James for cleanliness and cooperation, grumbling to third parties, and strained silences. Perhaps the most overt expression of the discontent and tensions came from a young New Guinean salesman trainee who made a brief appearance in the quarters. Recruited from Lae, he had come to Moresby for a period of initial training and was to return to Lae after completion of his training. After a week of living in the Old Office he left to take up more expensive quarters in a nearby hostel. As he did so he made no secret of the fact that he was leaving because of the squalid conditions in the house. But, after Lucian's formal complaint, no recourse was had to management. The state of the quarters continued to bring forth criticism from certain managers but most of this was applied indirectly through James, with whom officers of the company were in close contact through their work in the main office. Management was content to leave its intervention at this level, however, and to allow the residents to muddle through.

The cause of this domestic strife was a compound of many factors, including the ecology of the Old Office, clashes of personality, claims to leadership, attitudes towards authority and to Europeans, and broader self-conceptions. But the common elements were the ecological arrangements and the residents' low level of involvement in each other's concerns.

The physical conditions of the house were much superior to the company's other accommodation for single employees. But, although it was superior, it was not radically different in either conception or style.

In common with perhaps all other compound residents in the town the occupants of the Old Office, who had been thrown together by the vagaries of employment, were living cheek by jowl, competing for space and facilities, and trying to ensure a modicum of privacy in order to pursue their individual interests and activities. Both the official and unofficial occupants were sparring, whether overtly or covertly, for the same cooking, showering, toilet, and washing facilities. And not only was there a simple competition for common facilities; all residents were equally dependent on the cleanliness of the others and their guests. Thus community was a fact even for Vincent and John, the occupants of the two single rooms. They could retire behind their own doors for much of the time but were similarly affected by untidiness.

The ecology of the quarters involved the residents and their guests, then, in a web of dependence and competition. Thus the subsocial aspect of their living arrangements would, I argue, have been productive of strain and tension whatever the dispositions and sociocultural characteristics of those involved. But while this aspect of the residents' association provided a necessary background to the incidents, it was not a sufficient condition for the emergence of strife, nor does it explain the degree and the kind of strife which was experienced.

I have argued in the previous chapter that proximity may easily lead to other forms of association, and that these may include both relationships of intimacy and those of hostility. Similarly, we can see that proximity and the sharing of facilities in the Old Office might set the scene for both communal organization and solidarity as well as auguring strife and dissension. What was it then that led to the degree and the kind of strife experienced in the Old Office? And what was it that prevented the residents' realization of the fact of their community and organization of their activities so as to minimize conflict?

A major factor militating against the development of any form of communal organization was the residents' low level of involvement in each other's major activities. We have seen that each of the principal residents had been recruited independent of one another and, in most cases, without the advice or encouragement of other employees. Indeed, with the exception of James and Gabriel, the fellow villagers, none of the residents had any knowledge of their fellow occupants prior to employment with the company and residence in the quarters. This meant that on their arrival in the house, residents were thrown down among complete strangers. In some cases this initial strangeness continued throughout their sojourn.

There were certain relationships, however, which ran counter to this general pattern. Thus Bava and David had been acquainted with Old Office inhabitants while working at the plant and these acquaintance-ships had played a part in the subsequent residence arrangements and had led, eventually, to closer friendships. But, despite these exceptions, the overall quality of the house's social organization was that of an en-counter between strangers. This was due to the lack of common activi-ty and mutual obligation. Thus, even though certain of the residents could claim personal relationships with each other, these relationships were nonetheless at a low level and stopped short of major obligation or of common activity beyond the confines of the house. For the remain-ing residents, moreover, the lack of interpersonal knowledge and com-mitment was complete. It involved not only a lack of obligation and mutual involvement in major activities but a lack of day-to-day com-panionship as well. Rather than enabling these young men to disguise the competition of the symbiotic order by agreed communal action, their strangeness and lack of common commitment could only heighten it and translate it into overt conflict.

Despite the occupants' essential strangeness to each other, however, the social organization of the Old Office was not simply an accumula-tion of spatial juxtapositions. Indeed, the residents' very strangeness appeared to lead to a norm of privacy; a tacit understanding that resi-dents were entitled to privacy in order to pursue activities in which the others had no part and to entertain guests of whom the other residents knew little, if anything. Despite the provision of a central messing area and a table and chairs, residents preferred to retire to their rooms or to eat standing up in the kitchen rather than intrude on a half-full table where others were eating. This withdrawal to privacy became even more pronounced when the guests of other residents were present.

While the web of dependence and the norm of privacy led to a com-mon context for action, and while these factors help to explain why collective attempts to regulate domestic affairs did not develop, they do not account for the way in which individuals reacted to and conceptual-ized their situation. Thus, while certain residents reacted to the situa-tion by allocating blame, others did not. In some cases coresidence act-ed as a spur to companionship, but in others it led to further estrange-ment from fellow residents and their concerns.

To an extent these individual reactions were a function of personality. We have already noted the contrast in the personalities of Gabriel and Lucian and have seen that it contributed to their clash. But, even though in some cases the personality component of the relationship was clearly important, almost all the reactions and adjustments reflected social commitments and conflicts and were in turn expressed in culturally standardized ways. Thus Gabriel's and Lucian's clash was widely acknowledged to be a "Papua" versus "New Guinea" affair, and although Lucian himself attributed the primary cause of his irritation to the intrusion and chatter of unwelcome lodgers. Even though these factors may not have been the "real" cause of the dispute, they were nonetheless the ways the antagonists chose to conceptualize them. In this way they could justify and secure approval for their actions.

While there were important social themes in the individual adjustments to coresidence, these adjustments were not solely a function of the residents' involvement in the social web of the Old Office. They owed much to individual self-conceptions and to the residents' positions as migrants in a racially and ethnically divided town. To examine the interrelationship of ecology, low mutual involvement, and the various factors underlying individual adjustment for each of the principal residents would be impossible within the limits of this volume. Nor is it necessary. While certain events or attitudes were unique, others were more widely distributed, falling into broader themes or patterns. Thus it is possible to convey the sense of many of the reactions by describing one in detail and by merely suggesting the others.

Let me then turn to a detailed examination of the careers, commitments, enmities, and self-conceptions of the two fellow villagers, James and Gabriel. The wisdom of choosing these two rather than any other combination of residents is that their reactions to the conflicts fell at the broad extremes of a series of continua along which the reactions of the other residents could be ranked. Thus James' background and ties led to his almost complete withdrawal from the quarters, broken on occasion by criticism and forays into the ongoing activities when he was more than usually aggrieved at the disarray. By contrast, Gabriel was much less involved in ongoing rural or town-based relationships and activities. In time he developed closer and closer relationships with Patrick and Bava, the original occupants of Room C, until he spent most of his leisure time in their company and that of the younger Mekeos, the unofficial residents in that room. These were two contrasted modes of adjustment to the common situation. In addition, James and Gabriel differed radically in their personal styles and in their attitudes toward the racial division of the town. At the same time both James and Gabriel were closely involved in the strife in a way that Vincent, for example, was not. Thus in analyzing their own contributions and reactions to the disturbances and the way in which the other residents ascribed blame to them, we will come close to an understanding of the conflicting allegiances in the developing social character of the house.

Moreover, an analysis of their relationship to each other constitutes the severest test of my assertion of the overall low level of mutual involvement. These two young men were compatriots, acknowledging a diffuse sense of brotherhood, and had known each other's names, demeanors and affiliations before taking up residence and employment with the company. Thus, whereas the relationships between the other residents could be described, at least initially, as fully impersonal, the relationship between James and Gabriel could not. But although their relationship was exceptional and while they got along with each other they were never close. The fact that they were compatriots and were mutually involved in a web of village based ties and obligations set them apart as much as it united them: their primary allegiances were to different village sections and they were each involved in different networks of friends and kin. Thus, while they had a personal knowledge of each other and were to some extent involved in common activities and mutual obligations, they were far from united in their actions in the town or in the house. The same sense of social distance which characterized the encounters between the other residents also characterized their own encounters, although in their case it arose from different causes.

Let us now consider these two young men's careers and ties and examine the effect of these on the social organization of the Old Office.

James and Gabriel: Fellow Villagers, Fellow Residents

Although they were from the same village and even the same clan, James and Gabriel were from different "families," as they chose to describe units which would appear to be their immediate, personal kindreds, but which they often conceptualized as clan sections. Both of them were members of "X" clan (one of the three in the village), but whereas James was a member by birth, Gabriel was a member by adoption and by virtue of his mother's affiliation. By birth (that is, by patrifiliation), Gabriel was a member of another clan in an adjacent village. Their membership was not only distinguished according to their mode of recruitment to the clan, but also in terms of their primary affiliation within it. The "X" clan was divided into two sections, the senior and the junior. James was a member of the senior section and Gabriel was a member of the junior section. Each of these sections had its hereditary leader. Moreover, despite their membership in the same small, locally-resident clan, James and Gabriel had rather dissimilar school and work histories and were recruited to the P.M.D. labor force quite independently of each other.

James was about twenty-two or twenty-three years of age—some four or five years older than Gabriel. When he was about nine years old, James had left his village to go to mission boarding school on Yule Island. After two years there he was told that his schooling must end since he was not making sufficient progress to allow him to continue. Not content with his teachers' verdict, he came to Moresby and, after putting himself into the hands of the educational authorities, he was sent to a recently opened administration school in the Rigo Sub-District. After two years at Rigo he was sent to Sogeri High School where he completed his secondary education at the Territory Intermediate or Form III level, in 1965.

Upon leaving Sogeri, he applied to the Commonwealth Department of Works in Port Moresby and was appointed as a clerical assistant. A few months later he applied, from within the department and with the encouragement of a European clerk, for a position as a cadet hydrographer. He was accepted, and spent 1966 working in the hydrography section of the department both at the Port Moresby headquarters and camping and patrolling in the mountain areas of the Central District. Because of difficulties encountered with his studies and with supervisors, and after failing to return from leave on time, he was dismissed. Thus after one and a half years at "Comworks" he was out of a job. After seeing an advertisement in the local paper for clerks at P.M.D., he had applied and was accepted. When I arrived at the beginning of May, he had been working there for just three months.

In those months James had developed a few acquaintanceships with workmates, with people he had met in the course of his daily work routines, and with other residents of the Old Office. But his really important relationships—in terms of the effort he devoted to them—were with people he had known before joining the company. These relationships revolved around two major organized activities: namely, a sports club and an association of village people who had formed a business group.

The sports club grew out of discussions held in 1965 between Mekeo migrants working and living in Port Moresby. The expressly stated purpose at that time was to form a rugby football team to play on the oval at Bereina—the administrative headquarters of the sub-district —particularly at Christmas time when many of the young men went home on leave. The central figure in the preliminary discussions was a Mekeo who, at that time, was studying at the Administrative College in Port Moresby to become a local court magistrate. A meeting was called at Ela Beach to discuss the formation of the club, and he was elected as its first president. It was agreed that a team would be formed to play against *Huria,* a team made up of Mekeo and Roro people who were working in Lae. But for the accident of labor histories, which brought the *Huria* team together in Lae (a town in New Guinea), the match was purely a domestic affair. Nonetheless, some wag, with a hint of dry amusement, had listed it as a "Papua" versus "New Guinea" match.

In 1966 the European-dominated Papuan Rugby League Association decided to promote a Junior League, with both "Open" and "Under Twenties" sections.[1] The embryonic *Mekeo Sports Club*, having successfully organized its first match against *Huria* at Bereina, was approached by the association and it was agreed that a Mekeo team would take part in the competition to be arranged for the ensuing season. The first president, who by now had completed his course at the Administrative College and was attached to the town's sub-district office and court, recruited a senior member of the Port Moresby sub-district administration—a European—as patron of the club. This gentleman bought specially ordered sports shirts as his gift as patron. A well-known (largely European) club—Paga—supplied two coaches for the side. At the same time there was a recruitment drive for players, and several Mekeos, who had until then been playing Australian Rules football, ceased playing in order to join the new club. Both an "Open"

[1] Albert Maori Kiki reports in his autobiography that he had written to the Papuan Rugby League after returning from Fiji (in 1957) urging the president to throw the club open to Papuans and New Guineans and that this was "flatly refused." As a result he formed the Rugby Union Association (Kiki 1968:101).

and an "Under Twenties" team were eventually fielded, although to be able to do so meant drawing on the services of marginally-Mekeo and non-Mekeo players. Three "Bush Mekeos," four "Aromas," and six "Wanigelas" were recruited to bring the team up to strength and to ensure a modicum of experience in the side.[2] The three Bush Mekeos were already known; one of them, for example, had worked with Peter, the second Mekeo Sports Club president. The "Aromas" and "Wanigelas" (who were otherwise known as "Marshall Lagoon" people) came from an area to the east of Port Moresby and were introduced to the club through the offices of a Mekeo man, from Inawai'a, who was employed as a domestic servant in the town area and was married to a "Wanigela" woman. The Under Twenties team played under something of a misnomer: it was a second team made up of those players not good enough to make the first team but who, if they were not actually under twenty years of age, were reasonably likely to escape notice because of youthful features or small stature. James, although over twenty years of age, was a regular player and vice-captain of the second team.

Apart from the non-Mekeo and marginally-Mekeo recruits, the club drew its supporters from a wide range of Mekeo villages, but with a heavy predominance of young men from Inawai'a, the major village in eastern Mekeo, and a lesser predominance of people from Beipa'a, the major village in central Mekeo. Moreover, for much of the time, the president, captain, and vice-captain of the first team were all from Inawai'a. Some of the smaller villages—for example, Jesu Baibua and Oriropetana—did not seem to be represented at all. Inawabui and Bebeo, two other small villages, contributed one member each.

Despite the inexperience of its players, the club did extremely well in its first full season, reaching the semifinals for the Open section. It was eventually beaten by a more experienced Marshall Lagoon side

---

[2] The Mekeo area is divided into an "eastern" part and a "central" part by the St. Joseph's or Angapanga River. These two parts are sometimes referred to as the Inawai'a and Beipa'a clusters of villages, respectively. A third division, the "Bush Mekeo," is to be found to the northwest. The "Bush Mekeo" speak a different dialect than either of the other divisions and inhabit the middle reaches of the Biaru River. Seligman describes them as "an ethnographical annexe to Mekeo" (Seligman 1910:311). Their culture would seem to be basically Mekeo but they also resemble eastern Elema groups in their river habitat. I was told that a number of their villages—the most important ones seem to be Babongo, Piunga, Maipa, and Apainaipi—had long histories of trading and intermarriage with the eastern Elema.

and was denied the chance to appear in the finals.[3] But throughout the season hopes and enthusiasms were running high and despite occasional criticism of the president's and captain's selection, and the continuing problem of exacting subscriptions and financial support from certain members, the new venture ran very smoothly.

One of the perceived results of the formation and early success of the club was that it became a focus for the young Mekeo town dwellers. I was told on several occasions that previously, young Mekeos in the town had formed small pockets of kin and friends who met together only briefly, if at all. I was given to understand that Mekeos were a "no-good people" and that they were always quarreling. "Bad things were said" and these drove them into small mutually-suspicious groups. But the "MSC"—as the club was often known—had given them the opportunity to meet regularly and given them a collective solidarity they had never previously experienced.

Whatever the truth and extent of the supposed changed quality of social relationships among young Mekeo men in the town, the activities of the club, and his membership in it, did have certain implications for James and the way he spent his leisure time. Moreover, it became a focus for his leisure activities over and above the time he actually spent playing rugby or practicing. James' close matrilateral relationship with many of the more important players, and the strategic location of the Old Office, meant that James and his quarters become major attractions for players and supporters.

The first president of the club was transferred to Madang during 1967 and there was general agreement that Peter, an ex-apprentice, who had recently qualified as a carpenter, and working for a private construction company at Four Mile, was the obvious choice as the first president's successor. Peter, who was elected unopposed, was, according to genealogical reckoning, James' matrilateral cross-cousin. Both were in their early twenties and Peter was two or three years older than James. However, the discrepancy in genealogical generations was ignored or forgotten: in English they described themselves as "cousin-brothers." Peter was a regular visitor to the Old Office, often spending most of the weekend there, and bringing with them other members

3 The "Aromas," "Wanigelas" or "Marshall Lagoon" people on the Mekeo Sports Club team were surplus to their home area team's requirements and were, moreover, rumored to have quarreled with the Marshall Lagoon Club players.

and supporters of the MSC teams. Thus, during the rugby season, every Saturday a number of Mekeo visitors, after eating with James, would travel with him to Boroko oval for the game. After the game the same group, would be augmented perhaps by other players and supporters or reduced by one or two who had other arrangements to keep. Sunday would again bring an influx of visitors who had come from Mass at St. Theresa's Catholic Church in Badili. Often they would stay for the greater part of the day, chatting or going down to the market and taking advantage of the fact that the Old Office had its own refrigerator by drinking cold beer.

The most frequent visitors were five young men from Inawai'a village. Of these five, James' two closest friends, Peter and Ine'e, were from the same clan as James' mother—*Ungokapia*—although Ine'e was by birth of *O'aki* clan in Jesu Baibau village and had been adopted into *Ungokapia* while still a very small child. Thus James' most frequent visitors were all people with whom he had close relationships before the formation of the club and were the result of kinship, clanship, and close association throughout childhood. Nonetheless, everyone was unanimous that the club and James' new accommodation had resulted in their closer and more frequent association. The important change from James' point of view was that he had become the host to these gatherings and had far more contact with the young Mekeo men who were scattered around the town. The factors which ensured that James' residence became the geographical focus for these home-boy relationships were his own popularity, his relationship to Peter, and the fact that the Old Office was near Koke—the Papuan heart of the town—providing good accommodation together with "first class" facilities—a fan, a bottle-gas cooker, a refrigerator, and a bathroom.[4]

The other organized group around which James' most important relationships revolved was the village Transport Group. According to James, he had been the catalyst for the group's formation when, during his Christmas vacation, senior members of his clan section had been grumbling about economic opportunities and the lack of village development. He claimed to have berated them soundly and to have suggested that they would never come to anything unless they organized them-

---

[4] Another attraction was the availability of the younger Mekeo lads to wash sports jerseys for the club. Initially, the jerseys were washed by the wives of married players but when they tired of this "the small boys," as James called them, were an obvious choice.

selves into a business group. They had taken his advice and had decided to buy a truck.

Other catalysts, it seems, were the jibes of the junior clan section: that section was blessed both with a blossoming entrepreneur (who ran his own truck and had erected a new trade store constructed of European materials) and with his cousin (who, after secondary education, had become a cooperative officer and had gone overseas as a representative of the Territory's cooperative movement). James ruefully recounted how the junior clan section had laughed at their senior relatives as "no-hopers" and ne'er-do-wells who, moreover, lacked any members with the education and flair for success that would enable them to raise their heads in the world. Treasuring the insult, and flaunting it proudly before their tormentors' eyes to show their disdain, the Transport Group called itself "Something of No Consequence" and painted this on the doors of their large $3,200 truck when they finally purchased it.

Two resourceful and forceful middle-aged members of the section were chosen as president and treasurer, and James was appointed its secretary. As the best educated person in the section, he felt that the junior section's barbs claimed himself as its principal victim. Perhaps because of this, and almost certainly because of the prestige and status he was accruing, James threw himself into the activities of the Transport Group with great zeal.

The suitability of various trucks had already been discussed and an initial fund-raising had been held in the village when I first became aware of the group's activities towards the end of May. By the end of July the truck had been purchased for approximately $3,200 and a deposit of $1,600 paid. Throughout the negotiations with the Development Bank,[5] the vehicle agency, insurance and licensing authorities, and transportation agencies, James played the leading part.

These then were the principal activities and relationships in which James was involved throughout the time he lived in the Old Office.

---

[5] James applied to the Development Bank for a business development loan to finance the purchase of the truck. However the application took far more time to process than the Transport Group was prepared to wait and in the face of criticism for his tardiness in "bringing the truck out," he arranged for hire purchase finance. An interesting footnote to my discussion of James' extensive social network was his attempt to get information on the progress of his application to the bank. Although he had not see him for years, James encouraged a young Papuan, who had been at school with him and was now working for the bank as a clerk, to send him reports.

For the most part, they were entirely separate activities and involved him, in each case, with a different circle of people. In the case of the sports club, he associated principally with young men, many of whom were in skilled or white-collar occupations, with the benefit of secondary education, predominantly from his mother's village, and working permanently in town. In the case of the transport group, he associated with rather older men from his own village who were minimally, if at all, educated, and were permanent residents in Mekeo, but whose trips to sell betel nuts brought them to town for perhaps a month at a time.

Many of the discussions about the truck and transport group business were carried out at Hanuabada, where the village men were based while selling their betel nuts, and this took James away from the Old Office. But there were numerous other occasions when the activities of the group brought Mekeo migrants back, to the house. When the truck was finally purchased, for example, a party was held for the members of the group, and hospitality was extended to representatives of another Mekeo group also in the process of buying a truck.

Thus James' involvement in the activities and relationships of the transport group and of the sports club meant not only that his primary interests lay beyond the Old Office and its residents' pursuits but that there was a constant stream of visitors to the quarters. His sponsorship of these guests and of Aite, the young schoolboy to whom he was *in loco parentis*, and the other young Mekeo lodgers became in turn a principal source of strain within the residence's social organization.

The account has now turned full circle: having followed James' network of relationships beyond the confines of the plant and its accommodation, and beyond the town even, we have returned to the Old Office to hint at the consequences that his associations and actions had for the social life of his fellow residents. But before exploring, in detail, the background of domestic strife, let us undertake an examination of Gabriel's career and associational life similar to that which we undertook for James. By comparison with the extensive network of relationships and activities in which James was involved, Gabriel's own ties and pastimes were largely restricted to the Old Office. His educational and work history was also far less eventful than that of his older compatriot.

Gabriel had received his primary education at mission schools in his local area. On leaving school he applied and was accepted for pre-apprenticeship training at Idubada Technical College in Port Moresby. After two years at Idubada and on completion of his Form II in technical subjects he had been recommended to P.M.D. by the Apprenticeship Board for indenture. He had then been working for the company a little longer than James.

Like James, Gabriel had not maintained his boarding school friendships to any extent. While at the Technical College, Gabriel had associated mainly with young men from the Roro-speaking areas of his home sub-district. All of the closest friends he had made at Idubada had stayed on in Port Moresby. Some of them had stayed on as full-time students at the college to complete their classroom apprenticeship training, while others were already working for companies in the town. One friend, from the Gabadi area of the Kairuku Sub-District, had been a member of the Mekeo Sports Club for a season and was living at the Salvation Army Hostel in Badili, within easy walking distance of the Old Office: however, they made no effort to keep in contact with each other.

Unlike James, Gabriel was not an active member of any formal organization of Mekeo people, either in the town or in the home area. Although on occasion he supported the sports club, he never played. He had not been asked to play partly because he lacked experience and partly because he was thought to be too young—although in size and strength he appeared to be at least the equal of James. He himself showed little interest in playing, although he was a keen fan of the game and would often turn the conversation to a past or approaching contest. Furthermore, and again in contrast to James, he took no part in organized village activities. This was perhaps because of his youth and because his section of the clan was not organized to the same extent as James' section. But it was also, in part, because Gabriel was only a member of the clan by adoption; judging from various comments made by himself and James this meant that he was something of a marginal member. Perhaps of even greater importance in explaining his lack of participation in either village-based activities or of town-based organizations (and Gabriel himself readily pointed to this) was his occupational status and financial position. As a first-year apprentice he received just over $6.00 net per week. Moreover, while James' wage rose very quickly to just over $12.00, Gabriel's wage was fixed for the rest of the year, limited as it was to the annual increments of the Apprenticeship Ordinance. Whereas James could afford to pay the financial dues, the bus and truck fares, and other expenses of his membership in organized activities, Gabriel could not.

A further aspect of the contrast between James' preoccupations and pursuits and those of Gabriel was their different pattern of visiting whenever we went to Hanuabada to call on Mekeo villagers who were in town to sell their betel nuts. These traders lodged with their Hanuabada *varavara* (in this case, a fictive kin relationship arising through trade) or *turadia* (friends) either on platforms underneath the houses built over dry land or on the verandahs of houses built over the tide. James' immediate kindred based themselves in a house in Hohodae (owned by a Motuan married to a woman from Tufi in the Northern District) which is the first of the Hanuabadan villages on the road from Konedobu (the administrative headquarters). Gabriel's own "family" came to a house in Poreporena, the second village of this peri-urban cluster (cf. Belshaw 1957:12).

Apart from his occasional visits to village kin who were in town to trade, Gabriel's leisure time associations were almost completely restricted to the social and geographical ambit of the Old Office—either to visitors to the quarters or to other residents. On those days (mostly weekends) during which Peter, Ine'e, and other sports club members spent their time in the house, lazing, chatting, drinking beer, and eating, Gabriel would join in. But only one young man, Allan, a cross-cousin, who also played for the club, came to see Gabriel. Thus many of his associates were provided by the stream of visitors on transport group or sports club business, or who had come for an idle chat with James. Beyond the visitors to the quarters, and especially during the early weeks of my stay, Gabriel spent a good deal of his leisure time with Aite (James' parallel cousin) and with the other young Mekeos who lodged there from time to time. Later, Gabriel's general camaraderie with Patrick, with Bava, and with Aipela (another unofficial guest attending school in Badili and a younger consanguinal kinsman of Patrick) blossomed into a firmer friendship. This later development coincided with, and was reinforced by, Gabriel's move from Room D to Room C.

The fellow villagers, James and Gabriel, then, found themselves, through the vagaries of the labor market and their own preferences and scrapes, living in the same residence. Their relationship before joining the plant could never have been described as close, and activities which they pursued after joining P.M.D. involved them in very different ways with varying sets of associates. Yet, despite this lack of major commitment to each other's concerns and activities a common birthplace, supplemented by the accident of coresidence, entailed a certain degree of mutual recognition. Whereas it would have been singularly inappropriate for any of the other residents to intrude on the activities and chatter of James and his Mekeo guests, this was not so for Gabriel. Nor did he face the barrier of language that the other residents did. But James' and Gabriel's relationship to each other was exceptional. None of the others were so closely involved or shared so basic an identity as that of "fellow villager." Nonetheless, on those occasions in which he participated in James' gatherings, Gabriel was more frequently a hanger-on than Aite even, who, despite his youth, could claim close kinship both with James and with his more important visitors.

The account of James' and Gabriel's leisure time activities outside the house shows that they were principally engaged with groups of home people. In this respect they were fully representative of the other residents. Looked at *solely* from the viewpoint of their own enduring rural-urban relationships and their important recreational activities, the residents appeared as monads, sharing the same space and facilities but otherwise not involved with each other. But the residents' involvement with extra-house activities varied considerably. Thus, James' rising eminence in village affairs, coupled with his membership in the sports club, took him out of the quarters more frequently than anyone else. At the same time, his extra-house involvement meant that a major share of the visitors to the house came under his invitation. Gabriel's involvement fell at the other extreme. Only Sidney, the young Tolai from Rabaul, surpassed him in his lack of external friends and commitments. Apart from a "brother" at the University, whom he saw very infrequently, and a couple of compatriots at the apprentices hostel in Hohola, of whom he saw even less, Sidney appeared to be friendless. But for his limited companionships at work and with his fellow New Guineans, Lucian and David, Sidney would have been almost completely isolated. As it was he spent most of his time sitting around the residence, violently homesick, hating Moresby and its people, listening to the radio, and awaiting his posting to "the New Guinea side."

The other residents were all heavily involved in activities and relationships with their home people. In some cases these activities and relationships took place within the context of a formal association; in other cases they did not. Lucian, for example, was a member of a soccer team for people from his home area and this was a focus for much of his recreational life. On the other hand, Bava's ties with his home people found expression in informal visiting and in more casual association. Only Vincent and David participated in associations which were *not* manifestly related to village and other home ties. Both of them were, respectively, members of a military, and of a mission-based sports organization. But their memberships of these organizations were in addition to home ties and not in place of them.

So far the account of the careers and social commitments of the two Mekeo villagers has been used to document my assertion that lack of mutual interest was an important determinant of the social organization of the Old Office. But there was also a developmental aspect to its organization. To discuss the evolving modifications to the original pattern of anonymity we must probe a little further into individual reactions to the domestic strain.

To an extent these reactions were determined by the changing character of the residents' individual commitments outside the house. But whatever the "real" determinants, individual adjustment was often expressed in terms of attitudes and values which were basic to the individual's social identity. Thus aspirations and self-conceptions combined with the course of events, and these were in turn reinforced or modified by the residents' experiences in other sectors of their social participation.

The interrelationship of these social processes was often extremely complex and varied greatly from individual to individual. It follows that the analysis of this interrelationship can best be essayed, as before, by continuing the account of the two Mekeo residents and the part they played in the domestic strife. The themes which emerge from the discussion can then be used to characterize the reactions of their fellows.

Urban and Racial Styles

James was one of the two most outspoken critics of the domestic squalor; only John surpassed him in the vehemence of his criticisms. In part, the strength of James' criticism would seem to lie in the fact that initially he slept in the dining area together with Sidney and myself. This section of the house was the main thoroughfare and eating area and was a repository for all kinds of litter. Moreover, it was very noisy and prevented even rudimentary privacy.

In the third month, however, James and I moved into Room B, which had been vacated by John. John had been pressing the management for married accommodation ever since he had joined the company. But the months had rolled by and, irritated by what he saw as the company's lack of good faith, he moved his belongings from the house and into an empty unit in the Old Married Quarters. He was soon told to vacate his new accommodation. Management, angry at his attempt to force the issue and aware that the Old Married units (particularly the one John had chosen) were highly unsuitable for its senior employees, took an uncompromising attitude and told him to return to his previous quarters. But, by this time, James had moved both his own and my belongings into Room B and, thus, we were in full possession of that room. After some weeks of living in Boroko with his relatives, John moved back to the Old Office. This time, however, he had to take up residence in the messing area.

Despite our good fortune in moving into a less exposed section of the house, however, James' criticisms continued unabated. He was proud to have his own room but after a while the novelty wore off and he remained every bit as conscious of the house's untidiness and distractions. Moreover, he had a new source of discontent. With the company's encouragement and financial assistance with fees and incidentals, he had commenced a correspondence course in bookkeeping and commercial principles. The non-arrival of a textbook and the distractions of the messing area had delayed his initial attempts to study so that, with our move to Room B, he threw himself into the course with renewed vigor. But even the new surroundings failed to serve as a panacea for the difficulties of a new course of study and the distractions caused by cheek-by-jowl neighboring. James' irritation was primarily directed at the younger Mekeo boys who were clearly responsible for much of the exuberance of the quarters, although other residents were also subject to criticism.

Part of James' irritation was essentially practical. With his initial success in stimulating the formation of the transport group and with his appointment as secretary, he had developed a robust desire to become an independent entrepreneur. Thus, although he was aware that his completion of the course would help, in a minor way, his advancement in P.M.D. and in the European industrial and commercial world of Papua, his foremost hope was that it would further his "business" education. Although James was literate, and already reasonably familiar with much of routine industrial and commercial practice, "business" had for him an air of uncertainty and even mystique. He hoped to master this with his anticipated knowledge of bookkeeping and commercial operations. For this reason, he was intolerant of any household disturbance which interrupted his progress in the course.

But part of his irritation, I feel sure, was because he resented the fact that Gabriel and the young Mekeo guests (who by now had all moved into Room C with Patrick and Bava) did not take him or his studies seriously enough. James' studies were an important measure of his own self-esteem: his background of secondary education at Sogeri was very important to him and he was very conscious of being an ex-pupil of what had been for some years the Territory's undisputed premier high school. As he was also conscious of his position as the senior Mekeo in the quarters, and of his growing importance in village affairs, he became somewhat piqued when insufficient respect was paid to him or to his endeavors.

His education was also important to him as a necessary background for friendship with Europeans—another important source of self-esteem and prestige. James was a representative of that group of high-school educated young men whose facility with the English language and personal experience with western mores had given them a confidence in dealing with Europeans and European ways which few other Papuans seemed to possess. It was no accident that of all the residents management should have chosen him to sponsor my introduction to the quarters. It will also be remembered that he had been encouraged to apply for a position as a cadet hydrographer by an Australian workmate whose friendship he enjoyed. Another association arising from his employment at "Comworks" was his friendship with an Australian accountant. While they were both working there, James had regularly visited him at his house in Korobosea. When his friend left the Territory for Fiji, and when afterwards he returned to Queensland, they continued to write to each other. His friendship with these Europeans played a significant part in his self-evaluation. He was a rather uncritical enthusiast of the Australian way of life. While few Papua–New Guineans in the town would dispute Australian technical and material superiority, their enthusiasm for this aspect of the intruding culture was very often tempered by criticisms of the white person's hardheartedness, arrogance, and insensitivity. This was contrasted with the Papuan's generosity and kindness. But, while James characterized white men as hard and uncompromising, he did so in a way which was as much admiring as it was critical. For him, these traits were the reason for their success. Papuans were kind-hearted—a trait which he applauded—but weak and ineffectual.

James' particular assessment of the racial division of the town and Territory was reflected in many of his actions and attitudes. It could be seen, for example, in his dress and in his attitude to his fellow villagers. It was also evident in his attitude towards the Old Office. He was impressed by the fact that the Old Office had many of the facilities of a European house and took pride in his friends' admiration when they visited him. But he also grumbled about the untidiness and squalor of the quarters, arguing that certain of his fellow residents were ignorant and uncivilized. His targets in these attacks were Gabriel, Patrick, Bava, and the young Mekeo "passengers."

Thus, part of his reaction resulted from his use of a stereotype of European living derived from his earlier experience. But his attitude was undoubtedly reinforced by the nature of his continuing relationship with Europeans. My own presence in the quarters and the criticisms of members of management were of particular importance in this respect. As a European and living in the same room I could not help but make him aware of what he saw as the discrepancy between the actual living arrangements and the civilized ideal. Moreover he was eager to obtain the good opinion of the members of management with whom he worked. When they reminded him of the state of the quarters he felt it incumbent on him to goad people into tidying up.

On these occasions he called upon Gabriel and the young boys to help him, arguing that, together with Patrick and Bava, they were the primary cause of much litter and dirt. While berating them for their "bush" habits, however, he would also grumble privately that the New Guineans did nothing to tidy or to clean the communal areas and that their failure evidenced a lack of public spirit. But while he attempted to prod Gabriel and "the small boys" into action he never attempted to scold either Patrick or Bava or the three New Guineans. Between James and these young men was a distance born of similar experience, a total lack of personal ties and obligations, and, particularly in the case of the three New Guineans, cultural unfamiliarity. In James' relationships to Patrick and Bava this distance was occasionally tempered by a certain amount of gossip about areas of common concern—particularly rugby football, his relationship to the New Guineans was, however, characterized by silence and, at times, hostility. Moreover, leaving aside his attempts to study, James spent such little time alone in the quarters that there was little opportunity for his discontents (or his attempts at gossip for that matter) to develop into anything more significant. When he was in the house and not entertaining his Mekeo friends, preparing accounts for the transport group, or studying, much of his waking time was spent in routine activities which gave him little opportunity for intimacy. Eating was the only activity which necessitated his conversation with other residents. Even then, he ate with me and/or with Gabriel and the young Mekeo lads. This pattern of activity, moreover, was another reason why the brunt of his criticisms should fall on my ears and on the shoulders of his compatriots.

Thus we can see that James' reaction to the situation of the Old Office was compounded of various elements. His involvement in the affairs of the transport group and in the concerns of his town-based compatriots in the sports club meant that he had little time or energy to spend with the other residents. In turn his preoccupation with matters in which (with certain exceptions) the other residents could play no part and in which they themselves had little interest, reinforced the sense of social distance between himself and his fellows. This lack of mutual intimacy applied (with an amply-noted exception) to all the residents. But there were also more immediate components in James' reaction, in particular his self-conception as an educated person, his aspirations toward leadership and his assessment of the racial division of the company and of the town. It was these which gave his attitude to the house's social organization its distinctive flavor.

Certain of these characteristics and reactions were unique to the quarters, while others were more widely distributed. An instance of a unique reaction can be seen in James' touchiness on the subject of his studies. This centered, in part, on his claims to leadership over the young Mekeos. Only Patrick, who claimed the services of his younger kinsman, Aipela, could begin to rival James' pool of potential supporters and hence be sensitive over matters of personal allegiance and respect. On the other hand, the ideals of "educated" and civilized behavior influenced the domestic reactions and attitudes of a majority of residents and not just those of James. Only Patrick, Bava, and Gabriel seemed unconcerned by the possibility of being thought uncouth and uncivilized.

But even though we can isolate general themes and characteristics of adaptation and orientation, there were often significant twists to individual adjustment. Thus, for example, while the New Guineans were equally conscious of their responsibility as "educated" persons they would certainly not have accepted James' estimation of their public spirit. They thought the cause of the squalor was self-evident; it was due to the influx of inconsiderate and unmannerly visitors, and their hosts' insouciance and insufficient respect for others' privacy. In short, it was "the Papuans" who were to blame. James was singled out for especial criticism since a considerable number of the lodgers and visitors came under his sponsorship.

In this instance we can see that the New Guineans' reactions were variations on a common theme. The overall divergence in individual adjustments to the common situation of discord and bickering, however, was much greater, involving as it did very different self-conceptions and commitments. This divergence is nowhere more forcibly illustrated than in the contrast between James' reaction and that of Gabriel's.

Gabriel's personal style and certain of his ideals can best be described as "cowboy." "Cowboy" was used to describe a Papuan who had adopted a personal style, not only of dress but of stance and, to an extent, language which could be characterized as "cool" or taciturn. The explicit image was of the cowboy of the western movie—rugged, virile, laconic, and with a disciplined casualness. On one occasion it was used to refer to a young man at Koke who, in keeping with a current vogue, had torn the sleeves from his shirt exposing his shoulders and arms, leaving a jagged hole and, presumably, accenting his potential for violence (see also Ogan 1973:9).

This was an ideal which Gabriel tried hard to emulate; his attainment of it was hindered only by his shortage of money and, to a much lesser extent, by the competing claims of his involvement in a network of village-based social relationships and values. Whereas James' habitual dress was shorts and long walking socks and shoes, Gabriel wore tight-fitting trousers and thongs in his off duty hours. Whereas Gabriel was an ardent cinema addict, James rarely went to the movies. Despite his urbaneness, and the reference of his behavior to consumer standards deriving from an intruding culture, Gabriel was fiercely anti-white. On one occasion John, Patrick, and Bava, together with Gabriel, were discussing in my presence what national independence would mean for Papua–New Guinea. They were all of the opinion that the Europeans would leave overnight, secure that their savings were in Australian banks and leaving behind just their houses (which were rented anyway) and their cars. There would be violence between the native population and the retreating whites. At this point, Gabriel jumped up shouting and laughing bitterly that he would gun down the whites with a machine gun and would grab a car and a house for himself. On another occasion, we were discusing food preferences when he commented, with obvious relish, that whereas Europeans were anxious to eat pawpaws (papaya), his own people fed them to pigs.

His attitude towards Europeans was not altogether a simple product of previous experience and personal disposition. His initial attitude was continually reinforced in the work situation. Whereas James worked alongside senior managers, who had a greater stake in ensuring good racial relations in the plant and took an evident personal interest in James and his problems (one manager lent him $200 to service the transport group's truck), Gabriel worked beside European manual laborers, who were much less concerned with altering the prevailing racial attitudes and relationships. These men were typically on short-term contracts and were much less involved in the economic and political future of the concern. They were therefore much less concerned in the company's attempts to promote smoother racial relations, and moreover, were in closer economic and occupational competition with their indigenous workmates. Thus Gabriel would be much more aware of the disadvantages to himself of the prevailing racial division of labor, both in the company and in the town. In addition, whereas James worked beside a native clerk of the same age, who reflected many of his own attitudes and behavior, Gabriel worked with two older native employees both of whom were very bitter about current and past racial discrimination. One of these men, for example, on a visit to the house, pointed out that previously the Old Office had been supplied with hot water as well as cold, but that when natives had taken up residence the supply of hot water had been discontinued. He cited this as an instance of a more general attitude and injustice.

Whatever the balance of initial attitudes and subsequent reinforcement while at the plant, Gabriel's attitude toward the prevailing racial structure of the town and the company was in evident contrast to that of James. This contrast carried over into their attitudes toward co-neighborhood in the Old Office. On one occasion James tried to get

Gabriel and Aite to help him with the cleaning up, stressing that the Europeans in the main office had been scolding him about the state of the house. Gabriel retorted that he paid for his accommodation, swore obscenely at unspecified Europeans, and denied them the right to order him about in any way. On another occasion, I overheard Gabriel laughing and telling one of the Mekeo guests that James was sweeping because one of the Europeans had reprimanded James about the state of the house and James was frightened he would lose his pay.

It was evident, then, that Gabriel did not feel the same external pressure as James and that this was part of the reason for the contrast in their reactions to the house and its inmates. But I would suggest that these differences were not only because of a fear, or lack of fear, of external sanctions. Their attitudes about the racial issue were deep and emotionally based, and reflected their overall personal styles and self-conceptions. Whereas James' reaction to the situation was bound up with his self-conception as an educated and civilized person, and with his personal relationships to Europeans, Gabriel's reaction reflected a very different stance.

Ethnogenesis, Leadership, and the Lack of Common Purpose

We are now in a position to move from James' and Gabriel's "work's eye view" of the Old Office and return to the questions posed earlier in the chapter: why were there no attempts to deal with the domestic strain on a communal basis? and why did the relationships of distance and intimacy in the quarters take the form they did? So far we have seen separate individuals jostling for position within a set of constraints set by the policies and practices of the plant. These constraints on the residents' behavior followed almost inevitably on their decision to accept employment there. Was the social situation, then, a simple reflection of individual psychology and the spatial and functional arrangements of the company, or were there more explicit cultural factors at work?

The company's housing resources and its policies and practices of allocation placed these young men in close proximity and forced them to share common facilities. Thus the residents, who (with one exception) had been strangers to each other before their employment, and in some cases before taking up residence in the house, became enmeshed in a web of dependence and competition of the company's making. The pressures of this symbiotic order were common to each of them.

At this level of the analysis the oppositions and conflicts were purely individual in character: events and behaviors took the form of similar but separate reactions to a common situation.

This aspect of the house's organization stresses the competition of identical units. But the residents' commitments and ties outside the Old Office were by no means equivalent. Port Moresby is peopled predominantly by migrants from the coastal areas of Papua. Thus a Papuan living in the town is likely to have a more extensive pool of kin and other contacts than his New Guinean counterpart. Moreover, the home villages of the Papuans living in the house were closer to the town than those of the New Guineans. This meant that the Papuans were more available to people with strong claims on their resources. These claims were often pressed, and the Papuans were frequently called upon to accommodate and support kin and sometimes compatriots who were without a house or were out of work. Thus one of the most notable distinctions between the New Guineans and Papuans was that whereas the Papuans, with the exception of Bava, all had dependents living with them in the quarters, the New Guineans did not. Because of their additional commitments beyond the Old Office, the Papuans, through their dependents, made a greater claim on the common resources, and this became a principal source of strain.

In many cases the residents welcomed these guests, in others they did their very best to persuade the visitor that he should move on. Thus, in Aite's case, James did his utmost to keep the young schoolboy with him. At one stage, when management tried to force James to evict Aite, James had threatened to leave the quarters and live in Hanuabada, taking his young cousin with him. He argued that he was responsible for Aite and that Aite was not a "passenger" (with all the term's connotations of unemployment and parasitism) but was there for a legitimate reason—his schooling. The other guests in the quarters, although often very respectable and often welcomed by their sponsors, were much more like the "passengers" of conventional definition. Thus, by way of example, during the seven months I was living in the Old Office, Vincent had a total of three guests in residence. All of them were unemployed and depended on him to a large extent for their food during this period. They were all close kinsmen and were waiting until they could obtain the kind of employment they desired. The first two guests, who stayed some three weeks, were waiting to join the army: eventually one joined the army and the other the police. The third stayed for close to two-and-a-half months, having come initially, and officially, to care for Vincent and to cook his meals for a week when he was feeling sick. Welcomed at first, this guest became in time a source of embarrassment for Vincent who admitted that he was relieved when he left.

Whatever the complex, and perhaps conflicting, emotions that the Papuan residents had about their dependents the New Guineans' appraisal of their situation took little account of the Papuans' occasional embarrassment. The New Guineans almost certainly recognized that in different circumstances they might themselves be called upon to fulfill similar obligations. They argued, however, that the Papuans' fulfillment of their obligations to house kinsmen placed counter-obligations on themselves. The Papuans, it was felt, had the obligation to keep their guests quiet and to clean up after them.

Certain of the Papuan residents were singled out for especial criticism for their shortcomings in this respect. It will be remembered that Lucian blamed Gabriel for certain of his own irritations and discomforts while they shared Room D. Responsibility was also allotted to James. Yet despite their recognition of individual responsibility, the allocation of blame was often compounded into a single gloss. It was told repeatedly that the Papuans were the main source of squalor and untidiness in the quarters. "The Papuans are to blame" was a convenient shorthand; it allowed the New Guineans to describe the situation to their own satisfaction without having to go into boring detail. This gloss was not, however, a neutral description; it implied an emotionally-based stereotype of Papuan behavior and was an additional source of opposition in the quarters.

"Papua" versus "New Guinea" is a recurrent theme in Port Moresby social life. It derives largely from contrasted histories of administrative and economic development, and from current economic and political status. For most migrants from the Trust Territory, the opposition finds its most readily understood expression in beliefs about language differences and differences in economic ethos. It is almost an axiom of daily parlance that Papuans are people who speak Motu and no Pidgin, or at best a highly bastardized version of it, while New Guineans all speak Pidgin fluently and with a flair for idiom. Furthermore, almost every New Guinean I discussed the issue with believed (and was sure that all other New Guineans agreed) that Papuans were lazy. The Papuans' poor economic showing in the Territory was, ac-

cording to the New Guineans, due to their lack of application and a
lack of good soil. At times I felt that to have a deficient soil was itself almost a personal shortcoming.

These stereotypes (by their very nature) obscured individual variation. Nonetheless, the overall contrast between Papuans and New Guineans was real enough. There are certainly very pronounced differences in *lingua franca*, in history and in current economic position.
But much of the emotional force of the stereotypes seemed to derive
from the New Guineans' experience of strangeness in an alien town
(Deutsch 1953:185). As migrants from afar, they saw themselves involved in a radically different environment—an environment that was
bustling, alive with motorcars, and trucks, parched for much of the
year, thronging with many strange peoples and almost devoid of good
and inexpensive food.

These attitudes to Port Moresby and its residents were current
among many of the New Guinean residents in the town. The New
Guineans living in the Old Office were no exception. As we have
seen, Sidney's was the extreme reaction to the underlying "experience
of strangeness." He reacted to the strangeness of Port Moresby and to
the relative unavailability of friends by staying close to his bed, listening to his radio day and night, and bemoaning the fate that had
brought him away from New Guinea.

Lucian and David had made a less introverted adaptation to the
strangeness of their new environment. They had found support and
solace among circles of kin and friends. But they nonetheless resented
many aspects of their sojourn in the town; in particular, they singled
out the poor quality and high cost of the town's food supply, its harsh,
dry vista, and the uncouth behavior of many Papuans.

Thus part of the social distance that the New Guineans felt towards
the Papuans in the quarters was a product of a finely-cut "ethnic" stereotype. This was less true for the Papuans' attitude toward the New
Guineans. The Papuan residents' feeling of distance toward their
New Guinean counterparts can be described, perhaps, as *cultural* distance, or gentle ethnocentricism. It reflected a relative lack of common
interests and experiences stemming from their mutual unfamiliarity
rather than a rejection based on hostility, or clear images or stereotypes
of the behavioral potential of the other group. Herskovits' characterization of most ethnocentricism as "a gentle insistence on the good qual-
ities of one's own group, without any drive to extend this attitude into

the field of action" captures precisely the Papuans' attitude (Herskovits 1948:69; Banton 1967:317).

In part, the lack of hostility can be explained by the fact that the Papuan residents were more organically related to their surroundings. Although they were still migrants (with their bases, for the most part, in the countryside), all of them had spent considerably more time in the town and its neighboring areas than had the New Guineans. They were not subject to the same experience of strangeness. Yet, although more knowledgeable of Papua and the ways of Papua, none of them had had any intimate experience of New Guinea or its people. The little that they knew of the Trust Territory had been absorbed at school, gleaned from radio broadcasts and scant reading, or picked up from the tales of their more adventurous associates.

Some indication of the character of their association with New Guinea people can be gathered from their command of Pidgin. There are strong suggestions that the command of Pidgin is rapidly increasing among Papuans in the town (Wurm 1966–67:13).[6] Certainly many Papuans I knew had a fair command of the language and actively sought opportunities to speak it. But while the Papuans in the quarters, like their fellow territorians in the town, were by no means antagonistic to the idea of speaking Pidgin, their command of the language was very poor. All except John could manage a simple question and answer sequence but none could engage in sustained conversation with a native speaker. In the quarters, and among themselves, the Papuan residents used either their vernacular, Police Motu, or English. Occasionally they would call out and joke in a basic Pidgin. Yet when they addressed the New Guineans they used only English despite the fact that the New Guineans used Pidgin while speaking among themselves. The only Papuan who made any advance in the language during my stay was John. Unable to put together a simple sentence during the first months of my fieldwork, John encouraged his fellow resident Sidney to teach him Pidgin (at that time he was also learning Hula). By the end of my stay John had gained a similar proficiency to that of the other Papuan residents.

These language differences were often used to symbolize the social distance between the Papuans on the one hand, and the New Guineans

---

[6] The 1966 census states that 54 percent of indigenes over ten years of age claim to speak Pidgin. The equivalent figures for Police Motu and English are 77.8 percent and 64.4 percent, respectively.

on the other. All the residents spoke English and could have communicated in that language; but the New Guineans obviously preferred to speak Pidgin. It seemed that for them the use of English meant a degree of formality in a relationship, while Pidgin spelt affinity and intimacy. Just as they were uncompromising in their use of Pidgin so they made no attempt to learn Police Motu. We might say that the Papuans and New Guineans restricted their relationships with each other to those where English was spoken.

Although the Papuans and New Guineans were divided by language, by sentiment, and by enduring rural-urban and intra-urban social commitments, this division was not complete and did not lead to factions in the sense of enduring and continually opposed groups. The opposition between the New Guineans on the one hand and the Papuans on the other was undoubtedly a major reason for the solidarity of the three New Guineans in the face of the domestic incidents. But there was no such solidarity among the Papuans.

This contrast between the associations of the Papuans and those of the New Guineans was, in part, a function of numbers. The three New Guineans were drawn to each other as a minority in a strange environment. Two of them—Lucian and David—shared a room and all three of them were commensals. Moreover, Lucian had lent Sidney his spare radio and the three of them shared a mail-order catalogue and together ordered shirts and other clothing from Australia (those in Port Moresby, they argued, were not fashionable enough). In addition to eating together, they all tended to keep their distance from the Papuans at mealtimes; if any of the chairs around the table were already occupied, they tended to withdraw to the kitchen and eat standing up. The only hint I ever had of disagreement among the three of them was when Lucian and David, returning from soccer on a Saturday afternoon, had not waited to eat with Sidney, who for once had spent the day away from the quarters. They had prepared supper and had eaten without cooking him any. He was rather upset, both at this slight and at his companions' apparent lack of remorse. The incident clouded their relationship for several days.

The Papuans were too numerous to cluster or to eat together. They were divided broadly into four sets of commensals. James, Aite, and I tended to eat together, and often we were joined by Gabriel. On those occasions when Gabriel did not eat with us, he joined Patrick, Bava, and Aipela. For these two sets of commensals the pattern was always the same: the youngest members of the set did the actual cooking, and often the shopping as well, while the senior members provided the money for the provisions. Vincent and John ate either by themselves or with their guests. In the initial part of my stay, both of them withdrew to their rooms to eat. After he had vacated Room B, John was denied this option but continued to eat on his own or with a ne'er-do-well kinsman who had lodged with him in Room B and who continued to drop in every few days.

Their sheer numbers, then, set the Papuans apart from each other. Moreover, for them, there was not the same culture shock to draw them together and to counter the centrifugal pressures of ties with home-people. Additionally, there were other divisive factors in operation—style, opposed positions on race, and issues of leadership. These last were closer to their own definitions of their situation.

Thus, the contrast between "educated" and "cowboy" was not limited to the two Mekeo residents. It coincided, moreover, with the spatial arrangement of the quarters. The occupants of Room C were all "cowboy" while the rest of the Papuan residents were "educated" in their personal style. To some extent, this difference coincided with differences in standard and type of education, and with differences in age. It coincided exactly with attitudes toward the domestic squalor. The residents of Room C were apparently unconcerned by it. The others —John, James, and Vincent—argued that the squalor was regrettable, although Vincent never voiced his criticisms in public and withdrew as much as possible from contact with his fellow residents.

While differences between "educated" and "cowboy" styles may have been connected with the crises of adolescence, they also reflected images of occupational status current in the town and residents' evaluations of its racial structure. Thus John's and James' clerical positions were a matter for self-esteem. Accordingly, they adapted their dress to fit the Papuan image of the white-collar worker. John, in particular, was always very smartly dressed and took great pains to have a spotless and well-ironed white shirt at hand: on one occasion he had twelve ready in his wardrobe. No one else that I met in the whole time I was in Port Moresby was able to rival his sartorial standards. At the other extreme, Patrick, Bava, and Gabriel cultivated the dress and bearing of the manual worker. On weekends they wore more formal attire—long trousers, thongs, and a clean shirt—but never the shorts, long socks, and shoes like John and James. The residents' attitudes towards such is-

sues as personal cleanliness and mode of dress were often reinforced
by their association with European workmates. Thus James and John
associated with white office workers who had distinct standards of
dress and required similar standards from their Papuan assistants.
John and James internalized these standards and applied them to other
Papuan employees.

The influence of Europeans, however, was not restricted to clothing
and personal appearance. Nor was the opposition between those residents who were favorably disposed toward the racial structure of the
town and those who were not a simple function of the cowboy-educated
opposition. Thus John, the epitome of the educated and successful
white-collar worker, was also one of the fiercest critics of the prevailing racial relations that I met during my whole fieldwork. He argued
that the Europeans were "humbugging" the native people. Papuans
and New Guineans were told that they were receiving huge sums of
money as grants in aid from the Australian government, and that all the
political and economic development which had been achieved in the
Territory they owed to the money and skills of the Australians. Much
of the money the Australians said they were giving to the Territory
went back out of the country again in wages to the Europeans. As a
former wages clerk in the public service, with direct experience of the
administration of the dual wages and privileges structure, John told the
residents of the injustices to which Papuans were subject. He in-
stanced, among other things, the low wages and scant leave the Papuans
received and the high rent they were forced to pay for poor-quality administration housing. The Europeans, on the other hand, were paid
large wages, were given twice as much leave, and were asked to pay a
minimal rent for excellent housing.

John's attitude and the strength of his delivery won him the attention
of the young Papuans. Part of the attention was, I feel sure, because
the open discussion of racial relations before a European (myself) was
extremely cathartic for the younger residents. At the same time, John's
statements clearly articulated dissatisfactions which all the younger
Papuans gave evidence of feeling, yet which they could not express or
conceptualize at all adequately. His ability to articulate these grievances won him their respect.

I have only meager evidence to suggest to what extent John's leadership in these matters had ramifications for other fields of activity.
But I suspect, for example, that his stand on the racial issue further

limited James' ability to goad the residents into action over domestic issues. At the same time John's and James' opposition over racial matters may have reinforced the sense of rivalry between them and may have added a further barrier to their cooperation. Thus despite the fact that leadership in the quarters was almost a nonoccurrence, I am suggesting that we must consider to what extent it was at all possible. The point here is that the student of social life should pay attention not only to what does occur in a given situation but also to what does *not* occur (Merton 1957:60; Frankenberg 1966:294). By paying attention to what did *not* happen in the quarters it will be possible to conclude the discussion showing how the quality of social distance between the residents had implications for the domestic arrangements.

James' growing stature in village and town affairs was not accompanied by a similar influence in the house. He could command Aite's services, but Gabriel's services were less easily obtained and those of the other residents not at all. In the main this was because of the residents' low level of mutual involvement in rural or town-wide activities. There was no way in which obligations established in perduring fields of activity could carry over into the Old Office. The intercalary agencies, so to speak, were not available to effect the conversion of external influence into the currency of its internal counterpart.

At the same time, James' attempts at leadership within the ambit of the quarters were further discredited by his relationship to management. Thus Gabriel interpreted James' requests for help in cleaning up as due to the pressure of James' European coworkers, and discounted them accordingly. On another occasion Bava circulated a story he had heard from a kinsman which was more explicitly disparaging, although in a sardonic rather than a hostile way. It seems that James had sent home for some betel nuts which he hoped to sell among his fellow employees in order to raise additional money for the transport group. When the nuts arrived James visited the Old Married Quarters to deliver them to Hereva, a resident whose work as a driver required him to contact James each day, who had ordered some of the nuts. James arrival was greated by calls of "Eh, a white man (tau kurokuro) is coming" among the women who were sitting around the courtyard. They then called to James, "Why don't you give our husbands more money?" They were presumably referring to the fact that James was one of the clerks who distributed pay-packets on a Friday evening. James, moreover, controlled the petty cash of the plant, and if an employee wanted a loan against wages he had to negotiate, at least in the first instance, with James.

The story was warmly appreciated by the younger Papuans in the quarters and, as it made James' growing stature slightly ridiculous, presumably contributed to their lack of attention to his demands. I have no direct evidence, however, to suggest that John's racial stance was in any way responsible for James' discomfiture and the failure of his attempts at leadership within the quarters. Nonetheless, I think we can infer that John's authoritative statements and evident confidence and command when talking about the racial structure of the town and Territory must have reinforced the young Papuans' resolve not to pay too much attention to James' requests and whims.

While the conflict in attitudes may have set up additional barriers to James' attempt to influence the young Papuans, it may also have reinforced the sense of rivalry between John and James and may have added a further barrier to their cooperation.

The sense of rivalry between them was either not very strong or, as is much more likely, was very well controlled. At the same time, it was nonetheless very natural. While James was conspicuous in the affairs of the transport group, John was planning to set up his own business. Indeed, of all the residents, he was the most unabashed in his announcement of leadership aspirations; and these centered particularly on village and business ventures. On one occasion, he came into the messing area when Sidney and I were alone there and declaimed repeatedly on "How to be a big man; that's what I want to know. How to be a big man?" He answered his own question by stating immediately, "And the way to do it is to save your money."

At the same time as the transport group purchased their truck, John was devoting his savings, and time, to the construction of a trade store. He was building the frame of the store, and accumulating the building materials for its construction, outside the Old Office; when it was finished he was going to ship it to his village, erect it, and stock it with trade goods. Moreover, something of his "business" aspirations can be seen in his association with a policeman who was a partner in a trucking venture run by a group of Mt. Hagen migrants. John had first met this man at Popondetta and, now they were both in Port Moresby, was encouraging him to marry his sister. In return John was trying to get him and his compatriots to at least pay the deposit on a truck with which John could start his own business.

I am sure that, in view of James' evident success, John could not help but feel envious. The only explicit hint I ever had of envy, how- ever, was during the week after James had "brought out" the truck. During that week James and his compatriots spent much of their time riding around the town in the decorated lorry. John accused James of showing off. Moreover, John made no secret of the fact that he would never suffer fools gladly. He had a cutting tongue. On more than one occasion he lashed out at people in the quarters. He once arraigned Sidney before myself and a number of the residents for stupidity and incompetence while at work. He also criticized James, for throwing his money about. John was the only one, other than James who might have organized the house's domestic arrangements. But while he had a facility for drawing people to him, he had at the same time a facility for alienating them. His scorn and self-proclamation as the house's public moralist was more than the residents could stomach.

Unable to evolve a pattern of leadership or to settle their differences the residents drifted along in domestic turmoil. They remained, for the most part, as competing and separate individuals, making no con- certed or collective attempts to deal with the web of symbiosis. Com- mon employment and a similar classification by management, which might have helped to bridge the social gap, were unimportant. These shared characteristics were regarded as accidents rather than as signifi- cant bonds. The residents' important social ties lay elsewhere, and served to pull the residents apart. The social distances created by the centripetal force of these perduring ties was supplemented by the dis- tance created due to the contrasts in personal style, in racial attitudes, in ethnic identities, and in the residents' perceptions of their positions as migrants. There was thus no cohesion at the level of the quarters. But while these symbiotic and cultural variables divided the residents as a whole, they forged new social bonds at a lower level. Thus while the fact of community set Gabriel and Lucian apart, it acted on the un- derlying homogeneity of interests of Lucian, David, and Sidney to draw them together as New Guineans. A similar process was apparent in the grouping together of the occupants of Room C. In each case these new ties found expression in commensality and other joint activi- ties.

Social Adjustment to the Fact of Community

On the first page of this chapter, I used a quotation from Lévi- Strauss' "The Elementary Structures of Kinship" to illustrate the main theme of the discussion. The quotation was taken from a passage describing the situation of two strangers who are sitting together in a small French restaurant. These diners are faced with the problem of resolving the strain arising from the fact that they are at once together and apart. They are united by the objects and utensils of the meal—by the fact of community—and yet feel bound to maintain their reserve. The same tension was felt by the Old Office residents, demonstrating the force of the sub-social dependence involved in Port Moresby urban residence.

The fleeting but difficult situation of the two strangers in the small French restaurant is "resolved by the exchanging of wine. It is an assertion of good grace which does away with the mutual uncertainty. It substitutes a social relationship for spatial juxtaposition" (Lévi-Strauss 1969:59). Similarly, where the initial indifference between the Old Office residents was breached—as in the growth of relationships among the New Guineans and among the younger Papuan residents—it gave way to ties of friendship expressed in commensality and common-place exchanges. And although the exchanges were low-key, they were important in the eyes of the young occupants. It is also important, however, to stress the limitations of the ties involved. They rose to prominence in the domestic disturbances, were confined to the urban-located field of relationships and were largely abandoned when the residents moved on. Many Port Moresby associations show the same fragility. Towndwellers have contrasted rural commitments and customs and thus most urban relationships are tentative and hazardous. There are few established expectations of reciprocity and thus few residents fully trust their neighbours. Reciprocities are most easily established within the framework of ethnic labels, since these express perceptions of similarity in residential and educational careers and in the use of *linguae francae*.

Continuing rural commitments helped to set residents apart and maintain the pattern of anonymity. In the other P.M.D. quarters, however, anonymity was less pervasive since workers were often able to live with kinsmen and fellow-villagers or, in the married quarters, were able to set up conjugal households. But the presence of kinsmen and families only modified the worker's experience of unwelcome heterogeneity and urban symbiosis and did not dissolve it. Thus in the barracks which housed the bulk of single workers, isolated individuals were replaced by cliques or sets based on kinship and locality, but between the sets was the same suspicion and relatively normless antagonism. The cliques or sets, moreover, were not simply extensions of rural relationships. The social boundaries of the sets reflected the extension of reciprocity from kinsmen to previously unrelated compatriots within the context of the micro-history of the P.M.D. living quarters and broader patterns of ethnicity. The complex web of "ethnicities" reflected contiguity within the compound, kinship, locality, personal friendships and hostilities and cultural stereotypes.

*

4

Workers as Neighbors:

The Old Boy-House

It is evident, then, that space is not the only obstacle to communication, and that social distances cannot always be adequately measured in purely physical terms. The final obstacle to communication is self-consciousness. [Park 1926:16]

The morphological aspects of relationships between neighbors in the P.M.D. quarters were similar to the groupings described by Wilson and Mafeje (1963) for Langa, a black-African township on the outskirts of Cape Town. In the Langa barracks which housed the truly *migrant* males (those who regard their stay in town as temporary), corporate groups of "home-boys" emerged. In the flats and houses which accommodated the semi-urbanized and the townsmen the situation was very different. The corporate group was replaced by a network of friends, and no groups held together without some common tie other than the home tie (ibid.: 15, 50, 54).

This contrast between groupings in Langa finds many parallels in the P.M.D. compounds. These groupings were not, however, sufficiently sharp or tied so unequivocably to housing type to warrant following Wilson and Mafeje's clear distinction between corporate groups and networks, or to warrant the restriction of either of these forms of association to particular quarters. The contrast was rather one between a tendency for dense and multifunctional social networks to predominate in the barracks and for single purpose social networks with low density to predominate in the married quarters (Barnes 1969a and 1969b).

To some extent this contrast was related to the physical environment and the "household" composition of the various quarters. Thus the dormitory-like arrangement of the barracks was conducive to large domestic groupings, while the form of associations in the married quarters was in part the result of the conjugal basis of the household. As the residents of married units had their wives and families with them it was inevitable that the domestic organization should be one based on conjugal privacy and the family as the unit of consumption, militating against the growth of larger units. My aim is to describe and examine the processes by which such contrasts were given cultural expression. In this chapter I examine neighboring relationships in the Old Boy-House, the barracks for unskilled bachelors. In the next I move to the married quarters to examine the operation of similar processes.

THE BARRACKS

The Old Boy-House was tucked away behind the bulk-store and was bounded on its southern side by a garage and workshop, on its eastern side by a rainwater barret, and on the western side by the courtyard of the Old Married Quarters. But for the bright Papuan sun and clear sky the barracks' aspect would have been truly dark and satanic, occupying, as it did, a restricted site and hemmed in by other buildings. Access to the first floor was gained by two external staircases. One of these was situated on the eastern side of the building close to the rainwater barret which threatened to undermine it; the other arose more boldly from the married quarters' concrete yard. Access to the top floor was by an internal staircase from the floor below.

The interior of the Boy-House presented a uniform drabness, with its largely unpainted, corrugated iron walls and roof, and its long lines of unpainted stretchers standing on bare wooden boards. A general sense of airlessness and enclosure pervaded the second floor, mainly because the slope of the roof limited headroom and because the few windows on that floor were low—below eye level—or were left almost permanently closed. The first floor was much better ventilated and brighter because of the cross draught and light from two doors at the head of the external staircases. These were invariably left open during the day and evening.

During the period of my researches the average number of occupants was around fifty-seven. These residents were divided almost equally between the two floors. On weekends, however, the numbers sleeping there could rise dramatically. There was a far greater tendency for temporary visitors and more permanent but unofficial "guests" to be found on the second floor—possibly because its poor light and distance from the barracks' main thoroughfare gave a greater sense of concealment. There was always a fair degree of flux in the house, both because of the arrival of new residents and the departures and repositioning of those already there.

At one end of the first floor a wooden partition running the width of the building gave rise to a partially separate room accommodating —officially—six employees. The second floor had a row of six cubicles running along its eastern wall, a carryover from the days when the barracks was a store. Lines of beds occupied the nonpartitioned areas of the two floors. On the upper floor there was also a mess table.

Toilet and washing facilities were located outside the building in an ablutions block which backed onto the bulk-store. These facilities were shared with the families living in the married units below. Clothes could also be washed in the ablutions block, but many of the occupants preferred to use the sinks outside the Old Office. In doing so they incurred the wrath of any European supervisor who passed by since the overflow of water from the sinks fell onto the earthen yard and was churned up by forklift trucks and lorries coming from the bulk-store, thus making the area into a quagmire. Food could be cooked in the fireplaces provided in the middle of the courtyard on the western side —which were shared with the married workers—but most of the Boy-House residents cooked on kerosene stoves inside the buildings. With these spatial and living arrangements there was little privacy for any of the residents. The occupants of the cubicles and of the room on the first floor, however, were rather better off in this respect.

The usual daily routine was uneventful, marked only by people leaving or joining their shift. Some three-quarters of the occupants were involved in shift work—the majority working in Production Four. The second shift (the afternoon and evening shift, that is) came back from work just after midnight and the first shift (the morning shift) started at 6 a.m. With the exception of a Workshop Three attendant, the rest of the shift workers were divided between Production One and Two. All of these were on a seven-day-a-week, three-shift, rotational cycle, working either in the morning, the afternoon or the night shifts. These workers took time off during the ensuing week if they had worked over a weekend. This meant that, throughout the day, people could be found trying to sleep, playing cards, or just sitting around and talking. Occasionally someone would strum a ukelele or guitar. Musical talent, however, was generally poor. The two most proficient players lived in the Old Married Quarters. The resident working in Workshop Three bravely carried a guitar for some months but made little progress and provoked, from time to time, angry comments from people trying to sleep.

Often the main event of the day was the walk to Koke market and the subsequent promenade. Workers returning from the plant at 3 p.m. (or afterwards if they were day workers) would shower and then walk down to Koke. Often, on arriving, they would buy very little, aside from a few peanuts, *okari* nuts, or mandarin oranges. The aim was to walk around and to talk to kin and other friends. Occasionally, on the weekend or on some special occasion, native vegetables, fish, and other produce would be bought. But this happened infrequently; occupants of the barracks preferred a diet of rice and tinned fish, or very occasionally, tinned meat. The supplies for such a diet were cheaper, and easier to prepare and cook. Moreover rice and tinned food were relatively imperishable and easy to store.[1]

[1] On the basis of a survey of supply and demand functions at Territory markets, Epstein (1969:20–21) writes "In the course of one week about 50,000 individuals enter Koki [sic] of whom no more than 20 percent buys something." The modal income category for those surveyed was $10–$19 per fortnight, far higher than the modal category for unskilled workers at P.M.D. This also suggests that the purchase of native vegetables was beyond barracks' residents' means.

The occupants were, with few exceptions, completely unskilled. This also meant that the bulk of them were drawn from Production Four, and, to a much lesser extent, from Distribution—these two sections employing the vast majority of unskilled laborers in the plant. Indeed, many managers regarded the Old Boy-House simply as the living quarters for Production Four laborers. Work section membership and skill categories for the residents are given in Table 8. It will be seen that with only three exceptions they were either unskilled or semiskilled. The one skilled worker had recently been promoted from the ranks of the semiskilled and was on probation as a supervisor in Production Four. The two white-collar workers were the least formally qualified of the laboratory employees.

TABLE 8

RESIDENTS OF OLD BOY-HOUSE ACCORDING TO WORK SECTION AND SKILL

	White-Collar	Skilled	Semi-skilled	Un-skilled	Total
Production Four	...	1	3	28	32
Distribution	...	...	...	7	7
Production One	...	...	...	4	4
Other	2	...	3	9	14
Total	2	1	6	48	57

[A9797]

Despite the residents' lack of occupational skill, however, they were not quite at the bottom of the industrial hierarchy: they had a modicum of seniority. Employment at P.M.D. did not give automatic rights to company accommodation, and so an unskilled employee would usually have to give one or two months' satisfactory service before he would be considered worthy to take up a bed in the barracks. Nonetheless, despite the fact that they were not the most impermanent of the employees, a majority of Old Boy-House residents were only recent recruits. Some 55 percent had spent less than one year working for the company, and of these one-half had worked there for less than six months. The modal category of employment of all barracks' dwellers was six to twelve months. The two longest serving employees had been there continuously for eight and for seven years, respectively. (See Table 9.)

TABLE 9

RESIDENTS OF OLD BOY-HOUSE ACCORDING TO THE DURATION
OF THEIR EMPLOYMENT

Duration	Nos.
Under three months	11
Three to six months	4
Six to twelve months	17
One to two years	13
Two to three years	2
Three to four years	4
Over four years	6
Total	57

[A9799]

The age structure of the barracks' population was in itself partly responsible for the workers' length of service. Of the fifty-seven residents at the end of August 1967, I estimated that perhaps thirty were under 20 years of age, another sixteen were in the 20 to 25 year-old age range, and that the rest were over 25, with perhaps five bordering on 30. For many it was their first term of employment in the town.

It will be remembered that the plant garnered its labor force from most of the administrative districts of Papua–New Guinea, and, within each district, from diverse sub-districts and localities. Unskilled labor was drawn from fewer areas, but eight administrative districts were still represented among its ranks. Certain localities and subdivisions were considerably overrepresented with respect to the place of origin structure of the town population while others were underrepresented. Nonetheless, the overall picture for the plant as a whole, and for the unskilled and semiskilled labor force in particular, was one of heterogeneity. In all, seven districts were represented and within these, thirteen different sub-districts. The distribution of places of origin among barracks' residents is summarized in Table 10. The number from each district is given, together with an indication of the scattering from within the district. The final column gives the totals of semiskilled and unskilled bachelors in the labor force as a whole. These final totals represent a pool from which barracks' dwellers were drawn at any one time. As Table 10 suggests, however, the actual heterogeneity was considerably less than the total of districts and sub-districts represented would suggest. Thus the vast majority of the residents were from the Gulf and Northern Districts and within these from four sub-districts. Moreover, fifteen of the Gulf migrants were from the Kerema sub-district, and all those from the Northern District were from the same general locality immediately to the south of, and perhaps one-quarter of the way along, the road which ran from Kokoda to Popondetta. Residents from the Central District were almost completely absent, despite the fact that it contributed the second largest number of workers to the plant's unskilled and semiskilled labor force.

TABLE 10

RESIDENTS OF OLD BOY-HOUSE ACCORDING TO THEIR
PLACE OF ORIGIN

District	Total of Residents from District	No. of Sub-districts in District	No. of Sub-districts Represented in House	Semiskilled and Unskilled Bachelors Employed by Company
Gulf	25	3	3	27
Central	3	5	2	19
Northern	14	3	1	15
Chimbu	6	4	2	9
Southern Highlands	6	6	2	7
Eastern Highlands	2	5	2	2
Western Highlands	1	5	1	2
Morobe	—		—	3
Unknown or Uncertain	—		—	12
Total	57		13	96

[A9803]

The occupants of the Old Boy-House were allotted beds on the basis of occupational and "household" criteria and on the basis of certain minimum seniority requirements. Thus, in part, the distribution of residents with respect to area of origin followed inevitably from the distribution for semiskilled and unskilled bachelors as a whole. But it is also apparent from the very significant underrepresentation of Central District employees that other criteria were operating. Their access to other forms of accommodation was an obvious element in their choice, but the social arrangements of the barracks would also have made them rather anomalous.

Sets and Groups

Social arrangements in the barracks were marked by the clustering of individuals into spatially and socially distinct "sets" based, for the most part, on broad sociogeographic regions within the combined Territories.[2] All the residents could be referred to by using the name of the principal town or station in their home area, and (with minor qualifications) both floors of the Boy-House were divided into areas which were thought of as belonging to people from a given part of the country. These spatial and social divisions were important for much of the residents' daily activity. They were also important for the less mundane aspects of social life because they readily became emotionally significant symbols. These symbols could be used in the expression of many of the discontents and hostilities which, if not always overtly rife, were continually bubbling below the surface. Figure 2 shows the spatial distribution of the migrants at the end of August 1967, according to the most frequently used regional labels.

The use of regional labels as basic social identities within the context of the barracks, and the underlying spatial segregations, must be thought of as a set of statistical tendencies rather than a fully articulated system of named corporate groups, as my reference to Wilson and Mafeje's (1963) analysis of the Langa barracks might suggest. To see it as such would be to do less than justice, for example, to the presence of *wanpis*, that is, outsiders. These were people whose social centers

[2] The way I am using *set* will become apparent as the analysis proceeds. Anticipating it a little we can think of the set as a generic, and at the same time, dynamic concept by allowing it to take a range of meanings between a "simple aggregation" at one end and a "corporate group" at the other. The aim of the analysis will be to examine what factors impel a particular grouping to take up which form at any one time. For most of the time the concept will be used to refer to a social unit which is "a little more than category but less than group" (Frankenberg 1966:18). See also Mayer (1966) uses *set* to mean a finite set of linkages *initiated by an ego*. In my usage the specifically egocentric basis is seen as variable. The term "sociogeographic region" is taken from Fortes (1945:231).

of gravity in the town lay outside the barracks, but who nevertheless continued to sleep there. Within the context of the barracks itself, and compared to the rest of the residents, these outsiders seemed relatively

FIGURE 2

THE OLD BOY-HOUSE

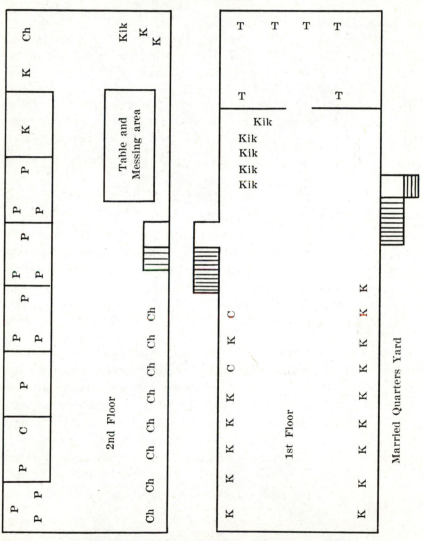

Key: P = "Popondetta"   C = "Central"   K = "Kerema"
      Ch = "Chimbu"   Kik = "Kikori"   T = "Tari"

[A9795]

friendless.[3] Thus, at the southern extremity of the second floor, and obscured by the large mess table which almost sealed them off from the other inhabitants, were a varying number of beds, usually four or five. These were frequently occupied by *wanpis* although sometimes they also served to accommodate an "overflow" from other sections. "Kerema" residents, for example, were concentrated on the first floor; but sometimes their numbers swelled and, although not *wanpis*, would be allocated to this end of the second floor.

To accept the adjective "corporate" for these groupings would be to imply collective responsibility and/or a sense of perpetuity (cf. Fortes 1969:279f) not always present. Rather, the sets were in a continual state of flux and incipient anomie as residents were dismissed, left of their own volition, moved to other accommodation, other employees were moved in, and everyone shuffled beds. To some extent these changes were merely those of membership, the boundaries remaining unchanged. On other occasions the boundaries were extended to include people of a rather different character than the core members; at yet other times they were compressed. And as the boundaries changed so too did the norms of aggregation.

The social processes underlying their formation, extension and contraction, however, were not readily apparent to the short-term observer. To him they were simply "groups." To understand how the aggregations might appear in this guise let us turn to a *wanpis* and to his view of barracks' social organization.

One of the most openly discussed and most irritating facets of life in the Boy-House was bedbugs. These were grumbled about continually and universally abhorred, but were largely accepted as an irremovable nuisance. The most vociferous complainant was David, a young, single New Guinean, from Finschhafen in the Morobe District, working in Production One. He was the only resident who appeared to do anything positive about eradicating the bugs, aside from spending fruitless half-hours picking them out of mats and mattresses as most others did: he borrowed my insect spray, and finding this only partly effective, left the plant.

---

3 *Wanpis* (from the English "one piece") is the Pidgin for "alone, without relatives, an orphan, without a mate" (Mihalic 1957:159). The term was usually used in a less encompassing sense to mean friendless or kinless in a specified situation, in this case, within the barracks.

David had had several jobs in the town but had joined P.M.D. from the army. He was not at all sure of his long-range plans and had decided to join the company as an interim measure. It was thought he had potential for training in production supervision and, because of this potential, management allotted him a cubicle in the middle of the line on the second floor which had just been vacated by a Western Highlander who had now joined the public service.

I met David quite by chance one night while we were both on the night shift, and for the fortnight he worked at P.M.D. he complained to me incessantly about the general physical and human conditions of his accommodation. Then, very late one Friday night, he arrived at the Old Office, obviously very drunk. He came, ostensibly to see me, and announced that he was leaving the next day. He told us he had been badly bitten by the bugs and couldn't sleep for the noise and stupidity of his neighbors. True to his word, he left the next morning.

David's complaints focused finally on bedbugs and the noise and foolish behavior of other unspecified residents. However, for much of the fortnight in which he worked and lived at the plant (during which time he conspicuously treated me as a trusted confidant—possibly because I was also *wanpis* and eager to listen), his continual complaints were about more general aspects of behavior and "the groups" than bedbugs. By "the groups" he meant the barracks residents' practice of segregating themselves both physically and socially, and the unfriendliness and loneliness this entailed for someone like himself. He was particularly critical and bitter about the exclusiveness of the coastal Papuans—including his immediate neighbors, the "Popondetta boys." [4]

Loneliness was not his only grievance: he was also disturbed by the practical difficulties that confronted a *wanpis*. Without cooking equipment and utensils, without friends from whom to borrow them, and unwilling or unable to buy them himself, he led a miserable exis-

[4] The resemblance between the nature of social relations in the barracks and in the dormitories of the government-controlled factory in Yunnan, China studied by Shih (1944) is striking. The study was based on participant observation, the author having slept in one of the dormitories. Shih (1944:101) reports strains in the social organization essentially similar to those in the Old Boy-House—talking after lights-out, excessive noise, lights left on while others were trying to sleep, etc. He writes that "one worker complained of the man whose bed was alongside his because he had lice and was very dirty. He remarked with humour 'It is said that lice do not recognise boundaries of sleeping quarters'. For reasons such as these, workers like to segregate into groups according to locality . . . ."

tence. He also expressed anxiety about his personal safety, arguing that fights were prevalent throughout the town and that he lacked friends to help him. Asked why he thought the Boy-House residents were unfriendly he said, "When you know more about this town you will see that *wantoks* stay together; they want to talk about their own things and find out about their own people . . . they don't trust other boys to help them and so they help only themselves."

This then was the view from the outside. It stressed exclusion and inclusion, an in-group and an out-group. But what of the "groups" themselves? How did they see their situation? Were the bonds within each set as standardized and uniform as David's comments would suggest? To answer these questions and to understand the lineaments of barracks' social organization it will be instructive to turn now to an examination of relationships within one of the sets themselves.

I have chosen to examine the bonds between Northern District migrants—David's immediate neighbors of whom he was so critical—and their relationship to other residents and employees as illustrative of relationships in the barracks as a whole. The network of ties between these workers was dense. They had appropriated most of the small cubicles on the second floor with the exception of one occupied by David and his predecessors and one occupied by one of the two Production Four boss-boys, a man from the Gulf District. Two other "Popondettas" lived in the space at the end of the row; this was almost a cubicle without a door. All the Northern District migrants were involved in ties of reciprocity and mutual obligation and thus spent much of their time together. They were also highly conscious of the spatial and social boundaries they and others had erected and made strong investments in their continuance. This heightened the other residents' awareness of them as a distinct collectivity. I look on the clustering of relationships among this category of residents as paradigmatic of the overall social organization.

"Popondetta Boys": The Background

Throughout my stay at P.M.D., Northern District migrants formed the third largest "regional" category: at the end of August 1967, some 12 percent of the labor force. They were even more evident in the barracks, however, than this figure would suggest; most of them were concentrated there rather than being widely distributed throughout the company's and other forms of urban housing as were, for example, the Gulf District migrants.

Of a total of twenty Northern District workers employed by P.M.D. during the first period of my fieldwork, eighteen were from the Kokoda Sub-District. Eleven of these came from three villages linked by affinal ties and grouped around a shared mission station at "Mbawe". Two other workers from the same sub-district were described as "Koro" people by those from "Mbawe": "Koro" is another mission station about ten to fifteen miles from the first. These thirteen were all native Orokaiva speakers. Orokaiva is a non-Austronesian language of the Binandere family of languages. Five others were from the Aomie-speaking area of Asafa. Theirs was also a non-Austronesian language but of a stock not obviously related to the Binandere family. Dutton has labelled this second non-Austronesian family as "Koiarian" (Dutton 1969).[5] The Mbawe, Koro, and Asafa migrants were all members of the same Local Government Council area.

The two remaining Northern District workers were from the Popondetta and Tufi areas. Vincent, who figured in the previous chapter, was a Kwarafe-speaker (Binandere family) from Cape Nelson in the Tufi Sub-District. The other was a Managalase speaker (Koiarian family) from the Popondetta Sub-District.

The first of these migrants to start work at the plant, in 1959, was William from the Koro area, for whom I shall use the cipher nA. (To avoid the confusion of too many proper names, each of the Northern District workers has been referred to in the account by "n" followed by a capital letter. "n" signifies "Northern District": the capital letters refer to the sequence of the migrants' recruitment—thus "nA" joined the plant before "nB". The principal figures in the account are referred to by name.) William (nA) had worked six years as an administration laborer in a rural area just outside Port Moresby. Unskilled and with only a minimal education, he had come to Moresby itself one weekend for a visit, had overstayed, obtained a job, and had been back to his village on only one occasion since then.

Humphrey (nB) started work at P.M.D. independent of nA. Having come from the Mbawe area, he had originally started work as an apprentice after graduating from Idubada Technical College. When

[5] I am grateful to Tom Dutton for his help in assigning these migrants to language categories.

the Australian Petroleum Company retrenched its labor force in the early 1960s, however, Humphrey had had to be transferred to another company. He said he was impressed by the small workshop at P.M.D. and felt that he would get a better training than he would have had with his former employer. He knew nA before he started work at the plant but said this had not influenced his decision to take up employment there. Vincent (nC) joined his former college mate, Humphrey, in the following year.

Paul (nD), from a neighboring village, joined the company in 1963 on Humphrey's recommendation. After these founding members of the set, other younger men from the home and neighboring areas made their way to the plant to join their kinsmen and friends already there or, in some cases, came quite by chance. With the exception of Humphrey (nB)—living in the New Married Quarters with his wife and child—and Phillip (nN) from Asafa—whose wife was living in the village—all were bachelors. Most were in their late teens or early twenties. William (nA) and Samuel (nK) were the oldest, in their early thirties. With the exception of the latter all had at least one year of primary schooling. The modal standard of education was Standard 5 or 6. As a category they were on the whole better educated than other (that is, district-based) categories at the plant.

Phillip (nN), the first of the Asafa men to arrive at the plant, worked in Workshop Three: the Managalase speaker, Hete (nE), was employed as a laborer in Workshop One. With the exception of these two, all were employed in Production Four. Humphrey (nB), Vincent (nC), and two others—nH and nI—worked as fitters or fitters' mates. Paul (nD) had recently been promoted to shift supervisor from the position of machine operator. As operator he had been assisted by his kinsman nF. William (nA) operated the same machine on the other shift where he was assisted by his affine nG. The rest were all Production Four laborers. Table 11 lists all Northern District workers involved in the events recounted in this chapter.

"Popondetta Boys": The Bases of Dyadic Relations

Having described something of the background of the Northern District workers' relationships and activities, we are now in a position to analyze their determinants. By doing so we will be able to see many of the mechanisms which established the spatial and social boundaries

TABLE 11

NORTHERN DISTRICT MIGRANTS AT P.M.D. BETWEEN
MAY AND DECEMBER 1967

Year of Arrival	Person	Vernacular	Locality	Skill or Task (i)	Living Quarters	Organized Leizure Activities and Memberships
1959	nA	Orokaiva	Koro	P. One Mach. Op.	Barracks	None
1962	nB	Orokaiva	Mbawe	P. One Fitter	New Married	PNGVR (iii) Mbawe Soccer
1963	nC	Kwarafe	Tufi	P. One Apprentice	Old Office	PNGVR (iii)
1966	nD	Orokaiva	Mbawe	P. One Supervisor	Barracks	Mbawe Soccer, Boxing
	nE	Managalase	Nataka	Workshop Labor	Barracks	Mission Soccer Club
	nF	Orokaiva	Mbawe	P. One Labor	Barracks	Mbawe Soccer, Boxing
	nG	Orokaiva	Koro	P. One Labor	Barracks	Boxing
	nH	Orokaiva	Mbawe	P. One Fitter	Barracks (ii)	Mbawe Soccer, Boxing
	nI	Orokaiva	Mbawe	P. One Apprentice	Barracks (ii)	Mbawe Soccer, Boxing
	nJ	Orokaiva	Mbawe	P. One Labor	Barracks	Mbawe Soccer, Boxing
	nK	Orokaiva	Mbawe	P. One Labor	Barracks	None
1967	nL	Orokaiva	Mbawe	P. One Labor	Barracks	Mbawe Soccer, Boxing
	nM	Orokaiva	Mbawe	P. One Labor	Barracks	Mbawe Soccer, Boxing
	nN	Aomie	Asafa	Workshop S/Skill	Barracks	Boxing
	nO	Aomie	Asafa	P. One Labor	Barracks	None
	nP	Orokaiva	Mbawe	P. One Labor	Barracks	Mbawe Soccer, Boxing
	nQ	Aomie	Asafa	P. One Labor	Barracks	None
	nR	Aomie	Asafa	P. One Labor	Barracks	None
	nS	Aomie	Asafa	P. One Labor	Barracks	None
	nT	Orokaiva	Mbawe	P. One Labor	Barracks	Mbawe Soccer, Boxing

(i) P. One = Production One

(ii) Only part of period in question: later part of the period spent in a smaller unit within the factory complex

(iii) PNGVR = Papua-New Guinea Volunteer Reserve

[A9813]

operating within the house. Let us look, first of all, at the way in which dyadic relationships when linked together helped to form the set.

Looked at from the individual standpoint of any one of the core members, a social universe can be thought of as a network of relationships, each line within the mesh denoting a relationship and representing different frequencies of association and various institutional and geographical settings. As we move along any path in the network from this given individual we will be moving from areas of "multiplexity" (Gluckman 1955:19), where relationships are frequent and involve a multiplicity of geographical and institutional settings, to those where the relationships are more limited.

If we allow the length of the line between each pair of points to represent the *intensity* of the relationship then we can abstract from the network a series of concentric circles—each circle defining a degree of social distance. The inner circle would encompass the relationships of greatest intimacy; those of close kinship and where exchanges and gifts would be phrased within an idiom of "generalised reciprocity" (Sahlins 1966:147). The outer circles would include relationships of lesser intimacy and would range from those of quasi-kinship status to those of simple companionship; this is the region where generalized reciprocity shades off into "balanced reciprocity" (ibid. 147). Around these circles would be a penumbra of diffuse camaraderie and, beyond this, zones of complete indifference or perhaps hostility and "negative reciprocity," where participants seek something for nothing (ibid. 148). The total configuration is the individual's personal *ambience* (see also Caplow et al. 1964:70).

Thus taking, say, Paul's position in the overall set of relationships we can see that he was involved in continual and close association with a number of the younger Mbawe lads. nM, for instance, worked on the same shift in Production Four, slept in an adjoining cubicle, went with Paul to the town's army barracks to take part in boxing tournaments, and played alongside him in the Mbawe soccer team.

The boxing was held at the army barracks for town residents interested in the sport. One of the instructors was a soldier from Mbawe. nF and a varying group of the younger Mbawe lads also attending the boxing with Paul and nM. The soccer team was captained by Humphrey (nB) and drew its players from the police, the army, and the tobacco factory, as well as P.M.D. Nonetheless, the bulk were P.M.D.

workers; all were "home-boys." The team had been formed at Christmas 1965 when the Mbawe set sent home to celebrate the marriage of Humphrey to a local Mbawe girl. The season I attended, they were "practicing" against other, mainly Northern District, teams. They hoped that in 1968, when they had sufficient funds to pay dues and provide equipment, they would be able to join the town's league. Eventually, however, Humphrey, Paul, and the better players joined a team which P.M.D. itself formed.

But more important to Paul and nM than these urban institutional settings was the fact that they were brothers and were jointly planning and helping in a village business enterprise with a third brother, nP, who worked on the other Production Four shift. Paul had originally come to Port Moresby in 1963, to earn and save enough money to take back to his home settlement—a settlement within the "Mbawe" vicinage —so that he could aid the "business" which his father and other senior kinsmen had undertaken. By 1964, helped by contributions which Paul sent from Port Moresby, the village people had accumulated enough cash to buy their first cow. By the time of my arrival Paul's "family" owned or had acquired shares in a number of other cows and had built and stocked a trade store. nM and nP, their schooling finished, had come to Moresby to earn additional cash for the family enterprise.

I am not sure of the extent of these operations or of the exact part that Paul and his two brothers played in them but they all talked of returning to Mbawe at Christmas 1968. Once there, nM and nP would help to look after the cows and Paul would supervise the operation of the trade store. They saw this as a permanent arrangement. For the time being they pooled their wages and sent periodic sums back to the village.

Beyond this small group of true brothers, cemented by bonds of sentiment, by ongoing exchanges, and joint business activities, there were further relationships with consanguinal and affinal kin from two neighboring settlements. Two of these men—Humphrey and Samuel (nK)—were mother's brothers to Paul and his siblings. The rest were all classed as "brothers," or, in the local English idiom, as "cousin-brothers." This set of people from Mbawe, subject to age (Samuel [nK] was thought too old to play) formed the pool of P.M.D.-based players from which the Mbawe soccer team was picked. All of them worked in Production Four and, with the single exception of Humphrey, slept in the Old Boy-House.

The Mbawe migrants were Paul's immediate and effective "home-people." Relationships between all of them were extremely close. They were linked to each other by kinship ties, shared the same fund of gossip and village stores, and recognized the obligation to help each other in need. They spent much of their leisure time together; paid each other's bus or truck fares and other ancillary expenses; had all gone back to Mbawe to celebrate Humphrey's marriage; had all contributed to the beer and food provided at the party which Humphrey gave for his small daughter on her first birthday; and had all helped entertain Paul's father when he came to town on a visit. Moreover, they all shared in the vegetable foods and nuts which this senior villager brought with him.

These links were continually reinforced by the group's everyday association and, for example, by their visits to Humphrey's house. His accommodation became a meeting place for Mbawe people in the town. Sunday would see not only the P.M.D. workers there but those from the army, police, and farther afield.

The frequency of their association and the multiple ties between them meant that they operated as a named, continuing, and cohesive group, through a great variety of situations, both inside and outside the barracks. All of them were kinsmen and in each case their relationships antedated either urban residence or employment at the plant. Indeed it was the recognition and utilization of these ties that led to many of them working there. Young men coming from the rural areas to find work had more often than not come to Humphrey and the other older men to seek their help. Joining their home-boys they could be assured of companionship, financial help, and other support.

Paul and his kinsmen were in turn individually tied to migrants from the other areas of their district. In each case there seemed to be a developmental aspect to the relationship. Starting perhaps from a chance encounter with someone from beyond Mbawe, or from being thrown together in the plant or barracks, in time the Mbawe people had established close relationships with certain district compatriots. Thus we can now pay less attention to Paul's ambience and begin to talk of the relationship of newcomers to the Mbawe group as a whole.

The two "Koro" migrants, William (nA) and nG were each classed as "brothers," despite the fact that no blood or affinal link could be pointed to. These quasi-kinship relationships had come about as the result of a long and continuing association at the plant and in the barracks between Paul and William. This had started when Paul began work at the company in 1963. I suspect that, recognizing the affinity of language and culture, their minority position in the town and plant, and with an acquaintanceship between Humphrey and William already established, they had seen their association as natural and inevitable. Certainly they had called each other "brother" for some considerable time. It seemed readily understood that nG, a recent recruit and William's affine, was entitled to be called "brother" as an extension of these long-standing ties.

Despite the use of such a close kinship term the two men from Koro were marginal to the core members. Neither William nor nG played on the soccer team and they spent many weekends away from the barracks and their Mbawe friends. At the same time, I had the impression, which was supported by Phillip's (nN) tattling, that the older Mbawe men disapproved of the two Koro migrants' heavy drinking. This was sufficiently serious to lead to nG's dismissal—he had been found drinking while at work—and to William's demotion from the position of a Production Four machine operator to that of ordinary laborer. Humphrey, in particular, a fairly quiet and sober sort of person, was reported to be disturbed by William's behavior. My impression was that William had once been much closer to the Mbawe people than he was at the time of my research.

Despite these differences and suspected disagreements, the Mbawe and Koro migrants were still frequent and close associates. They would share each other's meals, would go on shopping expeditions together, and I would often find them chatting and sharing news over a cigarette when I visited. There were a host of people whom they knew in common in the town and this, together with spatial contiguity, kept them together.

The Mbawe and Koro workers were all Orokaiva. The network of ties between them defined the limits of "kinship" within the set. But this should not be taken to mean that there was a substantial or sharp dividing line between the Orokaiva and the non-Orokaiva: the real division in the set was between Mbawe and non-Mbawe. Thus Hete (nE), although very much an outsider at first, had gradually been assimilated into the set on similar terms to William and nG. A new migrant from the Managalase area, Hete had arrived at the barracks as the result of a chance meeting with William who had then become, so to speak, his sponsor. In the course of time he came to sleep in the bed next to William and his initial association and obligation to this older man was therefore reinforced by spatial contiguity. Hete's relationship, however, did not end there: in the eighteen months he had been at P.M.D. he had developed firm friendships with the other members. A small quiet youth, and an outsider in many of the conversations, he was nonetheless accepted and liked by all. The most important measure of his acceptance is that he took part in many of the day-to-day reciprocities of the group. He almost always ate with them, gossiped with them, would sometimes take turns with William doing each other's washing, and, for example, borrowed a clean shirt from nM for weekend visiting.

An important factor in Hete's acceptance was the friendly patronage which the Orokaiva people could extend to him as "one of our bush people." Responsive to the style of the Orokaiva speakers, more particularly to the Mbawe men, and willing to accept their leadership, he was a fitting object of their aid and companionship. He did not, however, take part in any of their organized activities. Although a soccer player, he played for an Anglican mission team in the mission league.[6] Whereas the Mbawe's group's ties with non-P.M.D. kinsmen focused, to a large extent, on Humphrey's house and the Mbawe soccer team, Hete's were concentrated on a domestic servant's quarters at Boroko. Every weekend Hete would set out to visit his kinsman whose house this was.

The rather "patron-client" character of much of the association between the Mbawe group and Hete was also to be found in that group's relationship to Horae, an employee from the Southern Highlands. As in the case of William and Hete the mutual association had arisen from common employment and residency. A Huli-speaker from Tari, Horae was the boss-boy on Paul's shift. When the Mbawe people went back to Kokoda to celebrate Humphrey's marriage they had taken Horae with them. For a time after his visit he sent letters to an Mbawe girl, although she later transferred her affections elsewhere. While in Port Moresby, Horae associated mainly with the single Northern District migrants, both at work and in their leisure hours, but only on a casual basis, joining none of their organized activities. The formation and development of this relationship was almost certainly aided by the

6 It is of interest that David, living in the Old Office and from the Morobe District, also took part in these competitions, but as a member of a Lutheran mission team. A barrack's resident from the Purari area also played for the Everyman's club of the Papua Ekalesia.

pleasure of being able to lend a helping hand to a Highlander. It was a relationship that the "Popondetta" people and Horae himself never tired of discussing, perhaps because of its strangeness and novelty, and (a related point) because they may have seen that a relationship across the usual social boundaries was a measure of their sophistication.

Phillip's (nN) association was less firm. Previously a "farmer trainee" at Popondetta Agricultural College he had been befriended there by John, the occupant for some time of Room B in the Old Office. John had been studying at the college to become an agricultural officer. John was obviously fascinated by Phillip, a small elephant of a man, whom he described with a laugh as a *bus kanaka tru* (a wild "backwoodsman"), charging through *kunai* grass up to his neck without a thought or a care for decorum. Phillip, finding his way to Moresby after a series of jobs, had worked in the town for over a year when he met John again and they renewed their association. It was John who persuaded Phillip to apply for employment at P.M.D. Phillip already knew of the presence of the set of Northern District workers but had no personal ties to them.

When I arrived—he had arrived the month before—Phillip was sleeping at the end of the line of beds in the "Popondetta" section, having sought out his district compatriots after obtaining work in Workshop Three. But he was far from content with this arrangement and was engaged in a constant battle to obtain better accommodation. In this battle he had the support of the expatriate supervisor of his section but received little sympathy from the manager in charge of housing allocation in the Boy-House. Both Phillip and his supervisor took the view that as a trainee in Workshop Three he should not be housed with laborers; the manager took the view that these trainees were only laborers anyway. There seemed to be a stalemate for a few weeks until nH and nI, members of the fitters' work group in Production Four, were moved into superior housing within the plant itself. Phillip then took possession of the now vacant cubicle with the approval of his supervisor. Immediately, he introduced Baki, a recently recruited forklift driver and a fellow villager of John, Phillip's friend from the Old Office. Introduced to each other by John, Phillip had offered Baki a part share in his cubicle after Baki had illegally seized a vacant unit in the Old Married Quarters,[7] and had been evicted by management.

[7] With my unwitting connivance, I moved Baki's belongings from Hanuabada to the compound for him after he had flagged me down on the road from

At the time I found it strange that there were no overt reactions from the other Northern District workers at the intrusion, since that part of the barracks seemed like a "Popondetta" territory. Despite the segregation of the quarters, however, the social divisions were *not* autonomous territories in either fact or expectation: management would on occasion take part in the internal organization of the barracks. Thus the second cubicle in the section was alternately occupied by "Popondetta Boys" and by workers who were there because of managerial allocation. It must have been widely known that Phillip was angling for better accommodation and that he had the support of his supervisor because the management had jointly visited the Boy-House just before and on the occasion of Phillip's move. Thus the other residents in the section seem to have accepted the background to the new arrangements as part and parcel of barracks' life and of management's power to intervene in domestic arrangements. Certainly, they were powerless to remove either Phillip or Baki from the cubicle. Nonetheless, in those early weeks, Phillip was still very much an outsider to the set and was therefore largely autonomous. He was under no great obligation to his district compatriots in the barracks and was free to take advantage of the changed circumstances as he saw fit.

Unlike Hete, Phillip appeared to make no effort to merge his identity with that of the set. He was not, like Hete, content to be a relatively unobtrusive and dependent newcomer: he was already knowledgeable and experienced in urban living. Whereas Hete had come straight from mission school, after two years elementary schooling, his more ebullient compatriot had left school after Standard 5 and had attended schools in his home district and in Lae. And while in Lae, Michael had picked up a little Kwarafe—Vincent's vernacular—from "Tufi" boys at school. Moreover, he had been trained and had worked as a farmer; he had worked as a teacher for the Anglican mission at Kokoda; and had had three jobs in the last two years, one of which he was dismissed from for striking a supervisor.[8]

Hanuabada one night. The vacant unit was the one which John was to occupy and be evicted from (see chap. 3, Urban and Racial Styles).

[8] His attack on the supervisor may have landed him in prison for a while. John told me that it had. But there was a great deal of uncorrected contradiction in their various accounts. Thus John told me on another occasion that it was an attack at the college which had incarcerated his violent friend. Phillip admitted hitting a Malarial Service employee but denied that he had been imprisoned. Together they treated it as a huge joke but would never

Thus his greater experience of the town, his contacts, especially that with John, his greater material resources—during his working life he had accumulated utensils, a stove, a guitar, and enough money to buy basic supplies—all gave him an independence in evident contrast to Hete's initial dependence. Hete told me how, as a recent arrival with little money and no work for some weeks, he was completely dependent on one kinsman and a few other acquaintances. Their help had had to be supplemented, for the first week at the plant, by the generosity of his new workmates. Despite this initial contrast in the relationship between on the one hand, say, Paul and Hete, and on the other, Paul and Phillip, in time the differences were obscured by the bonds which united all three of them in opposition to the rest of the barracks.

Phillip continued in his exuberant and jolly fashion: he was the archetype of the good-humored, often rowdy, fool whom it is impossible to ignore but easy to love (as John had found) or hate. I can well understand how the other Popondetta workers would have had to include him in their conversations and offer him food if they were cooking; his banter and considerable presence forced one to take him into account. Moreover, with his knowledge of Orokaiva and the local area, his membership of the same Local Government Council, his vague linkage to them by marriage, and the integration brought about by a common church and administration, he could make substantial claims on their attention and help.

Thus, in the weeks following his move, Phillip grew closer to the other members of the set; he ate and chatted with them and on occasion made and received small loans of cash, food, and clothing. Although his associations with the others were never as frequent or covered as many institutional contexts as the associations between the core members, the banter, general camaraderie, and reciprocity which accompanied these meetings was as intimate as that between the Mbawe and Koro migrants and Hete.

Another important event which brought Phillip and the other members of the section together, and further swelled the numbers in the set, was the influx of three of Phillip's fellow villagers and a young man

share the secret with me. There was a double mystery as a kinsman of John's, a clerk, led me to believe that there was something disreputable about John's own hurried departure from the college. As neither of them would elaborate, and I could gain no other information, the matter had to be dropped.

from Mbawe. Following the appearance of a number of vacancies in
Production Four, the Northern District workers had told their kinsmen
and friends in the town and three had left their jobs, and one his unemployment, and had presented themselves for work at the plant. They
quickly moved into the barracks to eat and to sleep. With the greater
volume of interactions in the section Phillip became even more organically related to the other members.

But with the development of the Mbawe people's relationship to Phillip came an association with Baki. Just as it would have been hard to
have ignored Phillip's overtures of friendship, reinforced as they were
by spatial proximity, the accident of employment, and by regional affiliation, it would have been hard to have ignored Baki's own proximity and his claims to recognition based on his friendship with Phillip.
In accepting Phillip's association the other people in the set were in
turn recognizing certain obligations to his friend. And because of
these obligations Baki was, for many purposes, included within the
gossip circle and the circle of commensality.

We have now traced Paul's ties with his fellow-Mbawe people, the
relationship of the Mbawe people to other employees from the district,
and in turn, their relationship to Horae and Baki from outside the district. All except one—Humphrey—were residents of the barracks.
There were various bases to these associations. Some owed their origin to kinship and to an ongoing system of relationships in the home
area; others arose solely from urban residence and common employment; still others reflected differences in personal style. The strength
of some relationships was due to a direct bond between the participants; other relationships—such as those between Baki and the set—
were primarily those between "friends of friends."

Yet despite this variation there were certain clear distinctions. All
the Mbawe people were kinsmen and their relationships antedated either urban residence or common employment. Indeed, it was the recognition and utilization of these ties that led to many of the Mbawe people seeking employment at the company. Their spatial proximity
meant in turn that they spent much of their leisure and work time together, reinforcing the already existing ties. They became teammates,
neighbors, sparring partners, and workmates, and yet remained kinsmen.

In turn the Mbawe group was involved with other Northern District
workers. These ties reflected common employment and contiguity in

the barracks and the plant. Although we can point (as the Northern District workers did themselves) to potential or latent relationships between Mbawe and non-Mbawe workers existing prior to their recruitment, it was common employment which had articulated them. I am sure that there were other pools of people with similar attributes in the town but, lacking a point of articulation, they went unnoticed.

This is an assumption based on my general understanding of the urban society. But the point can be illustrated by events directly related to the Northern District workers themselves. Thus, on one occasion I was showing Vincent a set of photographs. These were of native New Guineans at work: the point of the exercise was to elicit attitudes about occupational prestige. We had leafed through some of the pictures without much reaction from Vincent when suddenly he started, saying he knew one of the people portrayed. It was a mechanic—a "Tufi boy"—whom he had known at technical college. Although Vincent knew him there was no continuing relationship between them. Their past association remained as a latent base which would almost certainly be used to reestablish a tie if they ever came in contact again, very much as James had utilized an old school associate to gain information on his negotiations with the bank. A more forceful illustration of the general point concerns nG who, it will be recalled, was fired for drinking at work. He stayed in town after his dismissal, but, despite the frequency and strength of his association with members of the barracks' set while at P.M.D., he appeared to make no effort to get in touch with them again. It seems that for the relationship to be maintained in any significant sense it needed the constant reinforcement of common employment and coresidence.

Aside from the Northern District migrants were relationships with people from other parts of the Territory, notably with Horae and Baki. These also reflected the bonds of common employment and contiguity in the barracks; indeed these were the *only* bases which could be pointed to other than personal compatibility.

Thus the more evident "egocentric" aspects of the processes by which Northern District recruits were assimilated into the social life of the barracks were coresidence and reciprocity. Workers were brought into association by spatial proximity which in turn was maintained by exchanges of commonplace items and services, gossip, and conversation. The major differences in the degree of incorporation of particular individuals would seem to lie in the duration of the association and the content of the reciprocity. Given a continuing association over time, and other things being equal, we would expect the relationship to move from an area of indifference or suspicion to an area of exchange. At first we should expect the exchange to take the form of a balanced reciprocity; finally it should move to an area of generalized reciprocity. And that is what we saw in the developing relationship between the core and marginal members. In the case of the Mbawe members themselves, each new recruit could assume a situation of generalized reciprocity from the start.

Dyadic Relationships in the Barracks

Each of the barracks groupings—not just that of the Northern District workers—could most aptly be characterized as a network of relationships. From the standpoint of any individual resident the network would take the form of a "star" (Barnes 1969:58) with lines, of varying length, radiating out from a single node (the individual concerned) and the length of each line representing the intensity of the association. Then, if each "star" could be matched with the "stars" of each of the other members of the set and the points of equal length joined, the result would be a complex spider's web of spokes and concentric circles —the individual's personal ambience. Pieced together to form a composite net the sum of these ambiences would describe the intensity of dyadic relationships in the barracks.

As we saw in the case of the web of relationships between the Northern District workers, in some parts of the net the mesh would be extremely large, in others extremely small (cf. Barnes 1954). The total barracks network, then, would resemble a complex patchwork of nets rather than a single net of standard mesh, material, and manufacture. And within this composite net the areas of closely-knit, regularly textured mesh would represent the association of individuals from the same broad sociogeographic region. There were, depending on the actual degree of density and intensity chosen and the activities involved, some eight or nine of these closely-knit areas with only fragile and loosely-spun threads linking them to the others. Members of the sets to which these metaphors apply were drawn from the Northern District, the Southern Highlands, the New Guinea Highlands districts, and the Kikori sub-district of the Gulf District. Somewhat less aptly these morphological statements also apply to the associations between members of the sets drawn from the other sub-districts of the Gulf District:

wanpis or outsiders occasionally left their marks on barracks' social life but its coherence and vitality was largely preempted by the sets.

Viewed sociocentrically, the sets might also appear as comparable and opposed segments, each aggregation informed by a sense of common purpose, unity, and responsibility. Yet viewed more critically, they were in fact quite varied in their composition and in the principles which informed their organization. For example, two of the sets, one involving the Southern Highlanders and the other involving migrants from the Kikori or Purari area of the Gulf District appeared equally homogeneous and intense in their internal relations and each involved six or so members. Yet, while the relationships between the Kikori migrants were firmly grounded in the rural social system and its urban offshoots (these ties, in turn, binding together workers who were occupationally relatively diverse) the relationships between the Southern Highlands workers owned little to perduring rural or rural-urban relationships while their unity owed a great deal to their occupational homogeneity and comparable work histories.

The coastal area of the Gulf District—between its most eastern limit at Cape Possession, and the Kikori River at the head of the Gulf of Papua—is settled by two ethnic groups. The people to the west have come to be known as the Purari or Kikori. Although composed of a series of separate tribes and recognizing no political unity, linguistically they form a unit of closely related and mutually intelligible dialects. Their cultures also reveal a basic similarity throughout (Maher 1967). F. E. Williams (1924) writes that "there is certainly a definite feeling that the Purari are *sui generis.*"

The six or so migrants from this area were spatially and socially distinctive. They occupied the row of beds which ran from the barracks entrance on the eastern side to the cubbyhole of the Southern Highlanders. They came from two of the Purari tribes—Koriki and Maipua. Occupationally, this was the most diversified of the sets. Thus while two were Production Four laborers, two were white-collar workers in the laboratory. Subject to the demands of shift work, they tended to eat together and spent much of their leisure time together. All had important ties to Rabia Camp, an urban settlement founded by Purari people (Oram 1967a). Sometimes known as "Kerema," after their District's principal township, these residents were more widely known as "Kikori" or "Baimuru" boys after their present and previous sub-district headquarters. They were occasionally even referred to as

"Daru boys" by the less knowledgeable. I refer to them as "Kikori" or
"Purari" people, reserving "Kerema" for the Elema peoples to the east
of them in the Gulf District. Their social centers of gravity lay in
Rabia Camp and the Purari area rather than the barracks or the wider
town. Even the two white-collar workers, who anticipated a lengthy
period of wage employment were firmly anchored in Purari continuities and intolerant of the barracks' and town's potential for social discontinuity.

We have already noted that the friendship between Horae, the young
Southern Highlander, and the Northern District workers was the most
obviously "inter-tribal" association of any of the barracks. Yet it was
also perhaps the most predictable since ties within the set of Southern
Highlanders were the most clearly divorced from a rural social system
and rural contiguity. Viewed from without the set they seemed no different than that of the "Purari" workers: the bases of the social relationships involved, however, were quite different. Relationships between the Southern Highlanders were intense and multiplex. There
were few of them—around six persons at any one time—and they all
slept in the small room on the first floor. They were, ostensibly, as
close to each other as the Mbawe and Purari home-boys—they ate together, played cards together, pooled their wages, and spent much of
their remaining leisure time in each other's company. Except for
Horae's relationship to the Popondetta people there were no significant
relationships with other residents, nor with many others outside the
barracks. Although all but one of the Southern Highlanders living in
the barracks during the latter half of 1967 were migrants from Huli-
speaking areas bordering on Tari sub-district headquarters, this did
not mean that they were "home-boys" in the same sense that the Mbawe
or Purari people were. Many of the ties between them had come about
solely as the result of common employment on plantations in the Central
District and a sense of diffuse clanship and common ethnic identity
due to a shared administrative division and headquarters. They were
referred to as "Tari" or "Mendi" boys. As their district was in Papua, and not in the Trust Territory, they often characterized their relative separation from their fellow workers from the adjacent Highland
districts in the Trust Territory as a separation between "Papuans" and
"New Guineans."

Horae, who began working for P.M.D. in 1964, was the first Huli
migrant to work for the plant. He came directly from a plantation in

the Rigo area of the Central District where he had worked for four years. In 1965 he was joined by two other Huli men from the same plantation, and toward the end of 1966, by two more young men from their local area. These last two had been employed on a rubber plantation in the Sogeri area and had been in town for six months. After meeting Horae and his friends they had joined the company. After this a number of their compatriots arrived on the scene, some only stayed a month or so and then were dismissed or found something better elsewhere. Others stayed and at the end of August 1967 there were six Southern Highlanders, all from Tari, living in the first floor room. All were laborers aside from Horae, a Production Four boss-boy. Personal loyalty and allegiance to Horae and shared plantation work experience were the important factors and lowest common denominators in the formation of the set rather than, for example, ties of rural locality, trade, or kinship.

The other Highlanders—those from New Guinea—appeared to be more aware of divisions within their ranks. And while their mutual association was more obviously related to rural commitments and statuses than that of the "Tari" workers, these rural commitments were as much a source of schism as they were of solidarity.

The New Guinea Highlanders were the most unstable in their residence: they shunted back and forth between the barracks and other accommodation in the town in an amazing manner. Only two of that category—both from the Chimbu Valley—lived in the barracks for the duration of my inquiries. The others were either dismissed or, without leaving the company's employ, made off for other accommodation, in some cases returning once more to the barracks. One young man from the Gembogl end of the Chimbu Valley changed his residence no fewer than four times within seven months. In each case he merely moved from one labor compound in the Koke-Badili area to another.

At the time of my census there were six workers from the Chimbu District—all from the Chimbu Valley itself—two from the Eastern Highlands and one Western Highlander. All nine slept in the "Chimbu" section facing the cubicles on the second floor. They were all laborers. The Chimbu Valley migrants were all from a small but very densely populated area: the valley is no more than fifteen miles long and yet between fifteen and twenty thousand Chinbu people live within it (Criper 1969). These migrants came from three "big-lines," as they described them in Pidgin, which may be translated as "tribe" (Brown and Brookfield 1959) or as "district" (Criper 1969). The three units were *Nonu-Yomane, Kewandeku,* and *Kukkane.*

The two from the *Kewandeku* district or tribe were first on the scene. They had joined P.M.D. in 1964. Although they had come from different localities—Yombai and Gogume—they thought of each other as clan "brothers." Three years of working at the plant and sleeping in the barracks had undoubtedly reinforced ties which antedated their employment. They were in their middle twenties and neither was married.

The three from *Nonu-Yomane* were from the same minor locality— Niglkuma: two were brothers and were linked to the third by affinal ties. These three constituted, under the supervision of a leading hand from an Elema group in the Gulf District, a distinct task group of laborers. They were much older than any of the other Highlanders working for P.M.D. I would estimate that two were in their middle to late thirties and one in his early forties; all three were married with children. The eldest was married polygamously. His was the strangest account I was given for being in Moresby: he had come to be fitted for a set of false teeth.

The *Kukkane* worker was from Womkama, the legendary place of origin of the Chimbu people (cf. Brown and Brookfield 1959:33). Also in his middle twenties, he was married, and had a child. Throughout his employment he worked in the bulk-store with a young lad from the neighboring district—*Inaugl.* When eventually he was fired for failing to report for work one Saturday morning, he was replaced by one of his workmate's clansmen.

The common association of these Chimbu migrants owed much to a town-located institution—a labor compound for workers of a local trucking company. This acted as a clearing house, staging camp, and information center for migrants from this part of the Chimbu District. It was here that the later recruits had learned of vacancies at the plant.

Contrasted work section membership, clan affiliation, and differences in age and marital status paralleled each other and accounted for differences in leisure time association within the set. They themselves contrasted those who came from the top of the valley (with administrative and geographical links to Gembogl patrol post) and those who came from the lower end of the valley (with primary links to Kundiawa station, the headquarters of the District). Certainly this distinction encapsulated almost all the others that could be drawn, those of age, work section, clan affiliation, and residence in the town. At the time of my census only one resident hailed from the upper end of the valley, although there had been others earlier in the research. This last man was later dismissed, as we shall see.

For certain purposes, however, particularly cooking and playing cards, the differences were unimportant. Moreover they were further obscured by ties between the Chimbu people and the other New Guinea Highlanders—two men from the Asaro and the Kainantu areas in the Eastern Highlands District and a man from Minj in the Western Highlands District. These three played a full and equal part in the common activities and would often join the Chimbu Valley people in activities outside the barracks.

The unity within the set can best be illustrated by events concerning the *kompani,* a rotating credit association (Geertz 1962; Ardener 1964) which at one time included all New Guinea Highlanders living in the barracks and a number of others from outside. Each member pooled a fixed portion of his wages; the pool then went to one of the contributors determined by general agreement, each week a different member receiving the pool. Everyone contributed, and each received equal amounts during a cycle. There were a number of these arrangements operating at P.M.D. The Chimbu *kompani* was by far the largest and most visible. Every payday all the Highlanders would squat on a small patch of grass outside the toilets exchanging money.

This unity of the *kompani* was broken when, following the dismissal of the *Kukkane* worker referred to above, it split in two. Urdun—the dismissed worker—had received the weekly payment at the beginning of a new cycle. When he was fired the cycle was just past the midway mark with half those involved having contributed each week but still waiting their turn to receive the pool. Urdun claimed he was unable to make the appropriate adjustments and asked for time to repay his debts. The *kompani* dissolved amid many recriminations. The older men argued that Urdun and his clan brothers—both of whom lived elsewhere—were tardy in their efforts to fulfill their obligations. The result was that they formed a new *kompani.* This included all those from the lower end of the Chimbu Valley and the migrants from other New Guinea Highland Districts but excluded those from the top of the valley. With Urdun's dismissal and the reformation of the *kompani* a new boundary was established for the barracks' set, and ties based on

equivalence of age and on residential and employment contiguity were
emphasized at the expense of ties based on, say, common language
and/or rural spatial proximity.

A set, or set of sets, with even greater internal differentiation and
with a more diffuse (but even then still important) sense of common
identity was the "Elema" aggregation. Including some 35 percent of
barracks residents, this set had taken over or been confined to the unin-
closed portion of the first floor. "Elema" was a name used by Motuan
sailors on their Hiri trading voyages to categorize the linguistically
and culturally related peoples inhabiting the coastal strip from Cape
Possession in the east, to the territory of the Purari people in the west.
Anthropologists have accepted this usage (Williams 1940; Brown
1957). The people themselves, although conscious of possessing a culture and language which distinguished them from their neighbors, were
never a single political unit and lacked a common name. In modern
Port Moresby the Motuan and anthropological usage has very little currency—migrants from this area are generally known as "Kerema" people.

The eastern and the western Elema are often distinguished from each
other. Ryan, who has worked among them, writes that the majority of
"Keremas" in Port Moresby are in fact from the eastern areas; these
can all be called Toaripi although for many purposes the eastern Elema
further distinguish between the Moveave, Moripi, and Toaripi proper
(Ryan 1968:60). At the plant, however, slightly under two-thirds of
Elema people were from the western areas. They were, however, distributed unevenly. In the barracks five-sixths were from the west,
whereas in the married quarters nine out of eleven were from the east.
Despite the broad homogeneity of "Keremas" in the barracks, spatial
and domestic groupings consisted of people from the same "subtribe"
or village cluster, modified by association between men of the same
work section and by age. One example will suffice. Thus the three
migrants from Uriri, at the time of my census, slept in adjacent beds.
Two were Production Four laborers and the other a "truck-boy."
These three ate and spent much of their time together in the compound.
But their "shifts" (the "truck-boy" was a day worker) failed, in certain respects, to coincide. This meant that for some meals they ate
apart—the "truck-boy" eating with two other employees in his work
section (a man from Hehere in the Ihu area and another from Koaru,
a village to the east).

The sheer size of the "Kerema" aggregation meant that even if a more intimate association with people from the same village or subtribe failed, a resident might nonetheless find support from a resident from an adjacent Elema area. But size might also imply a *lack* of discreteness because of the inherent difficulty of applying pressure toward group conformity in a situation where all members of the set would not be equally accessible to a given member due to their widespread physical locations and where, should an individual's "star" of associations include all others in the set, insufficient time would be available to nurse and tend the usual social abrasions. Thus, in view of the aggregation's size, while we should expect a fair number of Kerema-to-Kerema associations it is also surprising that so few members had relations with members beyond the set. During the whole time I was associated with barracks' residents I was aware of only two acquaintanceships between Kerema and non-Kerema men. One was between two drivers: the non-Kerema was from an adjacent ethnic unit, the Bush Mekeo. The other was between Samuel (nK), and a widower from a western Elema village: they worked together, were much older than the usual run of residents, and occasionally went on shopping trips together when off-duty. They were content to leave the relationship there. I argue, in the following chapters, that the lack of ties between Kerema and non-Kerema was the result of plantwide social opposition, and so, for the moment, we will leave it there.

I have used the metaphor of a web or network to describe the pattern of relationships within the barracks and in doing so have suggested that size and location, for example, played their part in shaping its structure. Also, as we have seen, part of the explanation lies in the selection and self-selection of the occupants. In many cases these processes of selection reflected already existing ties; those of kinship, clanship, rural contiguity, and friendships formed at previous workplaces. Occasionally these friendships and links had been formed within the town itself. In other cases associations arose more directly from common employment. When persons were thrown together by the accident of employment and other chance meetings, dyadic relationships were initiated and were kept in existence by reciprocity and propinquity in the quarters. These were almost completely limited to persons from the same broad region.

This still does not explain, however, why the boundaries of groupings were what they were. Why, beyond the circle of immediate home

people, and those with whom some personal friendship had already
been formed, did relationships not radiate out to link people from diverse areas?

In order to find a fuller explanation let me return to the account of
the Northern District workers to examine how their mutual association
was perceived by outsiders and how these perceptions acted as a further
set of constraints on the choice of associates. I turn, then, to a system
of cognitive categories and to the sociocentric imperatives of barracks'
social organization.

A System of Categories and Oppositions

As a cognitive category "Popondetta boys" existed on two levels:
first, as a means of classifying other people, and second, as a named
category with which an individual might identify himself. A short,
although extreme, illustration will serve to direct attention to the use of
this category as a means of external classification.

While discussing workers in the plant with the Production Four
trainee foreman (a man from the Hula area who described himself and
his own people as "Marshall Lagoon" or, somewhat awkwardly, as "K.
A.K." [9] people) I mentioned Horae (the Tari migrant and associate of
the Northern District workers) and Highlanders in general. He replied startlingly that Horae was not a Chimbu (Highlander) but was
from Popondetta. He said this even though Horae had been the boss-
boy on his shift until his recent promotion. Clearly, Horae's long association with the Northern District migrants and his visit to Kokoda
had led his immediate supervisor to categorize him with them. His
ability to speak Police Motu would also lead to such an identification,
since ability in that dialect would tend to imply that one was Papuan.[10]

9 "Keapara-Alikuni-Karawa." These are three villages on the Hood Lagoon
linked to each other by affinal ties, by a common mission organization, and by
economic interdependence arising from specialization—Alikuni is a fishing
village and the other two are agricultural villages.

10 Although the Southern Highlands District is technically part of Papua,
it is often regarded, and administered, as part of the Highlands region.
The region is composed of the Southern Highlands District and the three
"Highlands" districts of New Guinea—Chimbu, the Eastern Highlands, and
the Western Highlands. This association, together with certain physical and
cultural characteristics which the Southern Highlanders share with migrants
from the other Highlands' districts, has meant that Southern Highlanders are
often identified, in the public eye, as New Guinea Highlanders and therefore as
"Chimbu." Many coastal Papuans take it as an acknowledged fact that New
Guineans and especially "Chimbu" speak Pidgin and are ignorant of Police
Motu. (See letters to South Pacific Post 18.10.68) "Before you say Chimbu
think"; (15.11.68) "Not all Highlanders belong to the Chimbus."

The point here is that when someone referred to the "Popondetta boys" at the plant, they were referring not to a miscellaneous group of migrants from one of many administrative districts but to a set of workers who tended to associate with each other, possessing common social characteristics in addition to the location of their villages in one administrative unit. Indeed, the cognitive category might be used so as to include people from *outside* the proper administrative unit as we have just seen. There were important divisions within the ranks of this category but these were not likely to be immediately recognizable to outsiders. Some Papuans may have recognized the distinction between Orokaiva-speaking migrants and Managalase people but it was never referred to by them. William and Hete, for example, were both classed as "Popondetta." It is interesting to note, however, that a young Motu-speaker from Barakau in the Port Moresby Sub-District recognized that Hete came from the Papuan mountain regions and was a bushman by other Popondetta people's standards (possibly because of Hete's slight stature and their common employment in the same work section, or because of the Motuan's casual friendship with nH). He gave him an appropriate, although incorrect label—that of Kukukuku.[11]

This does not mean that the sociocentric classification of residents into gross regional categories was superficial. These categories were also used as stereotypes, with moral and emotional overtones. At this level they could be seen as an attempt to come to terms with the heterogeneity arising from coresidence and common employment. At times this heterogeneity was distinctly unwelcome.

Debate concerning the dangers of heterogeneous labor compounds was at its fiercest over an incident of theft. Bava, whom we met in the account of the Old Office, had washed his shirt and had left it to dry on a clothesline near the Old Married Quarters. When he went to recover it, it had disappeared. On making inquiries he was told by a woman in the yard that she believed William had taken it. Bava then fetched a European manager and together they interrogated William and found the shirt hidden in his belongings. William, for his part, stoutly maintained that the shirt had been taken by mistake. William was eventually reprimanded and threatened with dire consequences if it happened again, but no further action was taken. This did not stop the

---

11 Kukukuku is a generic name given to mountain peoples living in the area between, and surrounding, Wonenara (in the Eastern Highlands), Menyamya (in the Morobe District), and the northern strip of the Gulf District.

gossip.   Enough people had witnessed the interrogation and it touched a sufficiently sore spot in compound life to remain an intermittent topic of conversation for some three or four weeks.

"Shame" badly hampered my attempts to investigate the effects of this incident on relationships within the Popondetta set.   But such considerations did not restrict the comments of other people in the quarters.   Bava, the victim, and the young Production Two laborers who were housed in the Boy-House with whom I found him discussing the incident the same day, were suitably outraged.   Stealing, especially of clothes from washing lines or hoists, is a perennial problem in Port Moresby, especially in compounds and among large aggregations of single men.   Indeed it was largely for this reason that management consented to erect a wire fence around the Old Office.   Because of the frequency of thefts, shocked amazement would hardly have been appropriate but this incident—perhaps because it was so blatant and the culprit and article found so quickly and effortlessly—did produce a rich crop of stories of other thefts people had suffered or had heard of in the town.   Included in these stories were accounts given by two laborers from the Gulf District of thefts by "Popondetta boys," both of which had taken place at previous places of work.   These cases were cited as strong evidence that one should be very careful of one's relations with Northern District migrants.   As the five other stories I was given of major thefts, however, failed to implicate any group or person, perhaps the overall moral which people drew from the incident was that one should be careful of *all* relationships in a compound.   This was certainly the view which Bava and Patrick took.

Another issue of communal life which aroused strong comment was "sparking"—noise and the high spirits and tomfoolery which regularly followed drinking, especially on the weekends.[12]   There were various reactions to this kind of behavior: incidents laughed at by some were bitterly objected to by others and ignored by the rest.

Such was the case with the injury to a rather older man from the Chimbu District who, following some "sparking" among himself, his friends, and a group of Gulf District residents, was teased and harassed and then, rather more viciously, was chased onto the main road

---

[12] "They are drunk" (perhaps invariably with the implication of high spirits) would be in Pidgin *ol i-spak*, and in Police Motu *idia spak*. The idiom was included in the local variant of English. Andrew Taylor who has carried out a study of the Motu language, tells me that the term has been incorporated into Motu itself in the form *idia e'spaka*.

and into the path of an oncoming car. He suffered only superficial injuries and was soon back at work. At the time, however, with tales of *man in-dai long rot* ("a man has been injured on the road") it appeared much more serious than it actually was.

The news of the accident spread quickly and within minutes some twenty residents of the barracks and Old Office had congregated by the roadside. One—from Mailu—said to me sadly, "Kerema boys are very rough and fighting people." But to some the incident took on a comical aspect. James commented afterward that the Chimbu were "a funny people"; Bava laughed. Among the Highlanders themselves there were quite fierce criticisms at the turn of events, moderated to an extent, I felt, because the casualty was himself rather inebriated and had initially taken part in the roughhousing. The victim's clansmen made an idle threat to "kill" the offenders but this led to nothing. Samuel (nK) who joined the group also argued that the Keremas were too rough.

For the most part, however, the incident seemed to be accepted as "just one of those things" reinforcing, I suspect, the strongly held opinion of many that drinking was an activity to be shared with only those you could trust—namely, your home people. It is essential to add that the vast majority did not in fact take their own advice; there were frequent stories of friends and compatriots getting into scrapes and sometimes being beaten up in bar brawls. Nonetheless, the advice seemed well founded. During the course of fieldwork I witnessed several barroom brawls, each case involving others than the original disputants.

All these incidents show residents reacting to a situation of heterogeneity. It is important that we understand the nature and the basis of these reactions. Although many residents had been thrown together by the accident of common employment, the symbiotic basis of their association was not the same as that which we examined for the Old Office. In that situation one of the most important sources of strain was the residents' dependence on, and competition for, the public facilities of the quarters. Barracks' residents used an external ablutions block which they shared with the residents of the Old Married Quarters. Although they too were dependent on other users, and were concerned at the sometimes disgusting condition of these facilities the human cause of their dissatisfaction was not so obviously their coresidents: management tended to be blamed for failing to provide adequate facilities. Moreover, whereas cooking facilities in the Old Office were communal, the use of kerosene stoves meant that barracks' residents were not dependent on *all* other coresidents but only on their immediate neighbors.

At the same time the basis of their recruitment provided many of the Boy-House occupants with a natural focus for domestic grouping. In the Old Office recruitment left the residents as strangers. But in the barracks chain-migration and chain-employment meant that many residents, in adjusting to coresidence, could utilize ties resulting from rural social systems.

Nonetheless, although occupants were not obviously competing for public facilities, common residence meant that their actions did impinge upon their fellows. Thus noise, particularly when workers were trying to sleep between shifts, was always a problem. We can see from the incidents just described that residents were seeking to control their personal environment, either to guard against threats to themselves or to control their personal property and immediate surroundings. All of these gave cause for concern in an heterogeneous environment which gave little privacy.

Following the incident in which the Chimbu worker was injured after being chased onto the road, I was told by three people that the affair illustrated the dangers of fooling around with people from other areas: "You think they are friendly but if someone is bad tempered and if you say something to your *wantok* in your village language he thinks you are talking about him and then he might hit you" was the comment of one man from the Purari area.

Asked why they spent so much time with people from the same area as themselves, one-quarter of the fifty-two residents I questioned directly gave, as one of their answers, statements which might be paraphrased as "help from *wantoks* in the case of physical attack." Two residents gave this sort of statement as their first reason. Samuel's was the most forceful comment; He described fighting and drinking as "number-ten something"—presumably one of the very worst features of everyday living.[13]

In view of these attitudes and the incidents described it is a reasonable inference that the problems of guarding against theft and the ag-

---

[13] The Pidgin *nambawan* (literally, "number one") means excellent, the very best. *Nambaten* (number ten) means as far as one can get from being *nambawan*.

gressiveness of others in a heterogeneous environment could best be met by the type of adaptation which I have described for the Old Boy-House. Spatial and social withdrawal were obvious ways to deal with a situation of high density in which friction and competition were always latent, if not overt, and in which competitors were always highly visible. These adaptive mechanisms were largely effective, but, on occasion, hostility would become public.

This kind of adaptation—combined with the need of newcomers to attach themselves to other residents for certain domestic and leisure activities—explains why persons would tend to associate with a limited grouping rather than disperse their ties throughout the barracks. But it does not fully explain why newcomers, arriving without benefit of preexisting ties, should choose one set rather than any other. Why were certain social identities more important than others for the establishment of manifest relationships? Part of the answer to this problem lies in the operation, within the town, of broad regional categories with their often extremely vague and implied expectations of conduct and their application to the local context of the plant.

If we look at the incident involving the harassment and eventual injury of the Chimbu man we can see the way in which categories based on regional criteria were correlated with types of behavior. These correlations were not completely given by the incident itself but reflected stereotypes current in the plant and town. Thus the criticism that the Keremas were "very rough and fighting people" was by no means self-evident from the form of the actual incident. Nor was there any obvious reason why it should have brought forth the comical, or perhaps ridiculous, aspect of the Chimbu people.

In many parts of the town, perhaps throughout it, certain social categories have a reputation for violence. "Goilalas"—those from the Goilala Sub-District of the Central District—are most widely regarded as dangerous and disreputable. There does appear to be some basis of fact for this view (Hughes 1965:345–46). "Keremas" have a similar, though less widely or fiercely held, reputation. A comment by Samuel, from Mbawe, extolling the virtues of his own district and compatriots, must suffice to illustrate the quality of this stereotype. Samuel told me that his own people were a civilized people now, whereas before they had been *kanakas*. Today, Horae could now visit them and court a local girl, whereas before, it would have been "closed." He went on: "We people from Popondetta are not like the Keremas, Chimbus and

Goilalas. You [this was to me] always see them fighting and drinking
. . .. Popondetta boys have a few glasses and then go home to
sleep. These Keremas, they are always fighting, they are only rubbish
—they eat sago, a horrible food, and they let their hair and bodies stay
dirty."

"Chimbus" were also regarded as violent and aggressive, particularly
by Papuans and migrants from the New Guinea Islands. But my sense
of the stereotype was that their violence was seen as the product of
"bushiness" or backwardness in contrast to the viciousness and "bad-
tempered fighting," as I have heard it expressed, of the Keremas who
had been contacted for many years and who were something of an urban lumpenproletariat—hence, the feeling that the Chimbus were "funny." The picture of "the Chimbu" I built up from the attitudes of the
young Papuans in the Old Office, over an extended period, was that of
the amiable yokel. Plodding, thick-set and with extremely odd customs
—an announcement on the radio that seven-hundred pigs had been
killed at an exchange at the western end of the Highlands brought forth
squeals of laughter from those in the Old Office—"the Chimbu" was
also, on occasion, ridiculously quick to take offence. The comical aspect of the stereotype seemed to flow from an assumption of strangeness and unpredictability.

Thus stereotypes did help to form the spatial and social boundaries
of the sets. They led, in a situation where people were always coming
and going and where a regional classification was the only sure description of a newcomer, to adverse expectations of certain other
groupings. When skirmishes in the barracks involved members of
these stigmatized categories, the stereotypes could then act as self-fulfilling prophecies.

But recognizable stereotypes of this kind applied only to a few of the
regional categories in the town. All urban residents could be assigned
to a category, either on the basis of a known place of origin, skin col-
or, stature, physiognomy, dialect, associations, or their own self-classi-
fication. Very few of these classifications, however, seemed to imply
explicit expectations of conduct or any recognizable sense of antagonism. It is true that events can be cited in a local context to show that
"X" people are "bad"—as we saw when, following the theft of Bava's
shirt, other thefts were cited which implicated "Popondettas." But
only the three categories of Goilala, Kerema, and Chimbu, taken together, perhaps, with Mekeo (cf., for example, Sinclair 1957:6) seem to

have achieved a townwide notoriety.[14]   Thus many of the categories at the language group, sub-district, and district levels were neutral and carried no generally accepted connotations.   It was only at the higher level of Papua/New Guinea opposition that most migrants would be subject to stereotyping (involving regional criteria) on a townwide basis, and where expectations, of language and attitude, for example, were at all firm.

Thus the distance between many residents can best be thought of as *cultural,* involving not stereotyped hostility but a gentle ethnocentricism and lack of mutual experience and interests (mentioned earlier in Chapter 3 under *Ethnogenesis, Leadership, and the Lack of Common Purpose*).

Something of this self-identification has been seen in Samuel's comment on the virtues of his own set and the vices of others.   The rest of his conversation on that occasion was equally laudatory of the Popondetta set.   Rather self-deprecatingly he pointed out that whereas he was forced to use Pidgin or Police Motu to speak to me, the younger boys could all speak English;   moreover if I went to Popondetta I would find that all the young people knew English.

Samuel's vicarious pride in the achievements of his compatriots was extreme but it nonetheless reflected their general attitudes.   To them being "Popondetta" was an important source of self-esteem.   It meant prestige in the town and plant, common social and cultural interests in the rural area, a common administration, a common mission, common sporting and educational institutions, and an awareness that, although they came from different tribes, their peoples were closely linked, both traditionally and in more recent history.   These institutional frameworks had, in turn, channelled their developing experiences into a common mold so that "Popondetta" became intellectually and emotionally significant to them.   Moreover, Popondetta township itself served as a focus for many of their past activities and their aspirations.   All the younger members of the set talked of eventually leaving Moresby, returning home and then, after a while, taking jobs in Popondetta.   In this way they could be "at home," participate in "home" affairs and yet still take advantage of the urban wage economy.

---

[14] Sinclair provides an interesting deviation from the usual stereotypes. He states he was informed that " 'all Mekeos are rogues and thieves', 'the Orakaiva are aggressive', 'the Goilala are happy' " (1957:6).

This channeling of experience and interests into a regional framework was also true of members of the other sets. Indeed, in three—the "Kerema," "Kikori," and "Tari" sets—the members all came from the same cultural-linguistic group, and thus the ties of a common vernacular and culture were added to those brought about by more recent history. The difference here is of degree and not kind.

These relationships of cultural distance were in turn thrown into relief by the urban situation and the ongoing system of oppositions in the Old Boy-House. It may be that there were situations in the home area capable of eliciting a "district" identity. If so, the situation in town would not be in contrast to rural experience but rather a continuation of it. It does seem clear, however, that heterogeneity and instability accentuate tribal or ethnic distinctiveness. This point has been made, for Central African towns, by Mitchell (1956:29). He writes that "there is a constant flow of newcomers into the towns from the various rural districts . . . their own ethnic distinctiveness which they took for granted in the rural areas is immediately thrown into relief by the multiplicity of tribes with whom they are cast into association. Its importance to them is exaggerated and it becomes the basis on which they interact with all strangers." While talking about his experiences as a new technical college student in Port Moresby, Humphrey (nB) illustrated this point exactly. He described how he and "about twelve others *all from Popondetta, but some from different places*" (my emphasis) had had a difficult time and that seven had returned home during the first year. When asked the cause of their dissatisfaction he pointed to the strangeness of the place, food, and people: "We were given fish to eat but we hadn't eaten it before so that we didn't like to eat it then. But the Central people and the Kerema people they eat fish in their villages and so they are used to it and like to eat it very much. We looked at them and they were enjoying it but we went hungry because we only wanted to eat the rice. Now when we go to the market we don't like to pay big money for the fish . . . the Papuans here they sometimes spend two or three dollars to buy one fish."

It is from these kinds of experience that the feeling of regional or ethnic distinctiveness arises and that entitles us to speak of a system of cultural distances.

In Summary

We have now turned full circle—from an individual's personal ties to other members of the set, on to sociocentric forms of classification, and to stereotyped expectations of conduct and back to the individual's self-identification, shared experiences, and aspirations.   With this background we can now summarize the argument.   Within the spatial propinquity and functional arrangements set by management, dyadic relationships were formed by the transference to the town of perduring rural-urban ties, and by the need of newcomers to attach themselves to established domestic groups.   Those which referred to rural ties were stronger, multiplex, and more intimate.   They were largely independent of the urban social system and that of the barracks although urban residence and common employment threw participants together and entailed their association in terms of urban institutions as well as rural ones. Those that arose from contiguity in the barracks and common employment tended to be limited to informal leisure time within the local vicinity and to domestic activities within the barracks itself.   There was every indication that with the cessation of common employment and residence these latter ties would atrophy perhaps to be reactivated if the accidents of migration brought the participants together again.

While these variables explain one aspect of mutual support, they do not fully explain why people who had no previously acknowledged relationship were drawn to each other in the first place.   It is at this point that cultural distance, self-identification, and stereotyping enter the picture as variables structuring the choices of residents who were previously strangers, urban heterogeneity throwing their common identity into relief.   Once the requisite spatial boundaries had been established within the barracks they made the choice of succeeding newcomers more predictable.   These sets were not stable corporations: the boundaries were always subject to the flux of barracks' life and thus to redefinition.   Despite the movement and flux, however, ethnicity or compatriotism continued as the single most important basis of association. And although compatriotism owed much to kinship, and the importance residents gave to locality, the actual operation of compatriotism and the boundaries of the sets were determined by urban involvements.

The movement and flux of barracks' life was due to the age, aspirations, and marital status of the residents, as well as to the instability of urban employment and the residents' changing occupational prefer-

Plate 5   Town and Country cousins in Mekeo—bringing home a wild pig

Plate 6   Compatriots—migrants from Gumine on a weekend picnic

ences. Most residents were young and planning to return to their rural homes in order to marry women from their home locality. Indeed, many of the barracks residents, like other young men in the town, were trying to save money to contribute to a bride-price when they returned home. Others were contributing their savings to kinsmen for their kinsmen's marital purposes, secure in the knowledge that in turn their kinsmen would help them. Some older, single workers would almost certainly have had to accept a permanent bachelorhood, while others would have become stranded in the town through paying too much attention to their urban involvements. The majority of residents, however, would eventually return to their rural homes and marry, perhaps to return to the town after a period of rural residence.

Adjustment to urban residence for young, single residents was thus largely a temporary adjustment to cultural diversity and to the very visible inequality in the distribution of urban-industrial resources between the two major racial groups. The centripetal force of rural involvements was greater than the centrifugal force of urban involvements even though both were subject to change as urban residence lengthened. Those workers who married and brought their families to town, however, were likely to view their urban residence somewhat differently. Although they might all plan to retire eventually to their rural homes, most were planning to spend their working lives in wage employment in the town. These residents did not see their adjustment to urban residence as a temporary problem. Their adjustment, therefore, might give rise to a distinctive urban culture which would blend Papuan and New Guinean elements with elements imported by members of the colonizing society. As married workers were planning to spend their working lives in urban wage employment, their continuing urban adaptation also raises the possibility of their mutual identification as *employees* with common interests opposed to those of their employers. To examine these questions we will begin by looking at the adaptation and developing ambience of one newcomer. This was Mailala, a former taxi driver and migrant from the Madang District of New Guinea. His adjustments show that, like most residents, his associations and plans in Port Moresby were constrained by his dual commitment to both town and country. Bridging that dual commitment were ties based on a broad compatriotism.

*

5

Workers as Neighbors:

The Married Quarters

The town is another problem altogether. In the first place
it is not, as is the village, a single more or less homogeneous
social structure, the elements of which tend to repeat themselves
like a wallpaper design (fraying off at the edges) throughout the
whole countryside. Rather it is a social composite, and only partially organised coincidence of separate social structures . . .
[Geertz 1965:27]

A Visit to the "Babalau"

Very late one Tuesday night after I had gone to bed, Mailala, a truck
driver who had recently come to live in the Old Married Quarters,
came to the Old Office and asked for my help. Would I take him to
Hanaubada? He had no money for taxis and there would be few passenger trucks running at that hour. His wife, Elizabeth, had severe
abdominal pains and they wanted her to see a healer and diviner—in
the Motu language, a *babalau*. This *babalau* was the wife of a migrant
from the Sepik, a friend of Mailala's. I agreed to take them and on
the way, Mailala told me something of the background.

137

Figure 3. The Married Quarters

(not to scale)

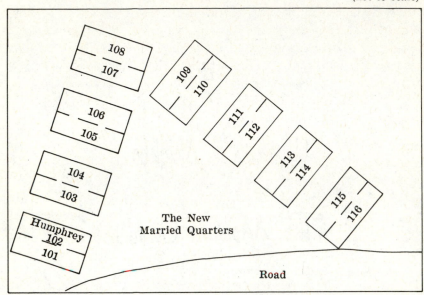

The New
Married Quarters

Road

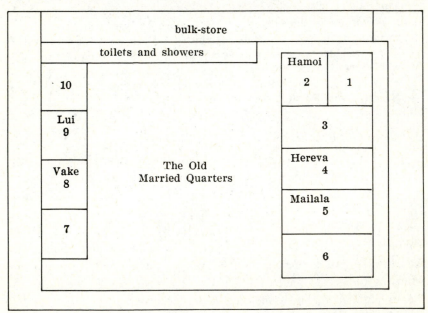

bulk-store

toilets and showers

10

Lui
9

Vake
8

7

The Old
Married Quarters

Hamoi
2   1

3

Hereva
4

Mailala
5

6

[A9839]

His wife had been in pain since the weekend. They both suspected a "Kerema" man, who had moved into unit 2 (see Figure 3) in the previous week with Hamoi, his married kinsman from Ihu in the Gulf District. Mailala and this new resident had argued violently at a party given by Mailala at the quarters over the weekend. The Kerema man, they suggested, had "poisoned" Elizabeth and caused the illness. There was therefore no point in going to the hospital; the doctors and European medicine were powerless in the face of "native sickness." It was better for them to consult Martha, the Motuan wife of Mailala's long-standing friend, Luke.

Luke and Mailala had known each other since 1958. They met quite by chance after Luke arrived to take up employment as a clerk with the public service. At that time, Mailala had been working in the town for two years, as a taxidriver, a job he was to hold, with one interruption, until he joined P.M.D. at the beginning of 1967. They had found that Mailala's father and Luke himself were from the Angoram area in the Sepik District. Mailala had never lived there—his parents were divorced early in their marriage and he had grown up in Bogia in the Madang District, his mother's home place—but the common tie and their situation as New Guinea coastal migrants in a strange town had drawn them together. Their friendship had continued beyond their marriages. Elizabeth was also from Bogia. Martha, the *babalau*, was from a village in the Hanaubadan complex. It was Martha's late father's house we were to visit.

On our arrival at Hanuabada, Mailala knocked on Luke's door and told him of our purpose. They spoke in Pidgin. After a long discussion about me and my activities, and a consultation with his wife, Luke agreed to let me attend the divination provided I kept quiet and agreed to leave when asked. But firstly, Mailala, Luke, and I were sent out in search of four betel nuts. These had to meet Martha's whispered specifications.

While we were away Luke discussed his wife's powers and their origin. As a girl, he told me, Martha had been "carried away" and set down in Koiari bushland. She had been shown many things by the spirits. "Returning" to Hanuabada, her kinsfolk had become aware of her powers and had invited people to see her and test them. She had been able to cure from that time to this and specialized in the sicknesses which "only native people experienced."

We returned to the house. After a matter of fact discussion about the betel nuts and questions (in Police Motu for the most part) about the weekend's party, Martha sat us down and commenced, cutting first into one of the betel nuts and knocking four times with it on the floor of the house. This was to summon the spirits. She then proceeded to interrogate Elizabeth in Pidgin [1] about her activities of the last few weeks, asking her repeatedly if she had argued with anyone or had reason to suspect anyone's malice. Several people unknown to me were mentioned, but uninterestedly: much of the interrogation centered on Mailala's argument with his Kerema neighbor.

At this point Mailala took up the story. He related how, early in the party, he had had an argument with "this Kerema man," who, he argued, had been trying to get beer without paying for it. The party had been held, ostensibly, for Mailala's daughter's first birthday. Mailala had provided a keg of beer and guests were asked to contribute twenty cents a glass for the little girl's "present." Helping him was Lui, the single man in unit 9, from Bush Mekeo in the Central District, and in charge of Production Three. Lui, eager at the news of beer and fun, had volunteered his help. As the number of partygoers swelled Lui took turns at serving the beer, and collecting the money. Mailala's irritation had first been aroused because Lui did not seem to be supervising the beer sales properly. Although he fussed around Lui urging him to pay attention, it was the Gulf District man whom he accused. At this they became angry, each accusing the other of being a troublemaker. There was no fight, however, mediators urging them to calm down. Later on, hostility had flared again but by this time I had left.

After most guests had departed Elizabeth provided food for a number of their intimate friends. Washing the utensils after they had eaten, she laid them to dry on a wooden stretcher outside the door of their unit. While they were drying, Mailala's adversary of the early evening passed by and upturned the stretcher, sending spoons and plates flying. Mailala had rushed out but his Bogia friends had restrained him, fearing an uglier incident, and the Kerema man had walked away.

---

[1] Luke and Martha both spoke Motu, Police Motu, English, and Pidgin; Mailala spoke English, Police Motu, and Pidgin; and Elizabeth spoke only Pidgin. The three New Guineans, of course, also spoke their local vernacular. Pidgin was used most frequently during the conversation, but occasionally Luke and Martha would use Motu. Mailala, understanding the gist of the Motu conversation, would sometimes interpose a comment in Police Motu.

Martha then announced she must examine Elizabeth. Mailala, Luke, and I were asked to leave the house. On our return Martha cut into another nut, knocked yet again on the floor, meditated, and then told us that the spirits accused the Kerema resident of sorcery. The agent was identified as Elizabeth's menstrual rags, which she absent-mindedly had left in the quarters' toilets on the day following the argument. She was told to beware of his sorcery in the future and to guard her behavior in the compound. Chewing the betel nut used in the invocation, Martha then breathed over a glass of fresh water, and gave it to Elizabeth to drink. We waited a few minutes and then left, Mailala paying Luke two dollars for his and his wife's services.

The next day Mailala pronounced his wife much better and, on Friday morning, completely cured. Surprisingly, the cure seemed to satisfy him. As the nighttime visit and his anger had been so spectacular, I asked him if he would accuse the sorcerer and ask him to stop. Might he not try to find another sorcerer to work countermagic to protect himself and his family? "No," he said, "that will make more trouble—what if he tries to 'poison' Martina?" (i. e. ensorcell Mailala's, daughter). Later on Friday, I saw Mailala with Vake, his neighbor from unit 8 just across the yard. They were pooling their wages —an arrangement they had started two or three weeks beforehand. After Vake had left I asked Mailala what Vake had thought about Elizabeth's illness and recovery. Mailala replied that they had not discussed it. But, I argued, couldn't he discuss it with Vake, or perhaps with Hereva? (Hereva was Mailala's next door neighbor and often came to borrow household and other small items.) I thought that since they had been living in the quarters for much longer than he had, they might be able to ask Hamoi to approach his kinsman. "No," said Mailala, "they won't want any trouble—better to keep it to myself." But couldn't he just ask their advice? "No, better not to have any trouble."

Mailala's apparent satisfaction, or fear of further trouble, however, did not stop a long discussion of the incident at the next of his regular weekend gatherings when half-a-dozen or so of his own and his wife's kin and friends would visit for the afternoon and evening. On the Sunday in question, three of their immediate home-people were present —all fairly distant kin but residents in the town for a number of years —one with his wife and brother-in-law, both from Talasea. I had eaten lunch with the family and was there when the guests arrived. All but the brother-in-law had been at the party on the previous weekend. After a few initial comments Mailala told them of Elizabeth's sickness and her successful visit to Martha. For their part, having congratulated Elizabeth on her recovery, they urged Mailala to find himself better accommodation to avoid such problems in the future. He to'd them he was hoping to get a house in the New Married Quarters and, if unsuccessful, would be applying for a house at Sabama, an administration low-cost suburb a mile or so away. At this, the subject was dropped in favor of a discussion of the housing of a visitor.

Discussion and Background

Accepting Marwick's argument that sorcery and witchcraft accusations serve as a social-strain gauge (Marwick 1964), this striking incident provides many clues to Mailala's residential situation and, by implication, that of the other occupants. In this incident, as in those in the Old Office and the Old Boy-House, we see workers adapting their behavior to the heterogeneity given by their decision to find work at the plant and to accept its accommodation. Mailala's excitement, the suspicion of sorcery, and the money and time he expended on the consultation are tokens of the importance of this kind of strain as a recurrent structural feature.

The best way of approaching the incident is to discover why, after such an exciting expedition, the aftermath was so unspectacular. What factors inhibited a more public accusation and why were the Sunday visitors the only people to be told of the consequences of the incident? The answer to these questions lies in a fuller examination of Mailala's situation and his consequent and ongoing actions in the quarters.

Mailala had joined P.M.D. as a truck driver in mid-January of 1967. Between 1954, when he left his mother's village, and 1956, he had worked in Madang as a taxi driver. Encouraged by a European officer to join the army he had made his way to Moresby only to find that he was unacceptable as a soldier. From 1956 until the time of the study he had been based in the town working both for the taxi service and as a member of the crew on ships on the Papua–Australian and New Guinea coastal runs. In 1963 he returned to his home area to find a wife and, after staying some eight months, returned with Elizabeth. He rejoined the taxi service and eventually became foreman, earning forty dollars per week, a princely sum by indigenous workers' standards.

He had been dismissed at the end of 1966, however, for arguing with and striking another employee. Replying to an advertisement for drivers, Mailala had presented himself at P.M.D. and was taken on at a basic wage of $16 per week. After a few weeks, however, he was able to supplement his earnings by normal overtime and by working a regular night shift taking Production Four workers living in other areas of the town home after they finished work at midnight. His total weekly earnings for much of the time I knew him were in the region of thirty dollars and thus he was among the half-a-dozen most highly-paid workers at the plant.

Many things about Mailala were distinctive—his distress at his lack of education, his wide circle of friends in the town, and his general amiability. The quality which struck me most forcibly, however, was his generosity. Despite the fact that he had been in the quarters for such a short time—he took up residence in unit 1 at the end of June and a month later moved to unit 5—I was struck by the calls on his resources. One evening two weeks before the party and divination, for example, while I was there, he had three calls; a visit from Hereva's wife (their next door neighbor in unit 4) to borrow cutlery; followed a little later by a visit from Lui, this time for cigarettes; and at the end of the evening a visit from Vake (from across the yard in unit 8) for some betel nuts and lime. After the first visit Mailala asked if his neighbors were never going to buy enough spoons. So, after all the other visits, I asked him why he didn't refuse. He replied that he had to be careful living among so many Papuans, otherwise they would say "bad things" about him. For the time being he had to stay there and so must have people like him.

At the time I missed the full significance of this remark, but subsequent conversations, his continued generosity, and the visit to Luke and Martha's brought it home to me. He continued to be available for these items, I judged, not only because he was naturally generous but because he was conspicuously more affluent than those around him and anxious about the consequences of his residence in the yard. Part of his anxiety was perhaps the fear of others' envy, but part, I am sure, was the product of a set of structural arrangements.

Mailala's initial situation was essentially the same as that of the young men in the Old Office. They were not linked to each other by any substantial obligations and reciprocities and yet the spatial and functional features of their immediate environment meant that they were continually rubbing shoulders. With few or no counter-balancing ties enforcing their cooperation, interactions between neighbors were thus potentially volatile. The levity of a party might break down the barriers but it might also serve, as in Mailala's case, as a touch paper to latent hostilities. Casting around for an explanation of his wife's sickness it was perhaps inevitable that Mailala should suspect the malice of a neighbor. Given his need to be tender in his dealings with co-residents, his reluctance to tell them of the divination is readily understood. So too was his obverse willingness to discuss the incident with his Sunday guests. To them he was bound by a more long-standing and intimate connection—by kinship obligations and sentiments and by a long association in the town. These ties were independent of the vagaries of employment.

Social Characteristics of Other Married Tenants

I have used the visit to Luke and Martha's as a way of highlighting Mailala's situation within the compound. And I have suggested that, by implication, the incident points to certain structural features of the overall residential situation. There is more to say about Mailala's situation and his continuing adaptation to it still to describe. But as these developments require a fuller understanding of the social arena within which he was operating, this is an appropriate point to consider some of the implications of his initial position by describing the ways in which it appeared to diverge from that of the other residents and those features they had in common.

At the time of my census, slightly under one-quarter of the plant's native employees were known to be married and living with their families in the town. Of these employees, twenty-four (or slightly under two-thirds of those who had families with them) were accommodated by the plant in its married quarters, leaving fifteen who were renting, had built their own accommodation, or were lodging free of charge with relatives. An additional twelve members of the native labor force were married but had left their families in the rural areas. With the exception of one man who was widowed and one who was divorced, the rest of the indigenous employees were single.

Living in the plant's quarters together with the married tenants and their wives was a single employee renting one of the Old Married units—he had claimed he was married—six other single employees lodging with their married kin and some fifty permanently resident children and infants. There was also some dozen less permanent residents, both adults and children, visiting their kin or lodging with them between jobs. Tables 12 and 13 place this material on "household" composition and residential distribution in a systematic form.

TABLE 12

HOUSEHOLD AND RESIDENCE

		No.	%
Married and family normally resident in town		39	24.4
a) P.M.D. housing	24		
b) other	15		
Married but unaccompanied by family		12	7.5
a) P.M.D. housing	9		
b) other	3		
Single, widowed, and divorced		101	63.1
a) P.M.D. housing	67		
b) other	34		
Unknown or uncertain		8	5.0
		160	100.0

[A9830]

TABLE 13

RESIDENTIAL DISTRIBUTION OF MARRIED EMPLOYEES ACCOMPANIED BY THEIR FAMILIES ACCORDING TO PLACE OF ORIGIN

	Central District		Gulf Dist.	Other Dists.	Total
	P. Moresby Sub-Dist.	Other Sub-Dists.			
New Married Quarters	2	5	8	1	16
Old Married Quarters	2	–	5	1	8
Hohola	–	–	2	1	3
Villages	5	–	–	–	5
Settlements	–	1	4	–	5
Other	–	–	1	1	2
Total	9	6	20	4	39

[A9829]

The twenty-four married couples accommodated by P.M.D. were assigned to the two married quarters according to their value to management: the less valued to the Old Married units, and the more valued to the newer units. Management's estimation of a worker's "value" to the industrial system reflected mainly educational and skill (and therefore to some extent seniority) criteria. In some cases distinctions between individual worth must have been very hard to draw. Capricious or not, however, managerial judgments on a worker's capabilities were strongly advanced and acted upon. Thus the two employees in the older units, who had joined P.M.D. before 1960, were both regarded as inefficient workers; one of them—Mailala's immediate neighbor—had recently been demoted from Production Two to Production Four for poor work. In selecting tenants for the new units the claims of both of these men had been passed over and much more junior workers accommodated. As a driver and recent recruit, Mailala was allotted to the older units. Whatever the "objective" skill-level of driving, individual drivers qua drivers were not of much concern to management. Turnover among drivers was high, and their skills were readily transferable.

The modal seniority of tenants in the new units was four years; that for tenants of the older units was one year. At first sight this suggests perhaps that the new section was rather like a settled residential community and the older quarters a staging-camp for transient workers. If so, the transient character of the older section would account for many features of Mailala's situation. At the same time such a contrast would point to a rather different set of relationships operating in the new quarters than those I have already suggested.

In fact, while something of the contrast holds, it was considerably blurred by the operation of other factors. The most important of these was the recent establishment of the new units. Erected in the second half of 1966, and largely occupied as soon as electricity and power were connected, the last occupant had not moved in until March or April of 1967. And, as only four employees previously living in the older units were granted accommodation in the new section, the majority of the new section tenants were newcomers to P.M.D. housing. Some were people who had taken advantage of the offer of superior accommodation and had left local villages and settlements. Others were more recent recruits to the plant, in two instances attracted to P.M.D. from other companies in the town because of the availability and quality of married accommodation. Thus, while Mailala was a newcomer to the married quarters, the recency of his arrival was a matter of degree and not of kind. But what of his ethnic identity? He was the only New Guinean in the married sections. Did this not make him an obvious outsider, an exception to the general rule of ethnic homogeneity?

Compared to the plant as a whole and to the single quarters in particular, the married sections drew its tenants from a much more limited part of the Territory. All but Mailala (from Bogia) and Humphrey (from Kokoda) were coastal Papuans—from the narrow coastal strip between Mailu Island to the east and Goaribari Island to the west. This area involved only two of the eighteen administrative districts— the Central and the Gulf. Furthermore, within these two districts, four sub-districts—Kerema (with three), Kukipi (nine), Abau (four), and Port Moresby (four)—had provided the vast majority of the residents.

A Dual Engagement

This suggests that Mailala's birthplace was indeed distinctive. And given the situation of substantial anonymity I have described, his identity as the sole New Guinean might easily have overshadowed all other considerations in interpersonal encounters. We have already seen that Humphrey (nB), the only other non-coastal Papuan in the married quarters, had admitted the strangeness of his experience when he arrived in town. May not Mailala's status as the only New Guinean have thrown him back, so to speak, on a regional identity? Thus we saw in the Old Office and the barracks that a person's place of origin was an important source of self-identification and a convenient mode of classification. And because these regional appellations generally implied the common association of home-boys and "*wantoks*", they operated in many spheres of behavior. They became, in short, primary social identities.

The capacity of regional categories to channel and direct behavior in this manner depended ultimately on the association between the cognitive categories, social characteristics, and modes of association. In the Old Office and the barracks the correlation was real enough and thus regional labels could serve as important mediators of social behavior, both in the form of external classifications and self-identification.

Mailala's situation was less clear cut. He certainly associated, often conspicuously, with other coastal New Guineans and was warm in his attachment to his home-people and home-place. Yet at the same time, he had been in town a very long time and his wide experience (gained in the taxi service, for example) had made him conversant with the town and its myriad peoples. During his time in Moresby, ties with other coastal New Guineans had proliferated, as parties I attended with him testified, but his lengthy residence had also given him an opportunity to associate with Papuans. This was not however just a question of opportunity. His increasing commitment and involvement in urban employment and residence increased his need for such associations, as we shall see.

A token of this development was his fluency in Police Motu and his contact with Papuans like Martha, the *babalau*. But perhaps I can best illustrate the dual character of his engagement in urban-located social relationships by referring to a song sung at one of his Sunday gatherings. I had arrived and chatted for a while when Mailala suggested I get my tape recorder and record their singing. When we were ready we moved out into the yard. A number of other residents were either in their units or sitting outside. Mailala then announced:

> *Dispela singsing olsem bilong mifela long Bogia sub-district Madang.*
> *Nem bilong mi Peter Samola, Radio Wewak, Bogia mala.*

> This singsing is one of ours from the Bogia sub-district, Madang.
> My name is Peter Samola, Radio Wewak, Bogia.

And then they began to sing the lament of a reckless young woman made pregnant by her lover. They sang, almost endlessly, *in Police Motu*:

> *Ya, Dahaka daina(i) lau lao kava,*
> *Lau lao kava, lau mai kava,*
> *Ya sinagu-ya, natugu-ya,*
> *Dahaka daina(i) lau lao kava* (etc.)

> *Lau lao, lau lao Koke market,*
> *"Popo" ya ya, lau mai ya ya,*
> *"Popo" ya ya, lau hamorua,*
> *Koke market Koke market* (etc.)

> *Dina ibouna(i) lau hamorua,*
> *Lau be lau be gorere,*
> *Lau be lau be rogoro(go)-ya,*
> *Lau be lau be siava mama* (etc.)

> (Why do I wander, wander to
> no good purpose?
> O mother! my child!
> Why do I wander?

I go, I go, to Koke market,
"Popo," I come,
"Popo," I tell him,
Koke market, Koke market.

Every day I tell him,
I am sick,
I am pregnant,
I am (? *siava mama*?)[2]

This was repeated time after time. After ten minutes or so, at the end of a verse, Mailala called out, *"Ahhh . . . Givim! Bogio i-longwe"* (Ahhh . . . Let's have it again! Bogia's far away). And as he did so he pulled Hereva, his next door neighbor (unit 4) into the circle of singers, and they began again, this time *in Pidgin*, singing essentially the same song. Finally, they broke into a Bogia vernacular, and, after awhile, the women too began to sing.

The point of this illustration is not the intrinsic content of the song but the manner of its singing and the supporting references. All the men were from Bogia Sub-District and the style of the song had originated (according to them, that is) in their home-place. Moreover, Mailala introduced it by referring explicitly to the Bogia context and by presenting himself as an indigenous radio announcer based in the home area. During the song itself there was the nostalgia of his cry "Bogia's far away." And yet, despite the New Guinea bias, the song was sung in a language they had picked up in the town, Police Motu, and the setting was Port Moresby's market. Mailala, moreover, deliberately pulled Hereva, a Papuan, into the group. It was a song of the home-place, and yet set in the urban environment, very much like the songs which accompany *kalela* dances on the Central African Copperbelt (Mitchell 1956:5).

Mailala was wedded to urban residence and employment, and yet was a New Guinean: this duality constrained many of his ongoing choices. His continued residence in town had long been decided. He would

[2] The English version is a free translation. The transcription was made after fieldwork was completed: I was therefore unable to check the meanings of certain references and words. *Popo* is the betel nut pepper but I am not sure of its implication here. Perhaps she has gone to Koke to find some; perhaps it symbolizes the feeling that the woman is dazed, intoxicated. *Siava mama* is meaningless. *Mama* can mean "jealousy" but *siava* does not appear to be Motu nor does it approximate anything that might make sense in the context. It may be that the phrase is in another language. *Ya* is a **rhythmical device.**

stay, he said, until his "children" had grown up and would be able to help him. But he had only one infant daughter and would sometimes admit to a hint of anxiety about his social security while staying there. Perhaps in part to keep ties open with his home village and, more explicitly, for sentimental reasons, he sent his wife and daughter back to Madang for an extended holiday while I was there.

Other areas of choice, however, concerned the proper balance to be struck between associations with fellow employees and associations with *wantoks* living in the town and the balance of associations *within* the plant itself.

Developments

I have argued that on arriving in the compound, Mailala was immediately engaged in a subsocial set of relationships with other residents. Yet, at the same time, he came with experiences of both the town and other places, and with already formed preconceptions of Moresby's peoples. Thus it was unlikely that relationships would long stay impersonal.

Moreover he was slowly becoming more involved in his employment with the company. His driving skills and knowledge of the town were almost certainly marketable outside the plant and thus, although wedded to urban employment, his commitment to his current job might seem less certain. Certainly he often dismayed of his accommodation and was tempted to apply elsewhere. But he also remembered the princely sums he had earned while a senior worker at the taxi service and was reluctant to change his employment again. He argued that, if he did his work well, the plant would "promote" him and give him better housing. Thus many of his goals and plans became increasingly focused on the plant and its network of relations. And as he did so, his and his wife's knowledge of the quarters and their fellow residents became, to use Merton's terms, less an abstract *knowledge about*, and more a concrete *acquaintance with* (Merton 1957:566).

We have already seen that Mailala singled out the "Kerema" as the cause of Elizabeth's pain. We have also seen that he had already formed, at the time of the visit to Hanaubada, a wage-sharing agreement with Vake in unit 8. Later he was to welcome Hereva to the circle of Bogia songsters. His relationships with these men were limited, however, never developing beyond their original base: Vake remained a neighbor with whom he pooled his wages, and Hereva a neighbor with whom he might chat or lend household items. The exuberance of a "singsing" could encourage a warmer emotion, but it seemed short-lived.

There were, however, other developments. The association between Elizabeth and Kone—Hereva's wife—was rather less restricted than their husbands'. They spent all day in the quarters and helped each other with the children occasionally. Even so, language was a barrier —Kone spoke little Pidgin—and the relationship remained casual. Like their husbands, their principal engagement was outside the plant. Elizabeth did, however, cultivate the friendship of the young woman in unit 1. Just married, this Toaripi girl's husband had lived most of his life in Lae. She spoke a basic Pidgin and Elizabeth took her under her wing almost as soon as she arrived, teaching her more of the language and helping her to adjust to married life and the compound.

The principal development in Mailala's own ambience occurred between my two periods of fieldwork, but the seeds had already been sown before I left. It started with Mailala's attempts to improve his living arrangements.

For some time Mailala had ferried Production Four workers back to their houses from the midnight shift. This meant that he was almost always to be found around the production line waiting for them to finish. After a while he asked Ephraim (nH) and Esikari (nI), two Production Four fitters from the Kokoda area, to make him a metal stand on which to mount his kerosene burners, to keep them out of the way of his young daughter. One night soon afterward, I was with Mailala in his unit when Humphrey, Ephraim, and Esikari came trooping in with the stand. Humphrey was embarrassed because he feared the stand was a little large and at the same time Mailala was embarrassed because Ephraim and Esikari had brought the "big man" into his shabby quarters without warning him. There were apologies on both sides, but Mailala's were the longest and most profuse; finally, he invited Humphrey to stay for some tea or coffee but Humphrey declined saying he had to return to the plant to finish something.

Despite the embarrassment, however, Mailala was obviously sufficiently encouraged to continue the relationship and in the following weeks sought from Humphrey information on the possibility of vacancies in the newer quarters. Humphrey eventually promised to mention the underutilization of unit 103 (the worker concerned had left his family in their village) and Mailala's interest to the Production Manager or Company Secretary if the opportunity arose. Any efforts he may have made on Mailala's behalf, however, were unsuccessful—eventually unit 103 fell vacant but Mailala's claims were passed over. By the time of my second fieldwork trip, Mailala was hoping to get a house at Sabama, and eventually a house at the new Gordon's Estate development. Nonetheless, by this time, the relationship between the two had become quite firm. Both had joined the plant's soccer and basketball teams. Humphrey was captain of the soccer team and many of the players were "Popondetta boys." Mailala was spending a good part of his leisure time in their company and had taken Hete (nE) under his wing; this young man was a regular visitor to unit 5.

But with Mailala's increasing involvement in relationships at the plant came further animosities; his eagerness to please and appear efficient was not always appreciated. On one occasion, he and the distribution section's boss-boy—from Kerema and employed since 1958—had a fierce argument, the boss-boy accusing Mailala of trying to usurp his authority in the section.

In the preceding chapters and in the account of Mailala, his developing ambience and his adaptations to the quarters, I have argued that the behavior of compound dwellers can best be seen as a set of choices operating within constraints set by the industrial system, managerial policy, and practice, the symbiotic features of the quarters and the worker's ties with his home village, and with *wantoks* and others in the town. In time choices were also modified by the relations developing in the quarters themselves. In Mailala's own case, I have so far argued that developments in his situation can be traced to his growing commitment to employment by the plant.

It is clear, however, that the analysis is incomplete. Thus I contend that it was not fortuitous that he should have accused a Kerema resident of sorcery nor that he should have allowed animosities to develop with the Kerema boss-boy of his section. These animosities were also a product of the ongoing opposition between Kerema and non-Kerema, an opposition which I have already noted for the barracks. To anticipate the argument a little, I consider that it reflected the more general antagonism between these two categories in the town and even beyond. At the same time, however, the contrasted situation of Kerema and non-Kerema within the plant itself was also responsible, feeding the already existing opposition.

THE P.M.D. QUARTERS AS SOCIAL SYSTEMS AND CULTURAL SEGMENTS

The necessity of recognizing that Mailala's disagreements were set within a wider context of "Kerema" and "non-Kerema" oppositions brings us back to the general issue of workers as neighbors and the paradigmatic nature of Mailala's "case" for the social organization of the married quarters.

As the events just recorded suggest, residents of the married quarters tended to lead their lives independent of their neighbors. There were a number of exceptions to this tendency but in all cases where there were established and generalized ongoing reciprocities—involving some five out of the twenty-five households—they were between residents from the same broad cultural area. Where the separateness of the quarters' households was bridged (over and above those cases just noted), the reciprocities or transactions attempted had either a fragile quality or had been precisely contained within narrow limits. Of the twenty households not involved in established and generalized reciprocities a further four or five had relatively sustained but limited joint activities, for example, pooling and rotating wages or common participation in sports associations. Yet there was little indication that these had or would lead to further reciprocities or associations.

These figures mainly reflect interactions on occasions when the male heads of the household were present. It was extremely difficult to collect reliable information on the associational patterns of the female residents because of their embarrassment and/or their lack of facility in the urban *linguae francae*. But even during the day, when a number of the men were at work and many night shift workers were asleep, my impressions and the information I did receive suggested that while there was a considerable amount of casual chatter and gossip in the public yards around the units, female residents rarely cooperated in common tasks or activities except in those five instances already noted.

Thus, despite Mailala's easy familiarity and initial attempts to strike up associations, his relationship with Hereva and Vake stayed at a mainly utilitarian level and, other than Elizabeth's friendship with the young woman in unit 1, there were no further developments until he began to associate with Humphrey and his friends nearly a year later. His unwillingness to be further implicated until then can be seen in the fact that the next time he held a party he purposely avoided holding it in the units, preferring Hohola. Other than myself, no one from P. M.D. was invited. Two other parties held by unit residents also emphasized the quality of this restraint.

Humphrey gave a party for his daughter, holding it in the New Married Quarters. Few were specifically invited, but the news spread quickly. Konemase, a worker from Pari village just outside the town and now living in unit 114, approached Humphrey "offering" him the Pari village string band—the Rainbows—which often played in the taverns around the town. So many people gathered for the party and to hear the band that Humphrey refused to serve the beer until they had gone. The final blow for Humphrey came when, several days later, the band demanded money from him, through Konemase, for the appearance: he had assumed all the while there would be no expense. The point of the illustration is not only the lack of communication between them, however. For when Humphrey told me of it later (I had already heard of it through Mailala) he couldn't think of Konemase's name! —notwithstanding their common residence for one year and their common employment for two years prior to that. It may have been a momentary slip but was still significant. The foreman of Production Two, living in unit 106, also gave a party, but he, like Mailala, held the party at Hohola to avoid unwelcome guests. As we shall see, however, it was also significant that he invited a number of other employees; most were unit residents who were Kerema as well as long-term workers.

The reason for restraint rather than pervasive strife or strain, as in the Old Office, lies, for the most part I would suggest, in the physical conditions of the "household." All the residents of plant accommodation had to adapt to heterogeneity. The Old Boy-House residents adapted by segregating themselves spatially, dividing the quarters into sections which the other residents usually respected: in this way they minimized competition. In the Old Office the attempts to deal with heterogeneity by moving to different rooms were only partly effective: competition for public facilities continued to sour relations. The married residents, however, had the advantage of separate units and doors minimizing visual contact. These latter residents, however, did continue to use a common ablutions' block and many were dissatisfied with their condition; but the few criticisms I heard were directed toward management for failing to provide adequate facilities, rather than toward fellow residents.

Thus, at one level of analysis, Hellmann's characterization of Rooi-yard, a Johannesburg slum in the early 1930s, is applicable to the married quarters. Writing mainly of women in the yard, Hellmann (1948:89) describes how:

> Social intercourse between the inhabitants of Rooiyard bears the stamp of utilitarianism and casualness. The men, owing to their absence from the yard during the day, are even less integrated than the women. But even among the women, who come into contact with each other during the day's routine, the bonds of friendship have no strength or permanence. Temporary friendships do exist, but are more frequent between women of the same tribe . . . (But the contacts) . . . are so fleeting that a family will depart from Rooiyard without informing its erstwhile friends either of the day of its departure or of its new address.

Yet the married quarters were not thereby a social vacuum in the sense of lacking all content and form. Nor are those "fleeting contacts," limited as they were, of only marginal importance to the overall analysis. The form of the married quarters, I have argued, lay in the spatial and communal aspects of the quarter's organization which entailed mutual dependence. The content requires further discussion. Before discussing that content directly, however, I turn to the question of the analytical importance of those limited and fleeting contacts since they serve to emphasize that while the quarters could be seen as relatively self-contained social systems, they were also segments of a wider cultural whole.

Epstein has argued that such temporary ties "do not emerge and die without leaving some trace upon the social fabric" (1958:v). Their importance, I suggest, lies in the fact that they serve to maintain and amplify the cultural viability of the town and its population and to incorporate what might otherwise be relatively discrete social systems based on, say, kinship, locality, industrial production, or racial statuses into an urban system of communication. To restate this, we can say that these fleeting contacts are important not so much because they are a codicil to a system of social positions and "direct acquaintanceships" based on established reciprocities as because their formation and death leave traces of underlying cultural understandings and conventions or "the knowledge about" which serves to give meaning and at least minimal coherence to the Port Moresby social process.

To illustrate this point I call attention to the fact that a major portion of Mailala's previous urban experience had been as a taxi driver. It is therefore interesting to discover that the previous tenant of unit 5 was not only married to the cousin of Hereva's wife, and was thus an affine of Mailala's neighbor, but that three months after being dismissed from P.M.D. he had gone to work at the taxi service. Both this man, "Township"—named for his infant attraction to a local administrative station—and Hereva—the occupant of unit 4—were Motu-speaking, and both were based at Barakau village, some twenty miles southeast of Port Moresby, although Hereva had been born in Tubuseraia (Barakau's legendary parent village) which lies five miles closer to the town. Township had originally persuaded Hereva to work at P.M.D. The two Motuans were to live next to each other in units 4 and 5 for another year until Township was dismissed.

Township had worked as a forklift driver, supplying materials to Production Four workers. Vake, from Gorohu (a Koita village to the west of Port Moresby) drove a forklift truck on the other Production Four shift. One night leaving work after midnight, Township, who was quite tipsy from drinking beer, went back to the quarters, pushed a hose under the door, turned on the water, and flooded Vake's unit. Waking up in the middle of the night, soaked to the skin, Vake's wife (from the Rigo Sub-District, with a reputation for a sharp tongue, and, it was rumored afterward, no friend of Kare, Township's wife) had gone to the company management and complained of Township's prank. He was promptly dismissed, as much, I suspect, for the prima facie evidence that he had been drinking at work as for disturbing a coworker's household. His dismissal left unit 5 vacant and Mailala moved in from the cramped and dingy unit 1 where he had been living since he had joined the company some five months before. Township returned to Barakau and was "unemployed" for three months before he sought work with the taxi service.

Township's employment with the taxi service was far from accidental. In all there were six households at the taxi service compound—one or more spouses being from Barakau. In two of these households Barakau women had married drivers from the Sepik area. Another driver was married to a girl from Kapakapa, the easternmost Motu village. The remaining three were all married to Barakau women and were compatriots of Hereva and Township. Further reinforcing the ties between the P.M.D. and taxi service compounds and Barakau was the fact that two young P.M.D. employees had, for several months at a time, been living in either Hereva's household in the Old Married Quarters or in a unit in the taxi service compound. Tau—one of these young men—was Hereva's wife's brother and had come to work at P. M.D. as an assistant to the workshop storeman after leaving Keravat High School on the Gazelle Peninsula of New Britain. Management hoped that he might one day localize the storeman's job. Tau's wife— an ex-typist with the administration in Port Moresby—continued to live in the village while her husband lodged first with Hereva and then with his classificatory sister and her husband, from the Sepik area of New Guinea, at the taxi service. But before he left the P.M.D. compound Tau had introduced another young man to the plant. This fellow, Mero, moved into Hereva's unit when Tau vacated it.

Mero—who worked as a machine operator, and ultimately as a shift supervisor, in Production One—was from Dabunari, an inland Koiari village some four miles by road from Barakau. Dabunari was his father's village. His mother was from Barakau; she was Township's classificatory sister. There was a close relationship between the two villages. Long-standing economic ties were supplemented by the ties brought about by intermarriage, by a common church membership (they shared a pastor and, on major occasions, the Barakau church), the schooling of Dabunari youth at the Barakau primary school, and by the fact that the majority of Dabunari residents were bilingual. Mero himself spoke his second language fluently. Before taking Tau's place in Hereva's household, Mero had also been living at the taxi service compound.

Thus there was a complex network of social paths linking Mailala to Hereva and predating their coresidence. This network of linkages was expanded when Township later went to work at the taxi service. Yet I emphasize that it was not perduring reciprocities with, or animosities towards, Barakau villagers or taxi service workers which Mailala brought to the P.M.D. quarters and his new-found relationship to Hereva. Rather he brought an intellectual understanding of his previous work experience and social ambience. Having left the taxi service, Mailala never returned to visit its employees nor did he maintain contact with them. Yet his knowledge of the role of Barakau villagers in the taxi service compound and his understanding of his place and the possibilities in the occupational structure of the town continued to influence his musings and actions while working for P.M.D. There was nothing in the events leading up to Mailala's dismissal which would have made continuing relationships impossible; it was rather that although relationships with his fellow taxi service workers had been necessary and even comforting while he had worked there, they had nonetheless been limited to occupational and narrowly-defined coresidential spheres and could now be cast off like coats which had outlived their usefulness.

Certainly, the knowledge that they had both Barakau and Sepik acquaintances in common provided a cue for Mailala and Hereva to associate. Yet since there were no perduring ties being transferred from one situation to the other, their common (but not shared) experiences and understandings—for example, as drivers and long-term urban residents—were far more important.

The fact that there were concrete social pathways between them predating coresidence was nonetheless important as an indicator of these common understandings. One such understanding was the idea of the town itself as a social ambience, small enough to be understood as an entity. There was one sense in which all town residents could perceive of the town as a unique entity—through its bustle and buildings. For many, particularly the recent migrants, the overall town also appeared large and impersonal and, in its broader features, remote from firsthand experience. But residents like Mailala and Hereva (and, almost without exception, the other residents of the married quarters) could, with their social pathways extending out into the town, portray it as an assessable and accessible unity with known social and geographic components. When conversation revealed that their images of the town and its social character were at times discrepant they were far less ready than newcomers to discard carefully ground cultural lenses. They were more likely to blame the arbitrary, Australian limitation of educational and occupational opportunity that had prevented them from finding a sufficiently high vantage point from which to meld a full-face version of the simple profiles provided by its public streets. These pathways might serve, moreover, to indicate to Mailala and Hereva that "Port Moresby custom" involved shared specific knowledge and enthusiasms about, for example, jobs, employers, hierarchies of preference for beer and cigarettes, prestige, personalities, aspirations for their children, and white authority. Thus, while actual associations within the married quarters were fragile there was also a social content which continued beyond their immediately visible life; this content, in turn, provided cues for associations elsewhere.

Underpinning these common understandings and conventions of discourse was the colonial matrix of the town: many of its key arrangements and activities were set by the colonial polity and economy. Certainly there were distinctive Papuan and New Guinean components or adjustments but these were not equally weighted across the range of institutions. While specifically Papuan or New Guinean components were often limited, components based on the authority and emulation of Australian values and predicates were strong.

Ideas about health involved both indigenous and Australian cures, causes, and practitioners, and these various elements were mixed in more equal measure than in most social spheres. Many sicknesses or states of distress were perceived as foreign to Australian understanding and experience, as we saw in the suspicions and findings associated with Mailala and Elizabeth's visit to the *babalau*. But in other cases indigenous practices were seen as at best additional and complementary to Australian practice: one had an injection and a wound dressed at the local clinic and only in those cases where it failed to heal would a local practitioner be consulted. For many migrants, moreover, Australian-introduced medical practices competed directly with indigenous practice because of the authority and perceived efficacy of all things Australian, the certainty and assurance with which they were administered, and the uncertainty and hesitancy of indigenous systems of belief when transferred to the town. Thus Highlanders I talked to clearly demonstrated that sorcery and magical materials were to be reckoned with yet showed great uncertainty about their operation within the town. Nonetheless, almost without exception, coastal migrants, and thus the bulk of the urban population, were emphatic that there was much still undreamt of in Australian philosophy: you could be ensorcelled as readily in Port Moresby as in Mekeo, say, while Samarai witches were magnificently adept at overnight flights up to the town.

In the field of public order avoidance and segregation were the only indigenous responses. Sometimes these were articulated into clear conventions and understandings—for example, the freely given advice "avoid beer halls unless you have compatriots with you." But in those cases where rights and the pattern of avoidance and noninterference were infringed, workers either sought private remedies, as in the case of Mailala and Elizabeth, or, as in the case of the theft of Bava's shirt and that where Township flooded Vake's unit, solicited Australian-backed authority. This second response was a general one: on many occasions police intervention was called for even when the disputants were close compatriots.

The *kompani*, or rotating credit associations were a wholly indigenous response even if they show similarities with rotating credit institutions elsewhere (see, for example, Geertz 1962; Ardener 1964). But they were also complementary to, not yet alternatives for, Australian savings institutions. They were structured very simply: the number of members involved was small, ranging from two to eleven with a mean of perhaps five; contributions and payments were fixed and equal, contributions ranging from approximately one-quarter to the whole of a member's weekly wage while payments were fixed by the wage period; contributor's roles were identical and there were no designated organizers; membership was decided informally. No sums were kept for group purposes such as entertainment, although in one of the larger *kompani* there was a recognized obligation for that week's recipient to treat his fellow members, while in another the recipient was responsible for all food purchases for the week. In roughly eight out of ten cases the recipient would then deposit the bulk of his receipts in an *individual* savings account. Given the small size of the *kompani*, the equivalence of indebtedness and lack of profit involved, and the channeling of receipts into banking institutions, there seems little to choose between the two institutions as far as capital formation is concerned. Moreover, while *kompani* membership could promise unwelcome group pressure and lack of financial flexibility, workers saw that it was finally Australian banking institutions which were protecting their savings for them and they were delighted that every week bank officers were present, with account records, at the end of the line of the workers who were collecting their wages. Nonetheless, even if the narrowly defined economic advantages were minimal, for many workers wage-pooling symbolized comfortable, ongoing (and also newer, tentatively-explored) solidarities and reciprocities within the prevailing environment of restraint and heterogeneity.

Perhaps the key idea in the overall urban-located cultural structure was indeed "money" and its importance for social relationships. Money was used both as an *idée fixe* to explain urban residence itself—"I came to work for money"—and also as the single most visible symbol of the implications of urban participation and of workers' leading sen-

timents about Port Moresby man's relationship to his fellow men. I
have more to say of workers' dependence on wages and employment,
and of their own reactions to their situation as *employees* in the next
chapter. At this stage I will simply note that most compound residents
would agree with one of their fellow's judgment and apply it to their
own experience: "The Tubuseraia people half of them are nearly every
time commenting on the life here. Some people they don't understand
but most of them are jealous—that's what most Papua-New Guineans
are—jealous. Money has come to take the place of the old life of Papua–New Guineans. From money everything else comes. It goes under
jealous[y]."

These New Guinea urbanites, that is, had accepted the premise of a
now minor embellishment within Western social sentiment—that "money is the root of all evil"—and had expanded it into a major theme of
their social condition and consciousness.

Port Moresby is a town of wage earners. One group of fishermen
still plies its ancient skills and trade, others develop commerce within
the interstices of the colonial economy—collecting returnable empty bot-
tles or running passenger-truck services—but otherwise Port Moresby
residents appear as workers and their dependents. Thus the above quotation points to the salience attached to money as a constraint on a way
of life which had been animated by quite different principles. Yet it
also points to a more pragmatic type of constraint: "money" figures as
a severely restricting factor in individual options, determining, for example, the number of bus fares available to visit kin and so on. These
later pragmatic aspects of workers' lives occupied a great deal of their
attention. But it is also necessary to stress that "money" was not only a
neutral, mediating object but that it took on expressive value. "Money," in contrast to "the old ways," called for regret and nostalgia.
Used in other contexts it also became a statement and indicator of prestige and thus a diacritical feature of interpersonal relations. Thus in
the events surrounding Mailala's wife's sickness and cure we saw fears
of sorcery focused not, as in "Old Melanesia," on out-of-the-ordinary
and envied success at gardening or hunting, but on out-of-the-ordinary
and envied success at earning a monetary income.

Another basic and widely-shared perception which we can list as a
key feature of the urban cultural structure concerned the urban household. Crucial here is an understanding of the urban dwelling as a resource and not just a shelter. As housing was in such short supply in

the town, simple supply and demand would suggest its high social value. Job instability would also suggest housing as a stable resource. But associated with these factors is the idea that urban residence took on an expressive, not simply an instrumental, value and that owning or renting an urban dwelling put one in touch with the advantages of urban living—principally, schools and entertainment—as well as a style of life which, although recognized as only a pale reflection, nonetheless emulated white patterns of living. Thus we saw Mailala moving from a dingy to a larger unit in the quarters, and striving to find a still larger and less encumbered house at Sabama. He aspired to live in a dry, permanent "European" townhouse with an iron roof rather than a well ventilated and much cheaper, but also impermanent and combustible, "village" house.

Important here is the knowledge that with an urban house one could act as a host to fellow villagers, kin, and compatriots, accommodating them while they were looking for jobs or housing or helping them to take advantage of the town's schools and, say, its market. As Table 14

TABLE 14

HOUSEHOLD COMPOSITION OF MARRIED QUARTERS RESIDENTS
BY DISTRICT OF ORIGIN

	Central District		Gulf District	Other Districts
	Port Moresby Sub-District	Other Sub-Districts		
No. of Households	5	5	13	2
Resident children in all households (*4 not in tenant's conjugal family)	22*	5	26	2
Range of children per household	9–0	2–0	4–0	
P.M.D. employees lodging with tenant	1	3	2	0
Visitors: "a" = adults "c" = children	0	4a+1c	6a+3c	0
Mean no. of persons in households	6.6	4.4	4.9	3.0
Mean no. of persons in households	5.0			
Mean no. of persons not in tenants' conjugal families	1.0			

indicates, one out of five persons in the married quarters was a visitor, lodger, or resident child not in the tenant's conjugal family. Furthermore, there was considerable discussion and agreement on desirable Port Moresby locations with their associated advantages and disadvantages for entertaining and access to important Papuan centers. These understandings (coupled always with the perceived generosity and income of a given householder) led many groups of compatriots to regard particular urban households as important centers of urban social gravity. This was certainly the case for the Barakau villagers. The taxi service, particular houses in Hohola, and Hereva's unit within the compound, became way stations and centers of gossip. Visits to the market, the weekly visit of the Barakau Ladies basketball team, and so on, meant that, for the Barakau villagers, the town was not simply a direct extrapolation of a rural social or cultural system but became itself an autonomous element in a wider unity. Villagers look as much perhaps to the town as town dwellers looked to the village (cf. Friedl 1962:66–67). While other coastal Papuans and urban residents may have lacked the ease of rural-urban communication brought about by close proximity which marked that of the Barakau villagers, the difference was one of degree and not kind. Representatives of almost all major ethnic or tribal groupings in the town could, and did, discuss urban households as nodes of town-to-village communication and as nodes for the transmission of urban mores.

Barracks accommodation did not and could not serve the same function, except to a limited degree. There was, first of all, the lack of privacy in the barracks which drove *wantok* in their most intimate moments to associate beyond its limits. Of far more importance was the concrete status attached to the married males and the assumption that meetings of urban and visiting rural compatriots could be held most appropriately within these men's bailiwicks. This applied both to those groups where separate men's meetinghouses were still in use (or still remembered) within village society as well as to those groups where they were not. To embrace barracks residence was to embrace the society of *young*, low-status males, "work-boy" culture, and the "big-line."

While there was much in common between the society of the barracks and that of the married quarters, there were also interesting differences. Recruitment to work-boy society was by individual choice and the circumstances of labor migration. While the cellular, or set-based constitution of the barracks was a continuing phenomenon, most

of its occupants regarded their continued stay in Port Moresby as necessarily limited: they would be returning to village society to reestablish and/or further their positions there and to get married, even
though they might find the "bright lights" very compatible for the moment. They might even have to return to Port Moresby, as it was the
nearest source of employment, but hoped that it would be neither as unmarried men, nor as "big-line" or other unskilled labor. Recruitment
to married quarters society, like that of work-boy society, was by individual choice and the circumstances of labor migration. But it was
also by marriage and birth. The massive growth of Port Moresby has
been sufficiently recent, and the relationship of Papuans and New
Guineans to the urban labor market tenuous enough to date, to have prevented the rise of a large urban "second generation." But its seeds are
present and the commitments and attitudes of the married workers reflected their recognition of the entailments involved in bringing a wife
to town and raising a family there. Married workers were much more
concerned with the long-term implications of town residence, education,
and urban "life-chances" than their unmarried compatriots.

Geertz's description of Modjokuto, a Javanese town, as "a social
composite, and only partially organised coincidence of separate social
structures . . ." (1965:27) is equally applicable to Port Moresby
and to P.M.D. compound life. The contrast between the barracks and
married quarters emphasizes the composite nature of the overall social
arena: the urban cultural structure was an important mechanism in the
organization of its partial correspondences. A major source of the
composite, rather than unitary, character of the married quarters themselves was the opposition between "Kerema" and "non-Kerema."

When associations were measured by common activities rather than
by employment, few could be found between Keremas and other employees. I mentioned two such relationships involving barracks' residents, in addition to the tie between Patrick and Bava in the Old Office. There were occasions when I saw Kerema and non-Kerema married residents passing the time of day but far fewer occasions when
they stopped for a more serious chat. Perhaps the strongest tie between a Kerema and "non-Kerema" in the units was between a Toaripi
man and a man of part Motu, part Orokolo descent; they could, on occasion, be seen chatting after work or outside the quarters. Most relations, however, seemed hesitant or even embarrassed. Kerema-to-Kerema associations, however, were far more intense than other associa-

tions: all of the relationships which I noted as counter to the general pattern of restraint were between Kerema residents.

Their exclusiveness stemmed not, I judge, from competition in the quarters but primarily from their situation in the town and the industrial structure. Ryan (1968:63) writes of the Port Moresby Toaripi that "although a large number of the migrants have lived in Port Moresby for more than ten years, they have little contact with people of other language or cultural groups. A Toaripi settlement rarely has outsiders in it: Toaripi who live in the Administration housing areas have little to do with neighbours who belong to other groups."

Earlier, Kerema people claiming trading links through the *Hiri* voyages made by Motu sailors had been invited to settle and build on local rightholders land. Ryan, however, notes the current antagonism of the Motu and Koita rightholders to the growing settler population (ibid: 61). That this antagonism stems more from the fact that the newcomers are "Gulf" rather than "settlers" is suggested by Oram's comment that whereas rightholders at Vabukori resented Toaripi settlers they were prepared to tolerate or even welcome settlers from Hula (Oram 1968b:13).

Here it should be pointed out that the Motu people's relationship to incoming migrants has shifted somewhat in the course of time. Pre- and early colonial period trading links between the Motu and the Elema effectively colored the Motuan's role as host and urban landholder when the Elema began migrating to the town in large numbers after 1946. Now, however, Motuan performance in the role of host, while continuing to be cast within the framework of traditional landholder to settler relationships is nonetheless colored by the Motuan's experience of the present urban and occupational structure and the increase in social scale. While most plant workers were jealous of the social boundaries they and previous workers had erected and were apprehensive of extending their contacts too widely, the Motuan workers were seemingly prompted by a desire to come to terms with the unfamiliar as they continually encouraged young New Guinean "backwoodsmen" working at the plant to visit their quarters.

To an extent there was an element of fascination in the strangeness of the New Guineans—the marked differences in sophistication and occupational level between them lending an added charm. Many of the conversations I heard were concerned with each other's exotic customs.

Thus, the contrasted marriage customs of the Highlanders and the Motuans, for example—on the one hand, the search for special bird-of-paradise feathers, on the other the enormous cash payments—were an exciting and never ending source of sustained conversation. But there was also an element of largesse in the relationships, with its counterpart of gratitude, reflecting the fact that the New Guineans were far from home and were not directly competing with their hosts for land or jobs, which in turn allowed the Motuans to demonstrate their traditional hospitality. In contrast, the Elema were now long-term urban residents who were competing with the Motu for jobs and land.

To account for Toaripi exclusiveness, Ryan herself has stressed their large numbers, pointing out that there are so many Toaripi that most are able to associate almost exclusively with those who come from the same cluster of villages (Ryan 1968:63). But this is a little too mechanical: size alone could equally suggest their distribution over a wide number of settings giving rise to a parallel opportunity for innovation in relations.

Perhaps something of their exclusiveness stems from Melanesian racial prejudice. Thus Chalmers casts them as "the terror of all the other tribes from this [the Motu] to Kerepuna or Kerpara" (1898:326; see also Seligman 1910:314). Malinowski notes, in "The Sexual Life of Savages," Trobrianders' criticisms of "Papuan Gulf natives" employed on one of the plantations: their dancing was admired, but not their physical appearance. In Trobriand eyes, "their ugliness is chiefly ascribed to their dark skin. . . . Their pronounced frizzy hair and their strange manner of dressing it in plaits and fringes is also regarded as very unbecoming. Unattractive, too, are their prominent thin lips and their large, aquiline, almost Jewish noses, set in a long narrow face" (Malinowski 1929:306).

Thus the cultural distance born of large numbers, overlaid with highly unfavorable stereotypes, undoubtedly played a major part in their segregation.

Contrasts in associational life undoubtedly added something to this tendency. Thus the worker-tenants of all the five, married quarters households between which there were generalized reciprocities were rugby union enthusiasts and it was common to find them setting off for Boroko to watch the game. Rugby union matches in the town were a predominantly "Kerema" affair. The sport had been developed in the town, through the efforts of a leading political figure from the Gulf, Albert Maori Kiki, largely in opposition to the European-dominated game of Rugby League, and to benefit his own and neighboring peoples (Kiki 1968:101, see also the discussion of the Rugby League in Chapter 2). Since its formation, two clubs formed of people from other coastal areas—"Daru" and "Marshall Lagoon"—had joined, as well as some four clubs representing educational, military, and police institutions. The bulk of noninstitutional players, however, were from the Gulf: four of the teams were from the eastern Elema areas and one from farther west. One other Toaripi team—Fari—had amalgamated with a European team—Colleagues—to form the composite "Colleagues-Fari." There were enthusiastic supporters of "Mirihea" and "Sevese Miro" in the quarters, and two players—one for "Moripi," the other for "Isoposa." All were "Kerema" teams. This participation and the exclusive gossip about the sport, which involved all Kerema workers, acted as a further wedge between them and the non-Kerema.

Ryan writes of the Toaripi that a little over two-thirds first left the village more than ten years ago. Moreover only 5 percent were married and yet did *not* have their families with them (Ryan 1968:62–63). The Kerema residents of the married quarters—both Toaripi and non-Toaripi—were also, with minor exceptions, committed townsmen. Many were also senior workers whose wage rates were based largely on skills acquired at P.M.D. and not easily marketable elsewhere. There were some non-Kerema employees in a comparable economic position (but not many), and many Kerema employees who were *not* in this position. Thus I do not wish to argue that Kerema residents were a completely different economic group with opposed interests to those of their non-Kerema workmates. But, given their numbers in the plant and dominance in certain sections, the mutual association of long-term, committed industrial workers meant, very largely, the association of fellow-Keremas. With similar economic interests, and similar cultures and language their mutual association was not unlikely. A further component of distance was the Kerema's economic position and sense of occupational solidarity as contrasted with people like Hereva and Mailala who, although committed to wage employment, were less committed to their employment at P.M.D. and were recently-recruited employees in ancillary sections and whose social networks tied them to institutions other than the plant.

Migrant Statuses and Cultural Distance

This discussion of involvement in wage employment and urban residence leads us to a discussion of the nature of the residents' migrant
statuses. Although these statuses have not been the principal focus of
this or previous chapters, it was impossible to analyze neighboring relations without taking them into account. I conclude this chapter by
underlining the salient points of the worker's position as migrant in
preparation for a more detailed discussion in the next.

In the chapter on the Old Office we saw how the migrant status and
rural aspirations of the two Mekeos, James and Gabriel, constrained
their behavior within the arena of the house itself. In addition, we
have seen in the last two chapters how aspects of Paul and Mailala's
ongoing choices could be related to their participation in rural social
systems—the rights and obligations of statuses in those systems carry-
ing over into their situation within the compound. In some instances
we saw workers discharging urban and rural roles simultaneously.
Thus James' bookkeeping studies could variously be seen as attempts to
adapt to the expatriate economy, to gain prestige in the eyes of his European workmates or those of his fellow-Mekeo residents, and, at the
same time, to qualify himself for his rural business aspirations and for
leadership in the village sphere. At other times his behavior in the
quarters can be seen as the unintended consequence of actions taken in
terms of wholly rural roles: thus, discharging his role of secretary to
the transport group, he invited villagers to the quarters and by doing so
aggravated the domestic strife.

Thus we can see the migrant statuses are sometimes important for
town-located relationships. Mayer's convincing demonstration that the
behavior of many Xhosa migrants in East London owed much to their
involvement in rural-located sets of relations sharpens this recognition
(Mayer 1961 and 1962). Furthermore, Oram has stressed the interlocking of rural and urban roles for the Hula in Port Moresby itself
(1968b:33). Specifically, he writes of a small group of settlement residents, that they "form part of a regional social system which extends
far beyond the boundaries of the town" (1967b:54).

While recognizing these interdependencies wherever necessary, I
have not, however, been concerned to analyze rural-urban interdependence *per se*. Rather, I have taken, as my starting point, Mitchell's advice to study the behavior of individuals in town within the social matrix created by its "external imperatives"—for example, density of set-

tlement, demographic disproportion, and heterogeneity (1966:48–49). Substituting "Papua–New Guineans" for "Africans" I have taken these external imperatives as a "limiting framework within which Africans must solve the problem of giving meaning to actions" (Mitchell 1960:171). This procedure involves an initial, analytical separation of rural and urban social spheres.

We cannot, however, leave our analysis there since the degree of separation of urban-located behaviors and rural statuses varies considerably even within Africa: *degree* of discontinuity is a crucial factor (cf. Banton 1964:133–35). Thus Epstein has argued of Gluckman's well-known aphorism—"An African townsman is a townsman, an African miner is a miner"—that while correctly inviting comparisons with urban studies elsewhere, it does not enable students of urban Africa to handle so readily the problem of variation in urban social systems. For my present purposes, however, Epstein's most telling point is that to lose sight of the town dweller's migrant status is to lose sight of the very process of becoming a townsman (Epstein 1967b:276).

Moreover, in the discussion of neighboring relations, I have relied, for the most part, on the concept of *cultural distance* as the only statement of their perduring rural-urban ties. It stressed the common experience and interests of migrants from the same area and their sense of group identity while in town. Thus I argued that despite contrasted ways in which they were absorbed into the set, both Paul and William were united in their sense of being "Popondetta" and that it was this self-identification which was the single most important principle of barracks' social organization. While adequate for the explanation of neighboring relations, it must be emphasized, however, that the concept is synchronic; it abstracts, at a single point in time, an aspect of several different processes. Thus on other occasions it has been necessary to probe a little further and to distinguish between the effects of urban heterogeneity, throwing into *relief* the migrants' common experience and interests, and the nature of those experiences and interests in themselves. At other times, it was necessary to distinguish the sense of shared interests arising from the accident of birth from the economic interests—in a broad sense and including social security—binding an individual to a rural network of relations. This second distinction is essentially that in the African literature between "tribalism" as a category of interaction in the towns, and tribal *structure* as an organized set of political relations (Mitchell 1956; Gluckman 1960). In the Melanesian context this contrast might well be rephrased as one between "localism" as a set of loyalties and oppositions in the towns, and the "local group" as a matrix of jural statuses and reciprocities giving rights to land and other resources.

As I have already argued, it was often possible for the analysis of neighboring relations *per se* to play down this distinction. Yet the account is thereby incomplete: thus, given that "local" or regional groupings were so prominent, we have yet to explain why individual ties based on localism were so limited and fleeting. Once the imperatives of common employment and residence were removed, most of these relationships ceased to function in an active manner, although they might be reinstated on a later occasion when the participants' paths crossed again, or a special need arose. As we saw, this in itself is significant. Yet it would be unwise to overemphasize this fact of latency in the relationships: fragility is marked and we must address ourselves to an analysis of workers' migrant statuses to understand why it should be so. In this way we will also understand why certain authors have stressed Port Moresby's lack of integration and coherence.

6

Workers as Migrants and Employees

Brown (1957:27) reports that "in answer to the question *A leva karu?* 'What person are you?' (i.e. of what origin) an Elema man will invariably give his village name" suggesting that the Papuan's primary commitment is to his village. It is because of this major commitment that Hogbin and Wedgwood (1953:252) have reported that "in labour compounds and in gaols, where persons from many places are gathered, there is a tendency for men of the same tongue to band together when major quarrels break out, but in daily life a man recognises bonds of fellowship with those who are kin to him or who come from the same settlement."

This suggests again the fragility of purely "ethnic" relationships once the imperatives of heterogeneity and compound life are removed. Thus an examination of the degree to which workers were committed specifically to village ties is a very necessary part of the analysis of urban-located relations.

Most workers were subject to a dual involvement: most were simultaneously villagers and townsmen. They aspired to a higher level of consumption and material benefit and were conscious that urban wage employment was essential to its attainment. Yet they were also highly

Plate 7   A coastal Motu village

Plate 8   At home for
the weekend—a young
worker and his wife

conscious of the economic, social, and emotional security that village life offered and continued to play their parts as villagers when opportunity allowed. I look on their attitudes and aspirations as, in part, responses to this dual participation.

But, whereas in previous chapters I have been able to deal with adaptations in some detail, in this chapter considerations of space and diverse material suggest a more general presentation. I have arranged the material, for the most part, quantitatively, and around a distinction between *commitment*—based on attitudes, plans, and aspirations—and *involvement*—based on decisions workers have already taken and on the constraints on choice which can be inferred from their surface characteristics. The utility of this distinction arises from the possibility of discrepancy between intention and realization. Most workers, judging by their plans and aspirations, are oriented toward their home villages and are anticipating an ultimate return. But all are dependent to different degrees on wage labor. And some, unable to realize their aims, are staying longer than they had originally intended, and are thus at least partly engaged in urban residence in an involuntary sense. The terms, and part of the distinction, are suggested by Mitchell (1964:14–15). Plotnicov (1967:296–98) makes the same point for Jos, Nigeria, but more strongly than I would care to for Port Moresby.

WORKERS AS MIGRANTS

> . . . such variations between individual Tonga as the length of their stay abroad, the amount of money sent home, and in general, the frequency and intensity of their contacts with the rural area, are differences of degree and do not alter the fundamental fact that the majority of the Tonga working abroad look to the economic and social system of their tribal area for their ultimate security. [Van Velsen 1961:160]

Sampling

Much of my information on workers' urban commitment and involvement was elicited in the course of normal interviewing. Indeed, I tended to ask most workers their reasons for migrating, reactions to the town, and plans when first encountering them since it was always an easy subject to broach. As fieldwork proceeded, however, it became apparent that I would need to collect more standardized and statistically-based information to supplement material gained from casually selected samples.

Accordingly, I prepared a set of standard questions on individual life and employment histories, plans, and attitudes, including a visual test of attitudes to occupational prestige. I decided to administer the schedules and tests to a sample of twenty-eight—one in three—unskilled laborers and to census each of the seventy-five workers in the white-collar, skilled, and semiskilled grades. My justification for this procedure was that the material I had already collected suggested that unskilled laborers were a fairly homogeneous category (except for a few surface characteristics such as "place of origin"). The other section of the labor force appeared much more varied, however, and I thought sampling would be hazardous.

This seemed a fairly modest undertaking at the time, but events proved otherwise. There were all the usual problems of gaining cooperation but, in addition, some who had appeared affable in less structured interviews seemed truculent when approached on this matter. Only one refused to cooperate but a number were evasive and continually pleaded they were busy or about to leave when approached. Workers living outside P.M.D. accommodation were particularly difficult to interview.

Eventually I collected detailed information on 68 of the 75 in white-collar and senior grades and 24 of the original sample of 28 unskilled workers. The visual test on attitudes to occupational prestige fared even worse but because even its "failure" reveals a great deal of the workers' cultural ambience I discuss it in some detail below.

Commitments and Occupational Prestige

I showed workers a set of sixteen photographs depicting Papua–New Guineans at work (or other gainful activities) and asked each man in one of Police Motu, Pidgin, or English to rank them in terms of the prestige assigned to each occupation by members of the "community-at-large." The method followed very closely that used by Xydias in a study of occupational prestige rankings among adults in Stanleyville (now Kisangani) in the old Belgian Congo (Xydias 1956:461–68). I laid the photographs before each worker in random order. He was asked to rank them and then to check his ranking and amend it as he felt necessary. The ranking completed, I asked each informant to explain his choice for the first three and the last three. As the testing proceeded I occasionally asked further questions about what appeared to be anomalous rankings.

Reactions to the protocols and an initial set of twenty-two plates were solicited from selected informants and sixteen plates were then selected from the actual test. The selection reflected my own intuition of relevance and the availability of suitable photographs. The plates and further explanation of the test are given in the Appendix.

One man complained afterwards that the test was irksome—"hard work." This opinion may well have been shared by others who refused to take part or pleaded other commitments. Certainly a number had heard of the photographs before I approached them and many saw me administering the test to their fellows. The test required me to make an additional formal visit or approach and thus some who were reluctant to take part may have resented my previous questioning or been bored by it. Perhaps some also thought they would be unable to understand my requirements and would appear unsophisticated. Thus two men listened politely to the protocol and then professed their inability to begin: they would "tell me later." I saw the test as supplementary and was thus reluctant to press too hard and endanger rapport. But reluctance to begin the test was not my only problem. Two men cooperated with good humor until guests arrived; they then abandoned the exercise in the middle and could not be persuaded to continue on another occasion. Moreover, enthusiasm also created problems. Thus I met my greatest difficulties in the barracks. Attempts to administer the test there would result in large congregations of men and suggestions from all sides. The attitudes of any one individual were lost or obscured. Enthusiasm was sometimes a problem in the married quarters as well—children in particular were quick to volunteer reactions—but was less acute.

Once started, in a favorable environment, there were still problems. One Highlander ranked all the photographs but completely misinterpreted my requirements; [1] five others responded by taking three or so pictures and saying, "I like these."

These difficulties led me to abandon random sampling and attempts to census a category. Instead I administered the test whenever practical. In all, fifty-two employees completed the test satisfactorily; they ranked each picture and were able to give more or less coherent reasons for at least their first and last rankings. The sample is small and nonrandom. White-collar workers and apprentices were overrepresented —fourteen and six respectively—while unskilled workers were underrepresented—only fourteen completed the test. The remaining eighteen

[1] This man was the first to respond to the Pidgin version, which was unsuspectly ambiguous. It used, as its key phrase, "man, wok bilongen *i-sanap* nambawan long ai bilong ol" [the man whose work "stands-up" first in everyone's regard]. The respondent thought I wanted him to choose those men who were the most *erect* and gave the houseboy as his first choice! After that I amended the phrase to the version given in the Appendix.

were skilled or semiskilled. In view of this distribution, weighted in favor of white-collar and other "educated" employees, the results are perhaps all the more surprising.

Because of the close association between occupation and general social standing in advanced industrial societies, studies of occupational prestige have usually been undertaken as part of more general inquiries into social stratification. Similar studies in the "Third World"—the less, if at all, industrialized nations—have been used in a similar fashion (cf., for example, Tiryakian 1958; Mitchell and Epstein 1959; Thomas 1962; and D'Souza 1962). The results have borne a striking resemblance to results achieved in the industrial nations—professional and white-collar occupations heading the list of rankings and unskilled and menial occupations appearing at the bottom.

Mitchell, surveying these studies as a problem in comparative sociology, has argued that even if certain of the societies are not industrialized they are still nonetheless ordered "in terms of a modern productive system and permeated by the same appropriate general set of values and motivations" (Mitchell 1964:80). He does, however, also argue that such rankings reflect various dimensions which need not operate in concordance with one another and that some occupations may be evaluated in terms of conflicting frames of reference. Each ranking needs to be viewed within its local situation. Moreover, he argues that "a general ranking of occupations seems possible only when there is detailed differentiation, functional specificity and a generalised reward system" (ibid.:87).

These qualifications to the theory of the inexorable operation of the "modern productive system" are very necessary for the New Guinea situation. Van der Veur's studies of occupational prestige in West Irian (Indonesian New Guinea) correlate very closely with findings elsewhere: political posts were given the highest ranking, but these were followed by the expected rank order of professions—skilled and then menial and agricultural occupations (P. Van der Veur 1964 and 1966). Epstein (1967a), on the other hand, found that on the Gazelle Peninsula of New Britain variation in evaluation was very high and the "don't know" category, large. Moreover, agricultural occupations were the highest ranking category of any. Arguing that the evaluations should be taken as an index of urban involvement, he suggests that lack of occupational differentiation was the crucial determinant of the response. Many of the respondents were Tolai people from within twenty miles or less of Rabaul. Access and proximity, taken with other factors, meant that any Tolai might be simultaneously a cash-cropper, subsistence farmer, truck owner, and driver, and yet still work for wages in the town. Tolai people as a whole were thus less dependent on urban residence and employment, and occupation was not such a critical indicator of social standing. Their situation and evaluations contrast to a significant degree with the small number of Manus in the sample who were far more dependent on urban residence.

My own results are less extreme: workers followed the usual practice in placing professional workers—the teacher and the doctor—at the top of the hierarchy and unskilled and menial occupations—the laborer and houseboy—at the bottom. But there were also interesting deviations from the archetypal industrial model. Thus the carpenter, an artisan, was ranked higher than the technician, who in the local context would be regarded as a white-collar worker. The electricity linesman, a semi-skilled occupation, was ranked higher than the mechanic, a skilled occupation. Most strikingly, the clerk was ranked tenth, lower than all these, and below the coffee grower. The list of occupations, ordered according to the mean rank, is given in Table 15. As well as the mean

TABLE 15

OCCUPATIONAL PRESTIGE RANKINGS OF A SAMPLE OF 52 P.M.D. EMPLOYEES

Plate	Occupation	Mean	Range	1st & 3rd quartiles	Interquartile range
IV	Teacher	1.2	1–6	1/3	2
IX	Doctor	1.9	1–9	1/3	2
VI	Carpenter	5.7	3–12	5/8	3
XIV	Technician	6.5	1–16	4/9	5
XVI	Agricultural Officer	6.8	1–13	3/11	8
XII	Linesman	6.9	1–16	5/10	5
III	Policeman	7.2	1–16	4/12	8
VIII	Mechanic	7.4	1–14	5/9	4
II	Coffeegrower	8.0	1–16	5/10	5
XI	Clerk	8.2	3–16	6/10	4
V	Oil company employee	8.7	3–15	7/12	5
VII	Driver	10.2	1–16	9/13	4
XIII	Betel nut vendor	11.5	1–16	8/15	7
I	Forklift driver	12.1	4–16	11/14	3
XV	Laborer	12.1	1–16	10/15	5
X	Houseboy	14.2	10–16	13/16	3

[A9827]

rank, the range, first and third quartiles, and the interquartile range are given to indicate variation and central tendency.[2] In the first column the number of the appropriate plate is given to facilitate cross-reference to the Appendix.

Variation in the response was marked. Thus seven of the sixteen occupations were ranked throughout the whole range (although the overall variation in the interquartile range is not markedly different than that given by Xydias for her African sample[3]). It should be stressed, moreover, that very few informants appeared to rank the occupations in terms of *community* respect as suggested to them. Some gave highly practical reasons for their evaluation; having given the electricity linesman the first ranking, one New Guinean responded, "bai yumi stap tudak i-no gut" (We wouldn't want to be without lighting). The overwhelming tendency was to cite purely personal factors. Indeed, of the five who were rejected because they took only three or so pictures, four were Highlanders and each took, as one of his choices, the driver. This was completely consistent with their job preferences: each was trying desperately to get his driving license. As one young, rather better educated Chimbu remarked of the driver, "em i-sindaun tasol long stia, em i-kisim bikpela moni moa" (All he does is sit down behind the wheel and [yet] gets big money).

The low evaluation of the clerk may, in part, have been due to problems of visual comprehension. He was shown thumbing through a filing drawer and many unskilled and semiskilled were unsure of this. As we discussed each picture and the task, however, before I asked for their evaluation, I incline to the view that this unfamiliarity played only a minor part in the ranking. Low social standing was far more important. As one Highlander characterized the clerk: "hap i-save gut, hap i-save 'fail'" (He understands half well, half poorly). One

---

[2] The overall variation is given by the range. The interquartile range is the remainder from the subtraction of the first and third quartiles. Thus a high interquartile range indicates a high degree of variation in the central 50 percent of responses. Xydias gives identical measures for her own studies of occupational prestige in Stanleyville (op. cit.). In view of the small size of my sample, and for purposes of comparison, I have followed her procedure.

[3] To obtain a measure of *overall* variation for comparison with her other samples, Xydias gives a mean interquartile range of 3. As she used only twelve occupations and I used sixteen, the mean interquartile range for my own material (4.56) should be multiplied by an index of 4/3. This gives a measure of overall variation of 3.42, comparable to that given by Xydias. See Xydias (1965) for further details and comparisons with other tests both in Kisangani and in America.

clerk ranked the occupation fifteenth arguing that it was not widely known by the people.   There was also an anti-white-collar sentiment in one of the comments of a young technician from the Central District who told me he wanted to leave P.M.D. and work with his body.

A high evaluation of manual compared to white-collar skills is also seen in the third place ranking given the carpenter.   This high evaluation is consistent with other New Guinea studies.   The carpenter is also ranked third (of thirty) in Epstein's study and appears, together with mechanic, teacher, doctor, and clerk as the most frequently mentioned in a study of job aspirations among settled workers and their children carried out in Port Moresby, Lae, and Rabaul (K. Van der Veur and Richardson 1966).   Part of the explanation is undoubtedly Papua–New Guineans' familiarity with woodworking skills: these are often encouraged by missions (cf. Oram 1968a:260) and woodworking traditions often form part of traditional cultures.   Thus a number of Papuans may work as carpenters at some point in their lives, alternating between this and other jobs as opportunity permits (Oram 1968b:19–20).

The territories' colonial institutions have always given high rewards to carpentry and artisan skills in general.   Artisans were among the best paid in the town: the highest paid indigene at P.M.D. was a carpenter.   Moreover, a perceived attribute of carpentry was the choice and autonomy it gave.   Of those five who gave third place to the occupation and of the three who were able to explain their choice, two argued that carpentry allowed one to choose his employer, one also stressing that, if he were a carpenter, he would return home and "make his business" building houses.   But it is also noteworthy that no one assigned the carpenter first or second place; the first quartile was no higher than that of many of the occupations; and the difference in mean ranking between the doctor and carpenter was great.

Generalized nondifferentiation, nonrecognition, and a multiplicity of individual attitudes were responsible for a great deal of scatter in the responses.   The respondents' detailed comments, however, suggest that the place of an occupation within the colonial society, the pattern of migrant labor, and the structural contradictions of colonialism, were also crucial.   Thus a reasonable interpretation of workers' comments suggests that the teacher and the doctor were ranked so highly because these were occupations which were analogous to prestigous Australian occupations in style, educational prerequisites, and income, and were firmly within the colonial sector of the economy yet also allowed scope for Papua–New Guinean leadership and autonomy from white direction. Those occupations which showed the inverse of those features—the houseboy and laborer—were unequivocally ranked lowest. Occupations in the broad middle of the range combined or expressed the desired features in an uncertain way and thus showed a high scatter and weak differentiation. This analysis is strengthened if we consider the "agricultural" occupations included in the test.

"Business" was one of the two most important criteria in the assessment of the coffeegrower. Surprisingly, despite the fact that the New Guinea Highlands are the center of coffee production in the combined Territories, Highlanders gave this occupation a low rating. One of those who failed to complete the test argued that "ol i-leba tasol" (they are only labor). My intention was that the people shown picking coffee should have been seen as smallholders and cashcroppers rather than labor: however, Highlanders may have been more visually discriminating. Others stressed national prosperity and prestige: John, in the Old Office, ranked the occupation second, after the teacher, pointing out the country needed more education first and then better agriculture. But more typical were the comments of Paul, from Mbawe, who ranked the coffeegrower fifth, and of a man from the Purari Delta, who ranked the plate first. Each of these emphasized that the coffeepickers were engaged in "business." Another response was that of two married quarters residents, both from Kerema. One ranked the agricultural officer tending rubber plants first, the coffeegrowers second, and the betel nut vendor third. These were all agricultural and therefore "business" and worthwhile; his last six—all menial or typically industrial jobs—were "bad," paying little and necessitating working for Europeans. The other, ranking the betel nut seller first and the coffeegrower second, made essentially the same criticism.

Thus professional occupations were unequivocally given first overall ranking and skilled manual occupations were not without their admirers, showing workers' involvement in the colonial, and for them largely urban, economy. Yet orthogonal to this general tendency was an undercurrent of rejection of urban wage employment on the whole, certain respondents preferring "business" occupations. These were seen as unequivocally centered in the rural areas. It should also be noted that the strongest response of this type came from two Keremas who had each spent over ten years working in the town, and over nine of these working for P.M.D.   I will take up these points again later in the chapter.

Plans and Aspirations

This brief survey of attitudes to alternative occupations lead me to consider the reasons people gave me for coming to town.   These statements were *ex post facto* and it would be unwise, therefore, to use them as indices of the actual decisions workers had made in migrating.   But whether rationalizations or fact, they do indicate migrants' goals and definitions of their urban situation.

Stated reasons for coming to Port Moresby were varied.   Some employees found my questions surprising: urban residence and employment in town appeared as "natural" progressions from school.   "It has all the jobs" was one comment.   One man from Marshall Lagoon replied, "I grew up here."

Sometimes, however, the intrinsic attractions of the town were mentioned, whether (inflated) economic or noneconomic ones.   Replies stressing the economic pull were "At home we heard many stories of Port Moresby; you can earn high wages (they say)—but I came and there was no money;" and "My *wantoks* told me, you can get high wages in Port Moresby.   They said Monday you get £10, Tuesday, £10, Wednesday £10, [etc.]."

But some gave it an almost mystical appeal.   Thus one young Highlander, after working for five years in the Highlands, had come just to see it—was it red or black or what?   Perhaps indicative too of the town's noneconomic pull was the desire which another Highlander attributed to his father, whose airfare he was paying to the town: "He wants to see Port Moresby and the saltwater before he dies."

But, despite the occasional "bright lights" element, reasons given for urban migration were generally pragmatic.   The typical response was, "I came to work for money."   Occasionally, specific targets were mentioned: those that come readily to mind concern a Chimbu man who had come to be fitted for false teeth; Hete, from the Northern District, "to fill two bankbooks" with his savings; and Phillip, Hete's district compatriot, to save enough money to help buy an £80 coffee pulper for a family enterprise.

I suspect that these last three may also have had other goals in mind; thus my use of "targets" may be questioned (see, for example, Dakeyne 1967:155). Phillip, for example, had spent a number of years both in wage employment and in the town and could presumably have returned before had he been sufficiently singleminded. Indeed, Phillip's father came to town, they purchased the pulper, his father returned, and yet still Phillip did not return for some five months. It would be unfortunate, therefore, to imply that workers had rigidly limited wants which, once satisfied, would lead to their immediate return home. But—as Elkan argues about the East African situation (1960:131)—while accepting that most labor migrants in Port Moresby aspire to a higher standard of living in general, and do not just want bicycles and sums of money, it is not necessary to dismiss the whole concept of the target worker. "Targets" imply that migrants see their wage employment as a means to an end lying outside the town. That is how, I argue, the *majority* of P.M.D. employees also saw it. And, although serving ends generated by urban residence itself, these were seen, on at least their first visit, as incidental.

Few had such specific goals as filling two savings bankbooks. Almost all, however, made regular deposits in their accounts when a bank officer called at the plant on wage nights. Many of those I questioned on these savings stated that they were planning to buy presents for rural kin; to send back money for their "businesses"; to help with a kinsman's bride-price. One, although saving for his own return, said that the next commitment on his savings would be to help his brother buy a plane ticket for the journey back to the home village. Moreover, although many—often the same people—said that they were saving to buy shirts, shorts, radios, and the like, it could be argued that, because they intended to return to their natal villages, these belongings would serve to mark them as men of wealth and thereby enhance their rural social standing. I must add, however, that workers were not very forthcoming on their savings and some thought my questions impertinent.

Overwhelmingly, aspirations were directed not towards life in Moresby but elsewhere. In some cases, plans to leave the town were coupled with the intention to try another center—"Port Moresby is too dear; next year I will go to Lae, I'm spending too much money here." One resident of the married quarters was planning to leave town but to go to college to study for the ministry. Yet the majority of workers were contemplating a more or less immediate return to their natal villages: one to pick coffee before it was rotten, one to get married, one because he was tired, one because his ageing mother had written threatening to comb the streets of Moresby to find him if he didn't hurry back, and still others because they had been away too long and just wanted to return.

In some cases, these plans seemed firm and fairly immediate. Thus, it will be recalled from Chapter 4 that Paul and his siblings, migrants from Mbawe, were going back to help with village undertakings at Christmas 1968. Other young men from the same area were also planning to return at or before that time.

The plans of others were less immediate and some were decidedly vague. Perhaps those who were less explicit reacted to questions which failed to touch their immediate experience with equally remote answers. Thus, one clerk, from a coastal village in the Central District, in his early twenties, married and with children replied, "I'm not sure what to do yet, but may go back to the village. 'What would you do there?' I could fish and garden and make toys—crocodiles and drums and those things—and sell them here. Yes, probably in ten or eleven years I will go back."

His response implied that, until I asked him, he had given little thought to the timing or context of his departure from town. But what is also evident, I would stress, is that he nonetheless failed to see any permanent future in the town. His eventual return was not in doubt, but the timing was. Even those workers who had spent years in wage employment and appeared rooted in the town nonetheless talked of retiring to their villages. Indeed, that they would do so appeared at times almost self-evident.

Those planning to stay in town *permanently* were few indeed. Three of those interviewed came from villages within the town boundary and thus had no choice: they envisaged working and living in the town for the rest of their days. But of those who could choose permanent urban residence in preference to returning to their natal villages, only seven appeared ready to do so. These seven included migrants from other districts, engaged for most of their adult lives in wage employment, and accompanied by their families.

The distribution of attitudes to continued urban residence is given in Table 16. The first line gives the responses of the sixty-eight white-

TABLE 16

Attitudes to Continued Urban Residence of a Sample
of 92 P.M.D. Employees

	Stay permanently in town	Stay indefinitely (5 years or more) but retire to home village	Leave within 5 years for another center	Return to home village within 5 years	Totals
White-collar, skilled and semiskilled people	10	31	6	21	68
Unskilled sample	–	5	2	17	24
Estimated percentage response of <u>all</u> P.M.D. employees	7%	33%	5%	55%	100%

[A9849]

collar, skilled and semiskilled workers who were formally interviewed; the second gives the responses of the complementary sample of twenty-four unskilled laborers. The third line gives the estimated percentage response for all employees: I feel justified in giving this since the responses of the samples are fully consistent with my other material. The distinction between those staying less than five years and those staying for longer was suggested by the material. Those who appeared to be firmly intending to return to their home villages within a specified period planned to do so within five years, many within two or three; those who gave a date for their return beyond five years generally appeared less definite. I decided on "five years" as a benchmark separating those who were definitely intending to return to their villages from those who would stay in town indefinitely but return on their "retirement."

What emerges from this table is that few saw urban residence as a permanent feature of their lives. Most were anticipating an ultimate return to their natal villages. This anticipation, I argue, played a major role in the determination of social relationships in the town, leading indigenous residents to maintain, above all else, their ties to kinsmen and fellow villagers.

Yet *complete* reliance on informants' statements and attitudes—particularly responses to schedules—may well be inadequate. There is always the possibility that some men will be constrained by force of circumstances (for example, insufficient savings) to stay longer in town than they planned. Others may falsify their intentions. Thus I now turn to an examination of involvement relying initially on inferences drawn from surface characteristics.

Measures of Involvement

Workers' recall of months in employment was extremely good—some even volunteered the actual date they had started employment some ten years previously—but they were rarely able to give a birthdate. So my estimates of age for each worker in the sample were obtained by working backwards through time and using periods of employment and schooling as the basis of my calculations. I took the typical response —"I left the village as a small boy and before I started shaving"—to mean that the worker left when he was 15 years old. This guess seemed reasonably consistent with the actual ages volunteered by the more sophisticated informants. Accordingly, I estimate that the mean age of workers was twenty-two years. Detailed results are given in Table 17. In coding this material, final figures on age, employment and residence were rounded off to the next three months.

TABLE 17

Ages of a Sample of 92 P.M.D. Employees

		White collar	Skilled and semiskilled	Unskilled
No. in labor force (p)		21	54	85
No. in sample (n)		19	49	24
n:p		1:1.1		1:3.5
Age	range	18 to 37 yrs	16 to 36 yrs	16 to 30 yrs
	median	20½ yrs	25 yrs	30 yrs
	mean	24.5	25.3	21.4

The indigenous population of Port Moresby is a youthful one: thus in 1966, of all adult indigenous males (i. e., those at least fifteen years old) 48 percent were twenty-four years old or younger. The P.M.D. labor force was even more youthful. Indeed, even the *mean* age obscures the boyishness of its members: the *median* age for unskilled labor, who constituted more than 50 percent of all employees, was only twenty years. The median age for white-collar workers was comparable. Older workers—by and large those in their late twenties—were concentrated in the skilled and semiskilled grades. A number of those in their late twenties and early thirties were white-collar workers, as the discrepancy between the mean and median for this category indicates. The major implication of this age distribution is that a significant section of the labor force were newcomers to both the town and to wage employment. And they had had insufficient time to develop firm roots in these sectors of the economy.

Table 18 compares the length of urban residence with the total time spent in wage employment for the same sample. Thus, assuming that the sample of twenty-four unskilled laborers was representative of all

TABLE 18

YEARS SPENT IN TOWN AND IN WAGE EMPLOYMENT OF A
SAMPLE OF 92 P.M.D. EMPLOYEES

	White collar	Skilled and semiskilled	Unskilled
No. in labor force (p)	21	54	85
No. in sample (n)	19	49	24
n:p		1:1.1	1:3.5
Years spent in town range	0 to 23 yrs	1½ to 35 yrs	0 to 6½ yrs
median	4 yrs	7 yrs	1 yr
mean	7.8	7.1	2.5
Years spent in wage employment range	0 to 18 yrs	6 mos to 16 yrs	0 to 11 yrs
median	2 yrs	5 yrs	3 yrs
mean	4.9	6.9	3.5

[A9848]

unskilled labor at the plant—and I have every reason to believe it was —we can see that the median length of urban residence for this, the largest category of workers, was one year. Indeed, taking the sample of ninety-two and inferring from their labor histories that of the plant's labor force, I estimate that nearly 38 percent had spent one year or less in the town.

The median years of urban residence for white-collar workers was rather higher. But a number of these had grown up in town or been educated at urban schools. This is indicated by the median years in wage employment for the same category: whereas the median worker had spent four years in town, he had spent only two in wage employment. We can also see that—as wage earners—the unskilled laborers were slightly more experienced than those in white-collar grades. This was because a significant minority had spent one or more years in employment in rural areas or in other urban centers. This tendency was much less marked for the skilled and semiskilled workers. In their case too the median years in town were higher than that for wage employment, but this may have been due to chance since the means are much closer.

In both Tables 17 and 18 it should also be noted that the means are generally higher than the medians, often significantly so. This indicates that, despite the youth of many and their brief urban residence, a sizeable minority were much older and experienced.

The age distribution and the short period that many had spent in town would suggest that workers' urban involvement was consistent with stated aims and goals. A further measure of consistency can be gained from examining their marital status.

Table 12 shows that 67 percent were single. This large unmarried element in the labor force is mainly responsible for what I have referred to as "work-boy culture." And because the society of young single males provides an alternative and viable design for living it may sometimes conflict with rural involvement. In the short term this was true to some extent for P.M.D. workers and, even in the long term, had probably led some of the older men in the barracks to become more fully involved in urban residence. But given the nature of the town and workers' preferences the long-term effect of their unmarried status is more likely to be a reinforcement of rural involvement.

Some laborers, through long periods of residence in labor centers, were perhaps obliged to remain unmarried. Such was probably the case with Samuel, the barracks resident from the Northern District, who, at the age of twenty-nine or thereabouts, had spent 80 percent of his adult life away from the village. Although he was coy about his own marital plans, his stray comment that "to buy a woman is no good —£20, £50—that's enough" points to the contraints likely to be operating on a man in his situation. Some found prostitutes and it may even be that some had adapted—as Hogbin (1951:190–91) suggests for work-boy culture in other parts of New Guinea—by finding homosexual partners, although I found no evidence to support it and, on the grounds of the barracks' and area's spatial arrangements, am inclined to discount the possibility in this case. The majority of single men were constrained by the sex imbalance in the town, their own preferences, and the tendency toward ethnic exclusiveness to find wives in their home areas.

Due to demographic exigencies and contrasting customs, the territorial range over which men traditionally sought wives varied greatly (Lind 1969:40). The normal practice, however, was to seek a wife in the natal, or an adjoining village. Thus of all marriages contracted by plant workers, only two crossed language lines and a further one, although within the same language group, crossed a major administrative boundary. Moreover, everyone I questioned expected to obtain a wife from home. It might be argued that the question was unreal as many were so young. Certainly some were embarrassed by these questions; but others could point to actual pressure from their village kin to marry local girls.

In some migrant groups, notably the Toaripi, there are sufficient females in town to insure that some of these young men will marry there. Moreover, because of distances, growing urban involvement and the shortage of women, some migrants will undoubtedly marry intertribally. Such was the case of the Sepik men married to Barakau women which I cited in the previous chapter: the Port Moresby Sub-District was now their only base. Similarly, one of the two intertribal marriages contracted by plant employees was the direct result of urban residence.

But the majority, I infer, would have to find their wives in the home-place. And as another 8 percent of the total labor force were married but unaccompanied by their wives, I estimate that nearly three-quarters of the labor force would be drawn back to their villages either to find women or to return to those they already had.

Despite the overall consistency between these measures and stated intentions, the degree of involvement should not be understated. Thus,

while few saw themselves as permanent town dwellers, a large number
nonetheless saw themselves as wage earners for the rest of their working lives; one-third said they would not retire in town but had no *immediate* plans to return home.   Van Velsen (1961) has stressed, for the
Central African literature, the necessity of distinguishing between involvement in urban residence *per se* and urban wage employment.
Thus although most workers are anticipating and depending upon the
ultimate security of their home villages—and thus less than fully involved in urban residence—many of the same workers were also heavily involved in urban wage employment.   That a minority were so involved is indicated by the *range* of years spent in wage employment
and in town, shown in Table 18.   That it was a *sizeable* minority is
indicated by the difference, for each category, between the mean and
the median for the same distribution.

Thus in analyzing the involvement of "the worker" we must bear in
mind that the work-force was composed of a sizeable minority of highly involved wage earners—many of whom were also long-term employees of the plant—and a majority who were less involved in working for the company and were also migrants circulating between town
and country, dependent for only part of the time on wage labor.   We
have seen something of this contrast in the contrast between the social
ambience of the barracks' residents and that of the married units' residents.   It can also be found in the frequency of rural visiting, an excellent measure of rural involvement.   In Table 19 I show the number
of visits paid, and periods spent, in the home village in the two pre-

TABLE 19

FREQUENCY OF VISITS PAID, AND PERIODS SPENT IN HOME VILLAGE WITHIN
PREVIOUS TWO YEARS BY A SAMPLE OF 92 P.M.D. EMPLOYEES

| | Frequency of Visits and Stays in Village | | | |
	none	one only	two or more	Totals
White collar, skilled, and semiskilled sample	19	32	17	68
Unskilled	8	14	2	24
Estimated percentage for <u>all</u> P.M.D. workers	30%	53%	16%	100%

vious years; an estimate is also given for employees as a whole. Since plant practice was to give two weeks leave pay in advance every two years, workers expectations of home leave tended to follow the norm set by the administration for its employees: public servants had return fares paid to the rural center nearest their "village of origin" every two years.

Table 19 suggests that the measures of commitment I gave in Tables 15 and 16 are largely consistent with the overall pattern of rural visiting. And yet, at the same time, it also suggests that the actual situation was not as simple as workers' attitudes might imply. While an estimated seven out of ten workers had visited their home villages at least once in that time, three out of ten had not.

The recency of arrival of many workers was an important determinant of the overall frequency. The estimated median of urban residence for unskilled labor—53 percent of the total work force—was one year. Thus I conclude that at least one-quarter of all employees had been in town for one year or less. Judging from the reported behavior of the sample, almost all would have stayed in their villages for at least a short time before coming to town. Of the remaining three-quarters who had been in town *more* than one year it appears that 60 percent had returned and 40 percent had not. The discrepancy between overall commitment to the village and actual visiting is even more pronounced when those in the sample—representing 47 percent of all workers—who come to town within the previous two years are eliminated. Almost all of these had stayed in, or visited, the village before coming. Their elimination from the sample would leave perhaps three out of five men, who were urban residents for two years or more, and when faced with a real choice of whether or not to visit their homes, had decided *not* to go home.

These calculations are crude and totally dependent on the representativeness of a small sample. Yet the pattern which emerges is consistent with impressions I gained from individual histories and attitudes. In part, the frequencies reflect the division between the true labor migrants and the sizeable minority whose attitudes indicated they would stay in wage employment indefinitely. But the division was not absolute. Perhaps—like the man helping to buy his brother's plane ticket or the one buying his father's—a number had arrived intending to hurry back, but had found that urban obligations and their economic position did not allow them to realize their aims. Some of these may well, through time, have come to redefine their situation and accept their place in town. Thus one man reported that his elderly mother had written threatening to walk the streets of Port Moresby until she found him. He recognized the obligation to return but found urban life too amenable.

Yet this case is exceptional. The vast majority were but poorly committed to urban residence. Some were prepared to accept it indefinitely as a necessary part of their dependence on wage employment: they aspired to a higher standard of living and must work to attain it. But even these looked to the home village as a source of economic and social security.

These processes of involuntary involvement and redefinition are not amenable to statistical presentation. Thus, to round off my discussion of workers as migrants, I illustrate certain types of ongoing choice by sketching, very briefly, individual adaptations to the dual system. We have already met the characters in the sketch in previous chapters.

Dual Involvement and Individual Adaptations

At one extreme some workers appeared to be merely biding their time in Port Moresby. Thus the young Mbawe men in the barracks presented the town as an unwelcome place. Their ideal was neither the town (which they presented as disreputable) nor the traditional-rural (which they presented as pagan), but "civilization." And contrary to the tendency, reported for some parts of Africa, to equate civilization with the town (see, for example, Little 1965:11; Pons 1969:12)—for these young men civilization was identified as being more educated and bringing modern goods and services to the rural area. The concrete expression of these values was the rural mission station, a center of relative affluence, social service, Christian values, and education. It is significant that these young men had taken the name of the home mission station for their soccer team. Denominationalism meant a lot to them, even if their actual church attendance was limited.

It will be recalled that these young men planned to return to Mbawe by Christmas 1968. True to their word all but a few had done so by the middle of my second fieldtrip, leaving only three Northern District employees. Only Humphrey and William were still there, together with one young man from Asafa. Samuel too had stayed in the area but had changed jobs. All the other "Popondettas" had returned, including Paul, much to management's chagrin at losing a shift supervisor.

Yet despite their evident rural commitment it should be stressed that it was not totally incompatible with urban involvement: they had found the town's employment opportunities essential to the realization of their rural goals. Moreover, by the time I left the town Paul's brother (nM), through problems at home, had returned to P.M.D. for another spell. And the two oldest men from the District—William and Samuel —were still in town, single and with no firm attachments to their home areas, but hoping eventually to retire there.

An emotional and ideological rejection of urban residence was by no means restricted to those with minimal stakes in the industrial system. Rural aspirations and lack of mutual involvement were also critical variables underlying the social tensions of the Old Office. John's cries of "how to be a big man" were aimed at the rural context as were many of James' strivings. We can see in these reactions desires for leadership and significance not met by the urban social structure. Until very recently few indigenes held positions of leadership in the largely European sector of social life. Nor are there many indigenous voluntary associations in which potential leaders can win recognition. Sports clubs and mission organizations may offer scope, but the achieving Papuan or New Guinean is rarely fully autonomous and positions are few. Moreover, there is as yet nothing of the welter of autonomous native churches, tribal, welfare, or educational associations noted for parts of Africa (Sundkler 1962; Little 1965; Wilson and Mafeje 1963, Chapters 5–7). The village community is usually far more hospitable, offering prestige to those who have achieved a measure of success in the towns and giving due credit to their wealth and achievements.

But the town dweller may easily misjudge the rural situation—either by underestimating village conflicts and antagonisms or overstating the potential for his talents—and so find his plans not feasible. I can best illustrate this point by examining James' developing adaptation to his migrant situation. As secretary of the transport group James became increasingly prominent in village affairs. The group ran the truck in town for a month and then James engineered its transportation back to the village. He played an important part in the village celebrations which I also attended. Returning to Moresby he continued to act as secretary, managing the group's books and organizing payments to the finance company.

After a few months of success his village kin urged him to marry a local girl. They argued he could not play such a leading part in the village while less than a full adult. James welcomed the prospect. In the first weeks of our acquaintance he had remarked that a man and a woman should "match characteristics" but that a man should not take an educated woman because "he [the husband] can't do anything": an educated woman would not be prepared to work in the garden, for example. He desired a wife appropriate to one aspiring in the traditional context.

And yet it was also apparent that he valued urban residence for its own sake. He was keenly aware of the superior material advantages that the town had to offer and at times presented himself as an urban sophisticate. On one occasion we passed a group of betel nut traders from central Mekeo, sitting in the dust by the roadside with their wares. James said to me and two other Mekeo urbanites, "Poor people!—look at them sitting there—they will never come to anything."

The conflict of goals and norms this implies was not always explicit; James was probably able to save himself much mental distress by selecting norms appropriate to each situation. But it often worried him as an intellectual problem. What should he do in the next few years—apply himself to his studies and then go to the technical institute to become an accountant, or should he direct all his efforts to the village scene? He asked my advice but supplied his own answer. He would go back in a few years and build his house and "make his business" near the local mission station. He would be of the village and yet not in it. This was no idle resolve since shortly afterward he asked a rightholder for permission to build there when the time came.

Events conspired against him, however. The truck broke down and the group failed to keep abreast of its hire purchase commitments. So James arranged, on his own volition, to have the truck brought back to Moresby: he arranged the transport; renegotiated the hire purchase terms; borrowed $200 from a manager to get the vehicle repaired; and subcontracted with the plant to help deliver its product.

The original marriage plans fell through but plans to marry another girl—the sister of the wife of the group's truck driver—were progressing well when I returned to Moresby in late 1968. James asked the company for married accommodation and was granted a unit in a new block of four some way from the other quarters. John, the other clerk in the Old Office, had moved there in the previous months. But James' marriage plans met further delay; the girl's father asked for too much money and James and his brother broke off negotiations. Unable to stay in P.M.D. married accommodation, James rented a two bedroom house in another part of Koke-Badili, from a European married to a mixed-race woman. He moved in with the driver and his family, together with a kinsman and rugby club teammate. In the following months this house became a center for Mekeo traders and other friends.

Now that the truck was back in town the group's affairs prospered. The subcontract with the plant proved lucrative. James was able to pay off the finance company within time and then to purchase another truck—second-hand, but much larger than the first. His rural kinsmen were resentful that the original truck operated in town despite the fact they bought it and were village-based. To pacify them, James wanted to send the new truck back, keeping the original one for his urban commitments. His kinsmen were delighted and proud of this double event; they had two trucks and a magnificent location for their urban operations. James' prestige—based as it was on his success in exploiting the urban situation to his own and his kin's best advantage—was high. It was at this time that a young man, not a kinsman, came to borrow $40 for his school fees.

I must leave James' story here. The important point which emerges is that although he had sometimes thought of returning and trying to establish prestige in a rural location he nonetheless became more fully involved in urban residence. His involvement increased as it became apparent that the truck would show a far greater return in town than in the village. Once a compound dweller thinking of building a house at home—albeit at the mission station—he now rented his own house, was bringing his wife there, and had control of a truck purchased through his own initiative. Perhaps in time he will try to buy out the contributions of his kin, take over the truck, and run the concern himself. As is far more likely, however, he will take care to keep his ties open to the village and maintain his dual participation. Businesses are hazardous, whereas rights in the village are secure. And at least for the next few years recognition of achievement will continue to be village-located.

Perhaps, as Elkan (1960: Chapter 10) argues for the East African situation, it is ultimately land as an unrealizable capital asset—and therefore ultimately the system of land tenure—which constrains the migrant to return. But, taking informants' statements at their face value, although land rights are the migrants' final security these are not mere abstractions. They are tied into the rights and obligations encompassed by kinship bonds (Watson 1958). For most migrants, that is, the complex of purely economic rights, bonds of sentiment and the striving for prestige and recognition formed an interlocking whole. But in some cases groups of kin developed in the town only minimally concerned with rural land rights. This was the situation of almost all those employees who saw a permanent future there.

Of the ten in this category, three were from urban villages, in none of which gardening or other agricultural activities were of any significance. Five others were from the eastern end of the Gulf District, an area of swamps, sago cultivation, and poor economic potential. Rights to rural land were less important to these men: they were long-term wage earners and urban residents. At the same time many of their kin, perhaps most, were also working and living in Port Moresby. Thus a network of kin and friends could grow up related only to the urban environment.

I asked one man in this category where he went when in need. It is significant that he replied, "The important thing is to stay well with your family and your wife's family—if you help them they will help you." The immediate members of these "families" were all based in town.

Leaving aside the three urban villagers, the seven who intended to stay permanently were, with one exception, all married with families. When they talked of their plans, all mentioned their children's future and the education and benefit they would receive in town: when they retired their children would support them. Few of the children were even of school age—Mailala's daughter was not yet two years old—but these responses do suggest another mechanism by which kinship bonds and the individual's social center of gravity come to be urban-located.

Workers as Migrants: Conclusions

Workers' low involvement in urban residence was a basic determinant of the impermanent and limited character of many urban-located relationships. As the overall social network in which they were embedded changed its shape and personnel in response to the circulation of labor between town and country, the sets and wider groupings emerging

in the plant were themselves subject to redefinition. In the case of the
Northern District migrants, their joint return to the home area radically changed the web of ties: in removing themselves they removed a
unit from the social system of the barracks. The anticipation of an ultimate return to the home village, moreover, meant that workers cher-
ished their home-boy ties (cf. Caldwell 1969:198), and were obliged to
maintain relationships outside the plant and town. These external relationships often competed with those internal to the plant and urban
complex.

Aspirations and reality, however, sometimes conflict. Some men
were staying longer than they had intended and no doubt were contributing to the very rapid growth of the town's population. It is hazardous to predict whether those who have only recently come to town will
stay or return. But it is clear that, through whatever process, their
predecessors have become permanent wage employees, although intending to retire to their rural villages. As we have seen from previous
chapters, involvement in urban wage employment did not mean the
abandonment of village or other *wantok* ties. Yet as men become more
fully immersed in the industrial system, we might expect them to throw
in their lot with others in the same life-situation. In short, we must
now examine workers' adaptations to their situation as employees.

WORKERS AS EMPLOYEES

> What [the laborer] sells when he sells his labor is his willing-
> ness to use his facilities to a purpose that has been pointed out
> to him. He sells his promise to obey commands. [Commons
> 1924:284]

Until now I have presented the labor contract as a wholly static element in the analysis. The variables structuring the selection and self-
selection of the labor force have been discussed, but only insofar as
they gave rise to a system of technical roles and labor exigencies.
This system was then treated as a set of parameters shaping the spatial
order of the plant and compounds.

But the factory is more than just a spatial pattern and a set of func-
tionally related tasks. It is also a system of command and compliance.
The worker sells his promise to obey commands concerning the direction of his effort and the manager or employer attempts to insure compliance by offering rewards. And thus the labor contract is a dynamic
bargaining over these efforts and rewards, however tacit. John R.

Plate 9 At Work—a worker from Bush Mekeo

Plate 10 At Work—two young men from the Chimbu Valley

Commons (1924:285) has expressed this nicely: "The labor contract therefore is not a contract, it is a continuing implied renewal of contracts at every minute and hour, based on the continuance of what is deemed, on the employer's side, to be satisfactory service, and on the laborer's side, what is deemed to be satisfactory conditions and compensation."

But it is unlikely that either side to the contract will be prepared to allow free rein to these competing interests. To start with—and to use Commons' terms once more—while each party to the contract has the liberty of not renewing it, each is also exposed to possible damage: the laborer to the damage of possible unemployment, and the employer to loss of production. Moreover, although each side may attempt to optimize its own advantage it will usually do so within limits set by the technical system, the market for the firm's products, and its relationship to its legal and social environment. Thus, through the search for a *modus vivendi* in which the excesses of competition are controlled, we may expect customary usages to develop concerning both the value of the "effort-bargain" (Baldamus 1961) and the authority relations necessary to insure workers' compliance to its standards.

At P.M.D., the demands of the manufacturing process, prevailing Australian industrial practice, and the legal and racial structure of the Territory have shaped cultural expectations about these fundamental features of the organization and have given rise to industrial customs. To the outsider these appear fixed and stable. Underlying these customary behaviors, however, the web of competition and dependence flowing from the impersonal labor contract—that is, the industrial system's symbiotic order—remained as a latent source of strain. And so, accepting the argument that customary behavior may best be studied in the breach, I now turn to a situation where employees were so dissatisfied with their conditions and rewards that they refused to concur in "the continuing implied renewal of contracts" so essential to the organization. I turn, that is, to the strike of late 1965. The stoppage reveals a set of ongoing authority relations at work, the racial division in the town and an additional group identity for indigenous townsmen.

From its incorporation in 1951 until late 1965, the company's industrial relations were uneventful. The emergence of the Port Moresby Workers' Association in 1960, and other industrial developments in the early years of the decade, left it untroubled (Grosart 1964; Hennessy 1964a and b). Few employees joined the association at that time and none played an active part in industrial affairs. Then in late 1965, 98 employees—out of a total work force of 120—came out on strike.

The strike came in a wave of industrial unrest in the town. One Monday one hundred drivers at the Administration Transport Pool had refused to start work and had stayed on strike all day. Wharf laborers employed by the two dominant shipping and commercial enterprises in the Territory had also failed to report for work. In the ensuing weeks and into early 1966 other strikes followed: these involved workers at the local brewery, carpenters at a joinery factory, construction site workers, garage employees, trainee teachers, and trainee male nurses. Other work forces were reported to be threatening similar actions (South Pacific Post; Metcalfe 1969).

At P.M.D. most of the day shift refused to start work and all of the night shift left refusing to return. At 8:30 a. m. the strikers moved off toward the market. Meeting them along the road, Department of Labor officials and the President of the Workers' Association persuaded them to select spokesmen for their case and to return to work. Selecting six of their more senior members—a number apparently suggested by one or other of the administration and trade-union officials—the strikers returned to work, two-and-a-half hours after leaving it. Later in the day, after mediating at another dispute, the officials returned to P.M.D. and there followed a four-way conference between representatives of each of management, the Department of Labor, the Workers' Association, and the striking workers.[4]

The strike was almost totally unexpected and many Europeans presented it as an exercise in irrationality. Asked to explain what had

[4] My knowledge of the events and causes of the strike and the subsequent settlement is gained from interviews with managers and strikers and from written records. Some thirty of the strikers were still working for the plant at the time of my inquiries. I interviewed the majority of these and, although some were not forthcoming, statements tally sufficiently to make me fairly confident of the course of events and workers' aims. Written accounts were gained from the local press and from documents compiled immediately following the incidents by Department of Labor officials. I am deeply grateful to that department and to the company for permission to consult them. Kiki (1968:134–40) gives a Papuan's reactions to the events.

Verbal accounts of intention and claims were made some two years after the stoppage. Thus it might be argued that this evidence merely reflected the current situation and not that at the time of the strike. I judge, however, that the lapse was not so long nor changes so radical as to make inferences drawn from one situation inapplicable to the other.

happened, one manager referred me to a paper written by a senior Department of Labor official and entitled "The Cult of the Strike." This was consistent with the consensus of European opinion which held that once employees in the town had started striking others had also decided it was a good thing and had followed suit. The manner and duration of the stoppage, it was argued, indicated that workers neither understood the reasons for striking nor the implications. Wandering to the market, they had appeared like lost sheep, unsure of where to go or what to do next. Moreover, many of the issues they raised were not plant matters, but arose from administration employment regulations and agreements made between "their" trade union and the Employers' Federation.

Much in this kind of explanation is true. The strike was far from the strategic show of strength in a bargaining process which managers thought a strike should be. Indeed, when judged by these standards the affair was almost meaningless. Workers had made no prior complaints and appeared unsure of themselves and their grievances when at the negotiating table. The strike achieved few concrete results and thus, it could be argued, was unnecessary and therefore irrational. Moreover, following a strike the previous Monday, it owed much to example and thus appeared imitative.

But even if an external event was necessary to crystallize discontent, the strike was nonetheless probably the most effective means available to workers to express their very real sense of grievance. Moreover, to stress its imitative aspects at the expense of its positive features is to belittle what, in the absence of established structures of leadership and representation, was a remarkable feat of organization.

The action of the Administration drivers on a previous Monday had attracted a great deal of attention. It was not the first strike in the town's history but was probably the most dramatic: at one point the drivers marched to Government Headquarters in support of their demands. It was by no means clear at that stage what, if any, results were to flow from the stoppages but it was evident that expatriate attention had been captured and directed to indigenous employment conditions in a manner never before thought possible.

Two Gulf District migrants living in P.M.D.'s married quarters had kin at the Transport Pool and so they and their friends were kept well-informed of the course of the strike and subsequent developments.

These communications, together with the knowledge gleaned from press and radio announcements, slowly percolated through the quarters. As far as I could establish, however, there was no really organized canvassing of support for any course of action until forty-eight hours before the stoppage, although knowledge of other strikes and the perceived feasibility of one at P.M.D. seemed widespread. When word reached the compounds, however, that another labor force was refusing to offer for employment, a group of senior workers living in P.M.D. accommodation began meeting informally and eventually decided to withhold their own labor. At least initially, this group was composed of Gulf District workers, the majority of whom were employed in the plant's production departments. Over the rest of the weekend the advice and support of other residents and of workmates living outside plant accommodation was also solicited.

Many of the actual links used to inlist further support are obscured by time and informants' reticence. But it does seem clear that to gain support workers relied on interpersonal networks arising from kinship, *wantok* links, coresidence, and common employment. It is significant that no one person claimed to have (or could point to any single person who might have) organized the stoppage. Many strikers argued that they had simply joined groups of *wantoks* who had discussed striking and had decided to stay away on the Monday concerned. An easy way of disclaiming individual responsibility maybe, but extremely likely given the organization of social relationships in the compound. At least some workers—mainly those living in other parts of the town—appear to have arrived at the plant before realizing what was afoot. Many joined the strikers, but a number joined those who, although knowledgeable of the strikers' aims, had decided to work on.

I want to emphasize, therefore, that the stoppage was spontaneous, a protest rather than a strategy. Moreover, the idea of striking, and support for it, were communicated through existing interpersonal bonds. These had been structured by somewhat different imperatives than those of the workplace—for example, by the needs of domestic social organization. No doubt, in the enthusiasm of the event, workers did form relationships based solely on a common identity as employees, but in preparing for, and in directing, the course of the strike these seemed much less significant than bonds already formed. What were conspicuously lacking were ties based on uniquely industrial imperatives, such as trade-union membership, the efforts of a shop stewards' committee, or any other plantwide system of representation and leadership. To some extent ties based on work section solidarity were operating, but even so, these were limited and had arisen from a more basic homogeneity—that of language and culture. Thus, to anticipate my argument a little, the strike was primarily a response to *like*, rather than specifically *common*, interests. The underlying attitudes were bitter enough but they lacked organization or coherence.

It is a fine point, but one which should be emphasized in view of the strike's apparently minimal effects on the system of authority relations. It was not—as was the strike which Epstein (1958) records for the Roan Antelope Mine on the Central African Copperbelt—a challenge to the existing structure of command. Epstein's analysis shows how the strike ushered in a new conception of authority in which the African Mineworkers' Union was to play a significant part in controlling employment conditions at the level of the organization. In its course the old system of representation based on tribal elders was rejected. The P.M.D. strike was a much tamer affair: it aimed at the righting of injustice, not at restructuring relations.

Eighty percent of all employees had stopped work—a considerable show of strength and therefore, one might argue, organization. But on the other hand no one had been able or willing to formulate a manifesto or even a simple set of demands, nor were there any undisputed leaders. Thus, although inspired to challenge authority, they were all back at work less than three hours later. And the manner of their return is also important. Some men spoke half-heartedly against returning so soon but, lacking positive and undisputed direction, the strikers had been responsive to the suggestions of officials. These latter men spoke as representatives of government authority and as Europeans—a powerful combination in the local situation. Se'ecting six spokesmen, the employees agreed to return to work without significant delay to the production process.

The lack of overt challenge to the prevailing authority structure is also to be found in the actual complaints which emerged at the four-way conference. Individual spokesmen were forced by their own lack of organization to relate, in piecemeal fashion, specific grievances. Many of these seemed trivial and of concern only to a few employees. The other parties to the conference concurred in this approach. They dealt with the grievances as isolated issues in which the legal obligations of management and the reciprocal rights of employees had to be ascertained and enforced. The officials had perforce to interpret their task in this way: their legally defined role was to insure that employment regulations were observed and industrial peace achieved. Workers' Association representatives seem to have acted largely as interpreters. Yet it is also clear that they were concerned to phrase workers' grievances in a way which related directly to the enforcement of employment regulations, and thus they maintained the Department of Labor officials' definition of the conflict situation. (Chapman [1965:20] gives a Workers' Association point of view on these events and issues.) Management, for its part, saw that its task was to get the men back to work as quickly and as economically as possible.

But although workers presented their case in a limited and piecemeal fashion their discontent was fundamental. Complaints made at the time of the conference were made to me in essentially the same form throughout my fieldwork. And in the vast majority of cases these reflected their sense of injustice. Their approach at the conference reflects not a lack of discontent and fundamental grievance but a lack of organization and, paradoxically, their acceptance of the effective authority and power of management and officials. To examine this paradox I turn now to a discussion of the grievances themselves, showing how management could interpret them as being trivial when workers could see them as symptoms of a more fundamental malaise.

Four of the grievances concerned the calculation of pay and the application of standard wage and overtime rates to particular categories of worker; two more concerned cases of failure to grant sick, and other forms of leave. The remaining issues were as follows: lack of transportation and rations for married men living in other than plant accommodation; inadequate and delayed compensation for one worker who had lost an eye in an industrial accident; failure to pay a tool allowance to certain men in the maintenance sections; and inadequate housing.

Of these, the last was the most easily settled; the basis on which tools were issued was explained and there the matter could rest. Other grievances were more fundamental in their origin. The legalism of the occasion, however, did little to uncover the cause of the discontent.

Thus workers' spokesmen pointed out that some men were receiving only $5.80 per week—less than the Urban Minimum Cash Wage. Management rejoined that, wherever appropriate, there was a 70 cent deduction for accommodation and that these deductions were perfectly admissible under the Wage Agreement. Officials then examined the company's wage rates and found that, although other rates were in order, those for packing and inspecting were wrong. Under Wage Agreement Determinations this work was defined as Grade B and merited an extra 25 cents a week: back payments were ordered. No doubt workers were glad to receive these additions. But the settlement of the issue was based on a false assumption about work in Production One. There were no packers and inspectors, only packing and inspecting positions. During the course of a shift as many as six men might man them and during a week perhaps two-thirds of all laborers in the section circulate through them. That some received back payments and some not could only have reinforced workers' suspicions that payments and conditions of work were often arbitrary.

Moreover, the settlement of the issue was doubly unreal to the strikers. Whereas management defined the grievance as one involving ignorance of permissible deductions, workers were almost certainly complaining about low wages in general. Two years later they still complained they were receiving less than the wage required for an adequate standard of living: a minimum wage, they argued, is a minimum wage.

Thus the strikers' disappointment was to some extent due to a lack of communication. But more importantly it was the result of an impasse: both sides, with different interests at stake, simply talked past each other. The strikers stressed their dissatisfaction but inappropriately chose minor grievances to make their points known. Management wished only to contain the strike and get the men back to work. Officials were constrained by their roles to enforce regulations.

Thus spokesmen pointed out that some workers had not received increments despite years of service with the company. They were stressing—as many complained to me on subsequent occasions—that with age men acquire additional responsibilities yet the company would not give them extra money. Management for its part reiterated its policy of only giving wage increments to those employees who could offer increments in industrial skill.

Workers' vexation, however, was more than a protest at employment conditions. Their sense of wrong involved, at its most fundamental, their position in the racial structure of the plant and town. Something of this can be seen in their complaint about housing. Inadequate housing was the one complaint which concerned a majority of workers. At the conference spokesmen pointed out that one hundred or so persons were forced to share six toilets and four showers and that only one cooking place was provided for all the bachelors in the barracks. Management noted their dissatisfaction and has since made strenuous efforts to improve standards of accommodation by building further quarters. At the time, however, they merely noted the protest. Officials for their part could do no more than ask for a general clean-up, make certain minor repairs, provide beds for all married workers and their dependents, and remove mess tables from the barracks. They also recommended that the quarters be painted.

Judging from the comments of the spokesmen and from complaints made to me during fieldwork, this was not at all what workers had in mind. However vaguely they expressed their aims, they were primarily protesting day-to-day indignities flowing from their status as "boys" in a racially divided town. Their status was most conspicuously symbolized in the contrast between their own living conditions and those of Europeans.

Some employees' housing conditions brought about in them a deep sense of "shame." Thus when I first met Mailala he was living in unit 1, in the older married quarters. Despite our developing friendship he refused to entertain me there until he had moved to unit 5; his shame at living in such conditions was too great. Even in unit 5, scarcely bigger but a little brighter than the dingy box he had left, he kept apologizing for his situation. His acute embarrassment was apparent when Humphrey visited him to deliver the metal stand he and other young fitters had made for the new unit. For many workers a tangible bitterness, rather than shame, characterized their reaction to the indignities of "boy-house" accommodation.

The racial contrast also underlay the strikers' grievance about transport. They argued at the time that it was difficult for men living in outlying areas to get to work. Bus fares were dear and it was too far to walk; why didn't the company provide transport? On the surface this was a simple request for better conditions. Management took it as such and refused to accept any of the implied obligations although promising to look into what might be done.

Reporting the events two years later, however, strikers tied their grievances to the racial situation. Stated in gross terms, they were complaining that Europeans had cars and they did not. As one man, who had both missed his bus and an hour's pay for arriving late, said of the manager in charge of his section, "He might miss his bus or his car might break down but he won't walk—the company will send a car for him." To cite just one instance of the general grievance, one white-collar worker complained, "Europeans see us walking on the road but they never stop to pick us up."

Again, consideration of strikers' grievances on the question of overtime largely missed the point and force of the perceived injustice. It was pointed out on behalf of certain production workers that they were ignorant of their overtime rates and the method of calculation and, moreover, that no overtime was paid for work on weekends or public holidays. Management and officials replied that the regulations specified time-and-a-half pay for normal overtime and double-time pay for work on Sundays. But they also pointed out that if shift work obliged one to work after normal hours or over a weekend, and if equivalent time off was allowed during the next week, overtime was not involved. Double-time, however, should always be paid on public holidays.

The workers concerned understood the argument perfectly yet nonetheless felt deeply resentful about their situation. Workers claimed that they alone worked weekends while Europeans went to the beach or watched rugby. Moreover, while the Europeans who had done their jobs before had been paid handsomely, they were not. At one stage in 1967 there was a rumor that the company was to establish sports teams. It was greeted with quiet scepticism by one shift worker. He wanted very much to play but doubted he would be allowed time off. Of a senior manager he reported, "He's a hard man, he will never let us [take time off to] play." And when I asked why he continued to work shifts he replied, "That's the only way to get enough money to live on —if we work all the time the Europeans might give us a little bit more money."

Although, superficially, the grievances expressed by the workers might appear as trivial industrial matters, they were, in fact, tied to their appraisal of the racial structure of the town. Every plantwide ceremony or custom emphasized the racial division rather than that between, say, officers and nonofficers, or manual and nonmanual employees. As was the practice in the town, there was a wages scale for each race. There were also dual arrangements for payment. Every Friday would find a large number of indigenes queueing beneath the time clock to collect and sign for their pay packets: Europeans received their own fortnightly envelopes more discreetly. Behind the time clock were other symbols of racial division—two urinals, one used by whites, the other by blacks.

Sections of management justified these and similar practices on the grounds that skill differentials were linked to cultural (that is, racial) characteristics. Thus at one stage the appointed indigenous representatives on the ineffective Works Committee—organized by management after the strike to act as a safety valve—asked for badges to confirm shift supervisors' authority. Initially, this was thought to be a good idea but, when the badges arrived, the Production Manager locked them away in a drawer arguing that the indigenous supervisors were competent but not as efficient as the Europeans they had replaced. To issue them with the badges might imply they were on the same level. He thought "shift controller" would be a better title.

I do not wish to imply that managerial policy was fixed and unchanging. Although the racial division was still firmly established at the time of my fieldwork, it was being questioned. Two events, occurring within an hour of each other, illustrate both workers resentment at ongoing practices and management's anxiety about its effects. Each event concerned a barbeque for white employees.

While in the plant one day, I stopped to talk to an old acquaintance; he was making a barbeque stand, and cursing. He told me he was building the stand for the Europeans to cook their steaks and enjoy themselves. Was I invited? No? Neither was he! Later in the morning a note was slipped to a new European recruit who proceeded to read it in front of me and his Papuan assistant. The P.M.D. Social Club invited him to the barbeque. But no sooner had he read his invitation than a workmate told him to keep quiet explaining that management did not want the Club's activities to be publicized. They might have to disband it because of possible racial trouble. These events also illustrate my point that management was well aware of worker frustration and grievance: their insensitivity to the impasse of the strike was rather that in the crisis their official roles led them to ignore all but surface grievances.

Yet why, if the division was so clear and attitudes so bitter, were the events of the strike so restrained? I now examine why, despite the radical change in existing arrangements promised by the scale of the strike and the underlying attitudes, its duration was so brief and workers' stated grievances so mild.

In reporting workers' resentment at injustice I have relied mainly on comments made to me, that is, on "disengaged" attitudes (Williams 1964:77). When face-to-face with the managers who were the object of their resentment, however, workers were more circumspect. Their behavior suggests nothing so much as the behavior of errant schoolboys who, justly indignant at heavy authority, rail amongst themselves but face-to-face with their masters feel guilty and unable to do more than feebly deny or justify their behavior. Support for such speculation is found in a case concerning a native policeman who had been in the force for over ten years and who was very conscientious, reliable, gentle, and remarkably compliant. He had been given anaesthesia for a minor operation and during induction "he swore, was physically aggressive and made violently anti-European statements, expressing the hope that all 'the bloody white men' would be driven from the Territory" (Sinclair 1957:19). I admit this is highly speculative but if true it would explain why, despite a strong sense of injustice, the racial etiquette was preserved and why workers allowed managers and officials to play such dominant roles. (For another view of "inarticulate workers" see Dennis et al. 1956:91). But even if true, there were nonetheless more overtly social constraints on workers' behavior, and it is to these that I now turn.

The workers' most severe external handicap was their lack of a continuing and strong organization able to provide leadership and a focus for their demands. The Port Moresby Workers' Association might have served in this role but it was weak and hampered by an unhelpful legal and social environment (Metcalfe 1969; Martin 1969).

Workers' Associations in the Territory were hampered, from the time of their formation, by procedural rules which effectively prevented them from calling a strike. Before a legal strike could be called a two-thirds majority of the association's executive was required, together with a 51 percent majority of votes cast in secret ballot by financial members in those industries affected. The "common rule" basis of wage awards also meant that all workers in a town or district received the benefits of union demands whether or not they were members (Metcalfe 1969). Moreover, inadequate finances have hampered forceful organizing by preventing the employment of full-time staff and officials (Martin 1969:162). Inadequate finances are in part determined by the fact that Papua–New Guineans are not used to groups which demand an annual renewal of membership—indeed two P.M.D. employees spoke of holding "shares" in it.

Other workers' associations in the Territory have labored under the same disabilities and yet have met with more success than their Port Moresby counterpart—by December 1967 its membership had fallen to 50 from a high of 1,700 at the time of the strikes (Martin 1969:141). Nonetheless, the association has experienced some problems common to all trade unions in a more acute form. Thus the tendency of top union officials to treat their opposite numbers in management or government as their primary reference group has been documented for unions elsewhere (see for example, Dennis et al. 1956:113–16). The senior members of the association's executive in Port Moresby, however, lacking any previous background in industrial relations, in many cases recruited straight from relatively senior positions in the public service, and often with aspirations to administrative or political careers, have been particularly susceptible to these pressures. Moreover, with their head office situated within the Administration complex at Konedobu, Government and Association officials had easy access to each other, and no doubt the trade union officials adjusted their behavior accordingly. Certainly it was claimed that, at the time of the strike, the Association's president was more responsive to the definition which officials placed on the situation than that of the striking workers. The expatriate General Secretary in 1965—an overseas volunteer—has acknowledged his embarrassment at the wave of strikes (Chapman 1965:20).

Nonetheless, despite these other factors, I consider that the critical feature in its failure, compared to associations in the other major centers, was Port Moresby's sheer size and its spatial, industrial, and social dispersal. Moreover, problems of communication already severe because of this dispersal would seem to have been heightened by official and other discouragement of representation based on ethnic or regional groupings, by far the most natural bases for group recruitment among indigenous townsmen. Any union wishing to organize the plant's labor force would have saved itself much time and effort by utilizing these links.

Thus the Workers' Association was unable, for a complex of reasons, to provide a focus for workers' demands at the level of the plant, even though general sympathy for its aims was more widespread than was actual membership (see also Martin 1969:142).

Moreover, by force of circumstances, it had to base its appeal to town dwellers as workers qua workers. As we have seen, however, P. M.D. workers were not often concerned with distinguishing these particular interests from those relating to their more encompassing status as "indigenes" in the structure of racial relations. In such a situation, it might appear that a nationalist political party, able to deal with Territory-wide issues, conscious of the racial division, and yet responsive to particular grievances at the level of a plant, compound, or neighborhood would have been a more appropriate organizational vehicle for workers' demands. At the time of the strike, however, no such party existed—with the exception of the New Guinea United National party which never left the drawingboard stage.

Lacking organizational supports, however, a striker's identity as "worker" or "indigene" remained embedded in his network of interpersonal ties. And even though the sum of all these individual networks—the total network between the strikers—could be used to mobilize support, the constitutive links were sufficiently complex to be divisive of singleminded loyalty to the strike itself. Moreover, given the underlying tensions and oppositions between the various sets in the plant and compound, and which were inevitably embedded into the total network, the strike also failed to provide undisputed leaders who might, by formulating a "package-deal" (cf. Barth 1963:14), have gained support for a more prolonged and forceful stoppage. The "Kerema" workers, those from the Gulf District of Papua were more closely associated with the genesis of the strike than any other category. "Kerema" workers were also more likely than other categories to join the Workers' Association.[5] Their initiative in the development of the strike, however, was too embedded in the networks and oppositions of everyday domestic life to allow them to act as acknowledged leaders in maintaining the strike. Thus, wandering along the road to the market, workers were responsive to the directions of men who, because of their occupational roles, and noninvolvement in the strikers' network, could

[5] Shortly after the strike, the manager charged with meeting the newly formed Works Committee suggested that the representatives should consider if it would be advisable to persuade all employees to join the Workers' Association. When they told him that almost everyone had already joined, he was so surprised that he wrote to the union asking for a list of employees who were also members. The list contained six names. All but one were Gulf District migrants: of the four Works Committee representatives, only the "Kerema" representative had joined.

offer effective leadership. I am referring to the officials who per-suaded the men to return to work.

Under the canopy of a conflict situation all strikers might temporari-ly achieve a sense of common interest and identity. But once Europe-an leadership had reasserted itself, and the enthusiasm of the crisis was over, the sense of shared grievance reembedded itself in the smaller units of which the total network was formed. As the employees were unable to utilize or generate a structure of leadership or representation, the oppositions which had molded the small-scale networks, and in terms of which they met their domestic and other everyday needs, also molded the duration and course of the strike. Although over time, workers' ability to forge a common identity at the level of the plant or town may have been increasing, the articulation of the identity within the interstices of a network of links rather than a continuing group militated against both cohesion and coherence.

*

7

Workers as Town Dwellers

The community with which this volume is concerned is nondescript; it is a place of unusual interest, but it has neither
the unity nor the charm of a place in which the common view
is set forth "in laws, customs, and all the arts of life" . . . .
It is, however, just this "nondescript" situation, so lacking in
"unity and charm" that gives this region its peculiar interest. It
is nondescript because it is in process of evolution. [Park, 1929]

Having explored workers' adjustments to the social arena of the plant
and its compounds, we are now in a position to move to the wider
questions posed earlier in the book. To what extent is the town's indigenous social organization akin to the passenger ship, to what degree
the cargo vessel? In other words, is Port Moresby social organization
merely a composite reflection of the societies of origin of its residents
or does it possess sufficient interdependence between its parts to allow
us to treat it as a separate social structure? In order to place the plant
within the context of Port Moresby urban structure we will therefore
have to discuss the role of the work situation and common employment
in shaping the overall process of change and adjustment. Our initial
conceptual framework, moreover, employed broad, generalized processes
—namely, individual strategies of choice within the frameworks of the
web of dependence and competition and of communication. It is now

time to abstract from those processes and delineate more specific propositions about the units of the urban structure and their interrelationship. As I have restricted my documentation of those processes to a very small sample of residents, extrapolations to the urban situation as a whole are necessarily tentative. I have framed them, however, in the light of my general knowledge of the town and my own and others' additional field studies and hope the reader will find them paradigmatic rather than reckless.

While African models have sometimes proved inappropriate for rural New Guinea conditions, African urban models, nonetheless, do provide useful entry points, setting the Port Moresby study within a wider comparative context. An important concept employed in the framework used by students of Central African Copperbelt towns has been "situational selection" (see, for example, Epstein 1958). It directs attention to the fact that while certain roles cluster into wider combinations, certain clusters—those of kinship and employment for example —may place contradictory demands on an urban resident who must, perforce, play roles in both sets. In playing roles, the town dweller thus selects norms appropriate to the one situation or cluster, leaving other norms in abeyance. This concept, then, directs our attention both to the combination of, and the incompatibilities between, the total constellation of roles and to the fact that changes in one cluster may be insulated from another. Thus Epstein (1958:232) advises us to treat the town as a composite of partly autonomous but also interrelated "sub"-systems of relations, with changes in one system "feeding-back" into another (see also Pons 1969:10–12).

Although their procedures differ in detail and implications Banton (1973) and Southall (1973) have also advocated that a theory of urbanization can best be essayed from an analysis of the overall structure of combination and differentiation within the assembly of roles and role-relationships available to town dwellers. The focus of analysis becomes, essentially, the degree to which an urban social system prescribes any combination of particular roles or allows flexibility in role combination.

Within the plant and its compounds certain interactions are phrased in terms of fully institutionalized principles of association; that is, they reflect well-defined expectations of, and sanctions for, conduct. Where innumerable individuals act in this expected manner we may think of them as playing social *roles*: the specific expectations of conduct which trigger and maintain the behavior are the norms and sanctions constituting those roles. A *role-relationship* "sums up the current experience of two persons who interact in terms of a certain [role]" (Southall 1973:80). The logical relationship of particular roles and role-relationships in time and space may lead us to speak of them as a *system*.

Following these basic approaches we can now abstract three types of social events—interactions between wage employees in the performance of productive tasks, interactions between kinsmen, and interactions between Europeans and indigenes—taking place within the plant's social arena. The predictable nature and logical interrelationship of these interactions allows us to speak of them as systems of *work, kinship,* and *racial* roles.

Of these, the system of work roles is the most highly specified in terms of the external details and timing of task performance. It is also the most limited and least encompassing, pervading only a segment of the day. Kinship roles are less specified in terms of external detail and timing but, unlike work roles, attempts are made to specify the mental attitude of the role player. They are also in one sense more encompassing, pervading all interactions between kinsmen, yet they are also more limited as they refer only to a small network of actual individuals and thus generate only a small number of role-relationships. Racial roles are perhaps even less specified and, like the performance of kinship roles, allow various interpretations, some of which, however, may be thought more satisfactory than others. That is, the role allows for various degrees of "role-distance" (Goffman 1961). But common to almost all interactions between indigenes and Europeans is the minimal expectation that the indigene will defer to the European. Whether the European actively requires this or regards it as an unfortunate barrier to a firmer human understanding is usually irrelevant for the overt form of the relationship. Racial roles are also the most pervasive and encompassing, generating large numbers of role-relationships. One in four Port Moresby residents is a European, and thus a Papua–New Guinean's identity as "indigene" is relevant in a variety of contexts—in his or her performance as consumer, churchgoer, sports club member, and so on. Even though many racial contacts are fleeting, they are nonetheless, in this core sense, highly predictable and prescribed; it is therefore still appropriate to term them role-relationships (but cf. Southall 1973:7, 80).

We can best understand the operation of these systems by identifying their principal referents. Following Barth (1966:5) we can identify these referents as *statuses*, that is, classes of positions giving fundamental, jurally binding rights within the distribution of human and material resources. The specification of these statuses will necessarily lead us beyond the industrial arena to the Territory and town as a whole.

Thought of in terms of statuses, racial relations in the town refer at once to the past and continuing distribution of Territory-wide resources made, and legislated for, by Europeans as members of the administering authority, and to the visually more evident allocation of resources in the town itself. The terms of the administrative distinction "expatriate" and "indigene" blurs the racial distinction, but only minimally: all Caucasians are "expatriate" and all native Melanesians are "indigenes" irrespective of place of birth or nationality. It is a system of subordination based on *genetic* transmission (Pitt-Rivers 1971:241). Although adjustments may vary, the racial division is such that no indigenes can escape it altogether. Indeed its spatial and material concomitants provide the dominant symbol system of the entire town. Europeans are the dominant group and the overt forms of the town reflect their possessions, their architecture, and other institutions.

The town dweller's performance of work roles reflects statuses arising from the Territory's labor determinations and ordinances, its commercial and corporate law, and administrators' and managements' ability to make rules of organization within the wide scope they set. In 1966 roughly 43 percent of all indigenous town dwellers were involved in wage employment. If members of schools and training institutions are included, the number of residents performing occupational roles in formal organizations is much higher. There are a very few town dwellers who are able to earn a living as independent fishermen and a few entrepreneurs in other fields of activity—for example, building subcontractors, and "boy-truck" and trade store operators. Yet very few of these completely escape the constraints of wage employment. The employment situation of subcontractors is very like that of wage employees (Langmore 1967) and other operators frequently have to support themselves by taking paid employment. They may achieve a measure of autonomy which other wage workers aspire to, but are as yet far from constituting a distinct entrepreneurial class. Moreover, even those not actively involved in wage or other functional roles are still largely subject, as dependents, to the pressure of wage employment and, if adult males, to the police patrols which try to force the migrant to leave town or work.

The primary reference of kinship roles is to the statuses based on the evaluation of blood and affinal ties which allocate rights to village resources—notably land—and other rights *in personam*. As we have seen, very few employees were actively prepared to renounce their involvement in the village sphere, and thus were more or less prepared to maintain village statuses. Some workers could return home for weekends, but many were based in town and so could only maintain their statuses from a distance—by writing, returning at Christmas, sending gifts, entertaining villagers visiting the town, and so on. Those who escape the network of kinship role-relationships are rare and usually from far afield and, I suspect, are likely to be "rubbishmen" in their local communities.

Having identified three distinct role-relationship systems and the statuses which support them, we can now turn to a fourth, and residual, set of events which can be thought of as nesting in the interstices of the racial, work, and kinship systems, but with its own additional determinants. Although it is residual, this fourth set of interactions is nonetheless particularly associated with urban residence *per se* and thus can be thought of as the *urban-residential* domain (Pons 1969).

Interactions in this sphere of town life at first seem particularly variable and uncertain. There are no obvious roles appropriate to all role-relationships in the sphere, in the same way that racial ro'es, for example, are appropriate to interactions between Europeans and indigenes. This is because a great number of urban-residential interactions occur between comparative strangers who are uncertain of each other's behavior. And although the statuses which structure the three role systems also set boundaries for the urban-residential sphere, these boundaries allow a great deal of individual choice.

Urban-residential interactions may best be thought of as initially subsocial. Typically, they flow from sets of spatial positions or webs of competition and dependence focused on common facilities. Norms may develop to meet the needs of the occasion but the fully social character of interactions flowing from these impersonal arrangements is rarely determinative. An analysis of their outcome usually requires a considerable knowledge of the attitudes and background of the individ-

Plate 11   At Work—a labor gang outside the House of Assembly

Plate 12   After Work—mingling with the crowd at Koke market

ual participants and of the arrangements themselves and a recognition of the scope for individual choice.

P.M.D. is only one of a number of highly specialized organizations in Port Moresby with tasks to perform and a consequent need for personnel. As each organization tends to exist in an environment created by the others, the town as a whole appears as a network of partly independent but also related occupational and other functional positions. This network, so to speak, requires certain skills and aptitudes and, in order to obtain them, offers rewards and "selects" personnel from the surrounding population. As the Territory is culturally highly heterogeneous, and as the required abilities are not randomly distributed but cluster in certain regions, the selection of these abilities entails, unintentionally, the selection of a culturally diverse town population.

At the same time, however, the occupational network's typical demand for young adult males creates a homogeneous, core population with respect to age and sex characteristics. Homogeneity is reinforced by the specialized demands of each organization and by housing arrangements. Some structures require predominantly scholastic ability, others require strong pairs of hands. Moreover, in order to house and attract individuals from far afield, agencies within the network have built various kinds of accommodation. This housing has been far from uniform. Some is reserved for personnel in particular organizations, while yet other housing is allocated according to family need and length of urban residence. Thus in order to attract more valued personnel, a proportion of the town's resources has been reserved for married men. Some married but unskilled workers have provided their own accommodation. But, by and large, men with families in town tend to be in either white-collar or skilled occupations. Moreover, because this type of labor is drawn from only certain parts of the Territory, they also tend to be "ethnically" and "regionally" distinctive.

Thus the occupational framework at once fragments the town dweller's urban experience and encapsulates him in small, typically less diverse and specialized milieux, at the same time as it thrusts diversity upon him at the level of the plant or town as a whole. This variation in milieux and the overall diversity give greater opportunities for choice than would be possible in the rural areas (Mann 1965:102–3; Southall 1973:82). While living in the town an individual may be, although not always, subject to the control of the same broadly comparable number of intimate others as he would be in the village, especially if rural-urban continuity is high. Nonetheless, the distinct possibility exists that in addition to those intimate ties there will be ties more limited in their duration and scope but otherwise able to constrain and channel his behavior. Schooling in urban standards may, after all, be as well provided for by the mass media, by fleeting relationships and by relationships involving high components of subordination yet limited face-to-face contact as it is by peer-group pressure (Southall 1973:82). The ability of the specialized milieux to "encapsulate" the Red Xhosa migrants in East London, South Africa and to effectively guard them against that wider diversity (Mayer 1961) is perhaps a function of the historical pattern of Xhosa-White relationships which caused certain sections of the Xhosa to set their face against the intruding white cultures. Papua–New Guinea race relations until the present, however, have been marked by injustice and attempts by indigenes to right the flow of European goods and relationships in their favor rather than by a rejection of their absolute value (Burridge 1960). Groups of "home-boys" in Port Moresby protect themselves and direct any xenophobia towards other groups of home-boys in narrowly-defined contexts: they tend not to protect themselves against the urban ambience *per se*. Thus it is in terms of a bipolar social density —areas of high moral density and solidarity nestling within a wider density of social interaction or role-relationships—that we must view "home-boy" sentiment or "ethnicity" in Port Moresby (cf. Banton 1973; Southall 1973).

We have seen that Papua–New Guinea peoples rarely had an inclusive name which distinguished them from other peoples. With the coming of the Europeans, and the increasing participation of the indigene in the colonial economic institutions, distinctions were drawn and titles found. Thus, in some areas, items of native usage were taken from their customary context to express group identity and a consciousness of own, or other's, kind. Epstein (1963: 182n) suggests that the people of the Rabaul area of New Britain may have come to be called "Tolai"—a name by which they are widely, although not exclusively, known today—because other New Guinea peoples seized on one of their forms of greeting and used it to distinguish them as a distinctive social category. The first occasion of this use, it is suggested, may have been on the New Guinea goldfields during the 1930s where the congregation of a heterogeneous labor force was likely to encourage the categorization of difference. In other areas it was not an item of culture which was fastened on but place names and names for regional features introduced by the Europeans. Thus F. E. Williams (1924) refers to regular intercourse between "Delta-boys" at work on the oilfields, that is, between the Koriki and like peoples and their neighbors to the east and west.

The significance of these innovations has not, however, always been obvious. Hogbin and Wedgwood (1953:252) imply that the use of such names is at best peripheral to the society concerned. They state that "such words as Orokaiva, Kiwai, Goilala, are used by Europeans to identify what appears to the European to be a distinctive cultural group, and to a limited extent these names are also employed by sophisticated natives with reference to aliens." However, other evidence suggests that their use was not so limited. As early as 1929, district and regional epithets were being used to point to a group consciousness which extended beyond the confines of the local group and alliance or even of the phyle. Mead records that just before the Rabaul strike "commentators on native life shook their heads, remarking that these natives were quite incapable of ever organising beyond the narrowest tribal borders overlooking the fact that terms like 'Solomons,' 'Sepiks,' or 'Manus,' when applied in Rabaul already blanketed many tribal differences" (Mead 1953).

Thus a Port Moresby newcomer's previous experience will have included not only relationships with kin in his own and neighboring villages and with villagers qua villagers but also relationships with people met at the local mission station and school, market, or administrative center. Some of these associations may have been with people from distant regions attending his school or working at the home station. Our newcomer will almost certainly have absorbed stereotypes, unfavorable or otherwise, about a medley of local or regional groups and may even have already extended his range of reciprocities while maintaining his principal associations with people in the general vicinity of his home village.

His arrival in culturally diverse Port Moresby will throw his own cultural distinctiveness into relief at the same time as he begins to grasp the town's cultural variety. Many people will appear very strange and alien to him but certain of those he sees on the bus and walking on the streets will appear familiar from his visits to his district center or from compatriots' stories. Perhaps he is from the New Guinea Islands and will recognize a hairstyle here as belonging to a

"Tolai" or another as belonging to a "Kavieng boy." Perhaps he will recognize certain facial markings as being "Manus." On the other hand, he may be from Papua and fear that this small wiry fellow is a "Goilala" or thinks that the exotic, bushy-haired man in the white vest and long, brightly colored *rami* (waistcloth) must be a "Mekeo."

In general, he will listen to the "tune" of any speech he hears and will pay particular attention to physique, physionomy, and to hairstyles as the most evident signs of "ethnic" identity. Our newcomer may also see men standing by a trade store and wearing smart white shirts, long white socks, and black shoes and identify them as "educated" people.

To some of these various people he will be drawn, of others he will be distrustful. But whatever his classification he is unlikely to feel threatened. It is a European center and during the day on its thoroughfares and in its principal gathering places he will expect the rule of law to prevail, people allowing other residents and visitors to go about their business quietly.

As he learns more about the town he will find out that, as he suspected from rural experience, some groups are rough and others are vicious, or that some are "funny people." But by and large he learns that most *wantok* groups are neutral—culturally distant and uninteresting but not necessarily threatening. Despite the appeal to "linguism" (Harrison 1960) implied in the term *"wantok"* (one-talk) he will increasingly use the term to identify sets of people who have common loyalties to a range of sociogeographic regions—from the dispersed homesteads of the clan territory and the village to the administrative division and even to broad regions such as "the Highlands" or "the Islands." Thus language and communication play their parts in the *wantok* principle but the indigenous conceptualization is one of *ples* (place).

In the "urban-residential" encounters in which he becomes involved our migrant will tend to be most aware of "ethnic" identities. This is not to say that he is unaware of townsmen's other characteristics. He may be very impressed by a smart shirt, a man's wealth, or another's "education" but, as the town's most visible characteristic is regional and ethnic diversity, he will give prime consideration to whether or not the other participant is a potential *wantok*, and thus able to share in his enthusiasms and other relationships. Before long he will have developed a network of personal relationships. Some of these will refer primarily to village statuses, others to previous association in the wider "home area" and some arise solely from urban residence even though they are cast in the idiom of "the home area." Nonetheless, although the referents of many of the relationships may appear to, or do in fact, lie elsewhere the migrant can utilize them to aid his own urban adaptation. Thus *wantok* links may be enlisted to help meet the migrant's domestic needs as a barracks' dweller or stressed to qualify him for sports club membership. In both these instances idioms with rural referents are generalized to serve as principles of association in uniquely urban contexts.

It must be stressed, then, that as the geographical range of *wantok* relations can vary greatly, extending far beyond the locality group and even beyond the *phyle,* this principle of association, although limiting, is also enabling. It carves out of the total town population a category of persons readily available for face-to-face engagements but, because the category can vary so greatly, also allows the individual migrant to sample a diversity of urban situations while still staying within the bounds of the *wantok* system. *Wantok* norms, although minimally specified according to the details of performance, are sufficiently basic to, and persasive of, urban social life to allow us to think of them as triggering a set of primary roles. *Wantok* norms, however, cannot be thought of as referring to statuses; rather they are "open-textured," generalized idioms. They have a core of common measure in their reference to space but allow a great diversity of right and obligation which can only be specified by the detai's of social context.

I have now delineated the relative autonomy of the work, racial, and kinship role systems and outlined a key theme of the urban-residential domain. It remains to show their interpenetration and the processes of feedback which relate them: to do so I use as an analytical benchmark a model of role domains and role differentiation based on Southall (1973) and Banton (1973).

There are roughly five possible role-relationship domains in any society: kinship; ritual or religious; political; economic and occupational; and recreational or leisure time role-relationships. In "tribal" society, kinship role-relationships and those arising from ritual and cult assemblies predominate and prescribe many combinations of political and economic role-relationships and, where these are at all visible, leisure and recreational role-relationships. As urbanization proceeds, not only does the number of role-relationships increase but economic and politi-

cal role-relationships proliferate making greater numbers of role-relationship combinations possible and also allowing greater scope for individual choice in constructing those combinations. To the extent, however, that urbanization is superimposed on a preexisting economic and
social base—as in the case of many towns in West Africa—rather than
starting anew and transforming the relationships between existing populations by industrialization and commercialization these tendencies
will be weakened.

In most areas of the Third World, industrialization and commercial-
ism are prevalent in the towns. Rural-urban continuity may still be
high, however, because of a circulation of labor; the coincidence of education, skills, and ethnic origin due to the variable impact of the colonial experience; and because urban housing and employment structures
fail to interdigitate the population and encourage the importation of rural ties. To the extent that this is so, as in Port Moresby, kinship and,
say, occupational role-relationships can be and are combined. Thus
workers may try to introduce a kinsman to an organization at the same
time as those in control may, to encourage a valued worker, allow him
to do so. It is true that employers may sometimes actively encourage
the recruitment of workers with preexisting kinship ties to facilitate
on-the-job training or indirect control through a system of "boss-boy"
responsibility. But this usually takes place only where worker-manage-
ment opposition is very weak or where the skill component of labor is
minimal and where, if ethnic solidarity leads to worker solidarity, a
large pool of unskilled labor will prevent workers from controlling the
concern's output. For the most part employers are indifferent: when
the specialization of urban milieux throws kinsmen together rather than
separating them, the power of employers keeps the performance and
norms of economic and kinship roles apart, even though many workers
may have succeeded in combining role-relationships associated with
these spheres.

A skilled or even semiskilled occupational elite—apprentices, white-
collar workers, and drivers, for example—will only rarely be able to
combine kinship and occupational role-relationships and, in many cases, will not be concerned with doing so, preferring to keep them separate. Town dwellers are urban consumers and workers, and at the same
time, are unwilling to dispense with kinship obligations and rights.
Any preference for separation of these spheres can be explained by the
growing desire to keep a firmer control over the degree to which role

rewards associated with urban occupational performance are brought within the ambit of kinship reciprocities and, among craftsman and senior white-collar workers, by a growing identification with their work roles.

Thus as (or rather if) commercialization, industrialization, and the bureaucratization of occupational structures proceeds, and creates new skills and positions, the number of separate economic and occupational role-relationships will increase and the total balance of role-relationships will move in that direction.

Port Moresby is not just "a town," however, reflecting the usual processes of role-relationship differentiation. It is also, most importantly, a *colonial* town.

In certain towns, colonialism has created a plural social structure: here the political role system prescribes all other role-relationships, hampering urban differentiation. Thus the urbanization of Fijians in Suva, Fiji, and their retention of Fijian cultural traditions (Nayacakalou and Southall 1973) must be seen within the wider political framework of Fijian, Indian, and European relationships and the unique position of Fijians as the autochthonous landholders within the legal pluralism set up by the protectorate and continued within independent Fiji. Equally, the fine balance in the pyramid of social oppositions in the Central African copperbelt towns studied by Mitchell (1956) and Epstein (1958) and the tendency for political-occupational role-relationships to usurp the pride of place hitherto occupied by kinship role-relationships and those of urban tribalism, would seem to owe a great deal to the crescendo of organized black-white opposition in the later days of colonialism in British Central Africa and which was focused around clearly articulated issues such as Central African federation.

In Port Moresby, however, urban differentiation has not had to cope with a vertical, fully plural social structure nor with an organized black-white political opposition but with an unorganized horizontal division between white employer/supervisor/administrator and black worker/territorial citizens lacking either a common focusing issue or political structures intervening between the national elite and its potential bases of support. The Chinese—the only intermediate cultural group—have been few in numbers and have been incorporated into the colonizers' occupational stratum as employers; into the colonizers' political-administrative system as Australian citizens; and, in indigenous

eyes, have become *Saina-masta* "Chinese masters." Colonial practice
in Papua–New Guinea has been to stress a common citizenry of administration—in part because of the extremely small-scale nature of
traditional political organization—with little attention given to intervening political structures until the growth of local government councils
in the late 1950s and early 1960s. Where intervening political structures did arise, as with the workers' associations in the early 1960s,
they were faced with the administrator's fear of social opposition and
an unwillingness to see that opposition could act as a tutor to wider, ac-
ceptable political action. The national elections of 1968, for example,
indicate that although Port Moresby residents were aware of issues
concerning race relations, political independence and employment
these were rarely articulated into clear political commitments except
where ethnic, local and personal loyalties were involved (Groves et al.
1971 :311–14).

Since there has been little indigenous political infrastructure in Port
Moresby—leaving the town's political arena as an extension of colonial
administration—and since the distinction between colonized and colo-
nizer pervades every occupational arena, political and economic roles
have not differentiated as much as they might have, but tend to be
merged into the structure of racial role-relationships. Although racial
roles within the town's economic organizations are partly obscured by
the specifically industrial division between "management" and "workers," or "expatriate" and "indigene," it is largely verbal. The cash and
other rewards offered in return for effort in the performance of work
roles are differentially related to the value of the task to management
and to competition for labor from other sources, but they vary only
within the broader racial structure. Occasionally, the work role pre-
dominates but, as all Europeans are also industrial supervisors, the
roles are more often mutually supporting. When, as in the strike of
1965, the normal functioning of the system is blocked, the underlying
processes are exposed. Our examination of that strike showed that indigenous workers are increasingly questioning the existing distribution
of racial/industrial resources but as yet lack the organization, sense of
common purpose and confidence to challenge it successfully. Even in
more harmonious periods workers commonly identify their industrial
activity as "working for Europeans."

But even though one system may predominate, dominant members of
the concern are both "managers" and "Europeans," and subordinates

are both "workers" and "boys." The two systems are thus interrelated in the persons of the participants, and a challenge to one system usually leads to modifications in the other. Thus following the strike, managers slightly modified the operation of the racial system to preserve the equilibrium in the industrial system—their primary concern as managers. The effect of these modifications will no doubt in turn modify the operation of the racial system. As indigenes gain increasingly senior positions in the industrial hierarchy they will come to appreciate even more forcibly the discrepancy in their own rewards and those of Europeans. Their struggle for better conditions will thus jeopardize the equilibrium in the racial system.

While the mundane aspects of daily life might suggest to the more skilled workers a degree of autonomy for their work roles, grievances and crises merged them and contrasted them as racial roles with the intimacy and equivalence of kinship relations. Heightened social opposition, that is, intensified the contrast between experiences in kinship role-relationships and those where racial membership set the pattern rather than subordinating kinship to political or economic roles. Lacking differentiated political and occupational roles relevant to the opposition, however, workers employed kinship (together with compatriot) ties to organize the strike. But the very basis of its organization doomed it to a limited life and to a theme of injustice and lack of reciprocity rather than political opposition.

The organization of the strike illustrates that Port Moresby is not just an extension of rural patterns of kinship or of the prevailing structure of racial relations. *Wantok* or compatriot relationships, which capture ingredients of both kinship and racial and work role-relationships, mediate between them. This mediation involves, in part, an extension of rural reciprocities. Parties held to honor children or kin pull in *wantok,* who are then enlisted for their support and help in the absence of kin. Yet the kinship component is very variable. Kinship does not indicate the outer boundary of the "ethnic group" as it does among the Toba Batak of Sumatra (Bruner 1973). And while there are occasions in Port Moresby when the content of *wantok* ties is very comparable to that of kinship (cf. Southall 1973:83), there are also many occasions when it is not. *"Wantok"* is used predominantly as a generalized idiom of friendship and may hold together acquaintances just met, or those met at a previous place of employment or at a soccer match, who now wish to promenade at the market or justify their association to others, and so on. It may also be used to evade the grosser features of a subordinate position in the town's racial structure. Through a network of interpersonal ties based on the broad compatibility of compatriots, a migrant may seek to incorporate himself in the town's villages and settlements or within a work group of friends. In doing so he meets the friends of friends and so extends the network's scope.

But whereas an individual experiences his own network over time, and in different locations, and draws distinctions between its various components, a stranger sees only the more public gatherings and discrete pluralities of persons. Viewed from this perspective the component dyads of ego's network are not sharply distinguished; instead, they are seen to cluster to form relatively undifferentiated sets. These are usually assumed to be sets of *wantoks* and ethnic or regional identities, such as "Popondetta boys" or "Chimbus," are used to describe them.

The importance of this process lies in the fact that when, as in a housing complex, individuals are linked in a web of competition for shared facilities the identities readily become foci for discontent and common grievance. As conflict develops, the identities and self-identifications crystallize and define group boundaries for sets of people previously linked by fluid and changing dyadic relations. Since a housing complex is not a closed system but involves individuals who also participate in other situations, we may assume that in turn the coherence of these oppositions "feed back" into the wider town. Unfortunate experiences in one local context would thus strengthen the participants resolve not to trust men from other areas and also provide specific examples to strengthen the force of verbal stereotypes.

The small scale and specialized nature of these milieux insures that, whereas in one situation regional or ethnic categories "X" and "Y" are opposed, opposition in another situation involves categories "X," "W," and "Z." Moreover, residential mobility flowing from rural-urban migration, employment turnover and changing housing preferences leads to fluidity of personnel, and thus to the fragility of group bonds where these depend only on *wantok* ties.

There are undoubtedly common denominators to many of these situations; the degree to which there are profoundly influences the force of stereotypes operating at the level of the town as a whole. Thus for many years "Keremas" have formed a large part of the town's labor force and, in order to get jobs and to be near *wantoks* and kin, have clustered in many of the town's organizations. Their domination of these functional settings has led to opposition and this has, in turn, reinforced unfavorable stereotypes about their exclusiveness and further led them to keep to themselves. They are involved in a self-fulfilling prophecy. And even though this process fails to generate a neat pyramid of social oppositions it strengthens the ability of the *wantok* idiom to cope with urban diversity and make it intelligible.

Many of Port Moresby's formal, voluntary associations lead a precarious life. Hungry for indigenous membership, but gorged with well-intentioned European officers, they figure as kindly but ineffectual extensions of the town's colonial structure. Only the sports clubs and the churches attract significant numbers of Papuans and New Guineans. The force of these associations derives from the regional basis of membership. Some teams arise from the sponsorship of large territory institutions such as the army or the police, but the majority arise from *wantok* ties. The pattern of missionization in Papua–New Guinea has cut it into denominational blocks, mirroring or suggesting administrative diversions. Ties based on church and administrative routes and obligations have largely coincided with ties based on traditional trading patterns and ratified the developing pattern of *wantok* friendships. When Port Moresby's sports associations began to develop in the late 1950s they fell into line with these established patterns. Since linguistic or cultural boundaries are flexible and lack sufficient scale, *wantok* ties came to be focused on *ples* (place) rather than *tok* (language).

While "educated" and "cowboy," for example, serve as vague norms setting standards for dress, bearing and attitudes, their role as a relational reference standard has been limited. *Wanwok* (one-work), *wan-lotu* (one-church) or *poroman* (one of a pair) might have served as idioms of friendship, but *wantok* has proved the most encompassing and best able to steer urban diversity within manageable boundaries.

The interrelations and processes of "feedback" between the functional and spatial settings, the role systems, and the more generalized principles which govern urban-residential interactions are complex and numerous—so numerous that the town is in continuous change, in a state of endless becoming. It is no longer, as it was between the wars, a small European town with a fringe of native villages and compounds. It is now a complex network of functional and spatial positions creat-

ing distinctive settings for social life while it gathers a culturally highly diverse population to fill them. Most participants come initially
as tourists with few commitments to other residents and with a desire to
return to their home areas after a working holiday. The town's internal dynamics thrust these new residents into association and yet also allow them, within partly insulated settings, leeway to create their own
way of life and to use urban resources for their own ends. To do this
they utilize relationships which refer back to the home area but which,
with their developing experience, gradually take on new functions and
involve residents as, for example, coresidents, fellow employees, and
sports club members. The relationships may retain their rural idioms,
but they involve the participants in new networks of functional positions not given by rural referents.

The urban-residential sphere of modern Port Moresby, then, rests on
the twin processes of generalization and symbiosis by which rural referents are recast as generalized principles of association to deal with
the impersonal interdependence created by the town's network of functional positions. Its form resembles a kaleidoscope of small groupings
which fall and change their pattern as circumstances press on their
functional framework (cf. Geertz 1965:144). They are sets of small,
semipermeable *Gemeinschaft* responding to a wider *Gesellschaft*.

Thus Port Moresby is neither a wholly separate set of common tasks
and activities nor simply a collection of people in limited association:
it is neither a cargo vessel nor a passenger ship, but both. Papua–New
Guinean conceptual polarities are as prone to overstate the issue as
those social commentators who would collapse the town in favor of the
countryside or the nation at large. The town clearly exists within a
wider cultural and colonial context. It is also a distinct social arena
with its own internal dynamics. But its residents do find it brown,
patchy, and rather inefficient, and there has been some talk of making
Lae the capital. If that day comes, I hope Port Moresby will not foun-
der.

Appendix

A Visual Test of Attitudes to Occupational Prestige

Certain workers were presented with the following sixteen photographs f Papua–New Guineans at work and asked to rank them according to the prestige attached to each occupation by "the community-at-large." They were presented in random order (and as they are in this Appendix) subject to the need to group them into "vertical" and "horizontal" plates to aid manageability. (Plates I through VIII are approximately one half (½) the size used in the test). Each man was asked to identify the occupations before beginning the ranking to give him confidence and allow me to check for any ambiguity.

I then asked each man to take the occupation with the highest prestige and hand it to me, then to take the next highest, and so on, until all the photographs had been ranked. They were then laid out in the order chosen and each man was asked to check his ranking and amend it as he thought necessary.

The concept of "prestige" is not easily translated into the local languages. Thus I used the following substitute words or phrases: in the local variant of English—"very important;" in Police Motu—"edana tau ia ena guakara be taunimanima ese idia hematauria bada herea idia henea;" and in the Pidgin version—"man, wok bilongen i-stap nambawan long ai bilong ol, kain man i-no save paul nabaut." Reasons for the first and last three rankings were then solicited.

Originally twenty-two plates were used, but this proved unwieldy and informants quickly tired of the task. Of the sixteen plates finally selected for the test, fifteen had been selected from the picture library of the Territory's Department of Information and Extension Services. I am grateful to its director and officers for their cooperation and for providing me with two sets of each plate. The pictures were not ideal for my purposes, but I had no resources to produce my own. I did, however, take Plate X as it was impossible to obtain a photograph of "a houseboy" from any other source.

I

II

III

IV

V

VI

VII

VIII

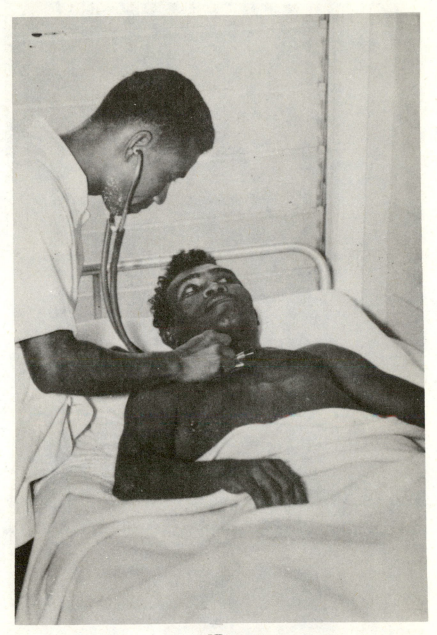

IX

X

XI

XII

XIII

XIV

XV

XVI

Bibliography

Ardener, S.

    1964 "The Comparative Study of Rotating Credit Associations." *Journal of the Royal Anthropological Institute* 94: 201–29.

Bureau of Statistics, Konedobu, Papua

    1966 *Population Census, 1966.* Preliminary Bulletin No. 23. Central District and Port Moresby.

Bureau of Statistics, Konedobu, Papua

    1970 *Population Count:* Port Moresby Urban Area.

Baldamus, W.

    1961 *Efficiency and Effort: An Analysis of Industrial Administration.* London: Tavistock.

Banton, M.

    1965 "Social Alignment and Identity in a West African City." In *Urbanization and Migration in West Africa,* edited by H. Kuper. Berkeley and Los Angeles: University of California Press, 1965.

    1967 *Race Relations.* London: Tavistock.

    1973 "Urbanisation and Role Theory." In *Urban Anthropology: Cross-Cultural Studies of Urbanization,* edited by Aidan Southall. London: Oxford University Press. pp. 43–70.

Banton, M., ed.
  1966   *The Social Anthropology of Complex Societies.*   London:
          Tavistock.

Barnes, J. A.
  1954   "Class and Committees in a Norwegian Island Parish." *Human
          Relations,* VII, No. 1:39–58.
  1969a "Networks and Political Process." In *Social Networks in Ur-
          ban Situations,* edited by J. C. Mitchell. Manchester: Man-
          chester University Press, 1969. pp. 51–76.
  1969b "Graph Theory and Social Networks: A Technical Comment
          on Connectedness and Connectivity." *Sociology,* 3, No. 2:215–
          32.

Barth, Frederik
  1966   *Models of Social Organization.* London: Royal Anthropologi-
          cal Institute.
  1968   "On the Study of Social Change." *American Anthropologist,*
          69, No. 6:661–669.

Barth, Frederik, ed.
  1963   *The Role of the Entrepreneur in Social Change in Northern
          Norway.* Bergen: Universitetsforlaget.

Belshaw, C. S.
  1952   "Port Moresby Canoe Traders." *Oceania,* XXIII, No. 1:26–39.
  1957   *The Great Village.* London: Routledge and K. Paul.
  1963   "Pacific Island Towns and the Theory of Growth." In *Pacific
          Port Towns and Cities: A Symposium,* edited by A. Spoehr.
          Honolulu: Bishop Museum. pp. 17–24.
  1965   *Traditional Exchange and Modern Markets.* New Jersey:
          Prentice-Hall.

Bettison, D. G.
  1961   Census of Indigenous Population: Port Moresby and Environs.
          (Unpublished typescript)

Bettison, D. G., Hughes, C. A., and van der Veur, Paul W. eds.
  1965   *The Papua–New Guinea Elections 1964.* Canberra: Australian
          National University Press.

Bevan, T. F.
  1890   *Toil, Travel and Discovery in British New Guinea.* London:
          K. Paul, Trench, Trubner.

Brown, H. A.
1957 "The Eastern Elema." Diploma of Anthropology thesis, University of London.

Brown, P., and H. C. Brookfield.
1959 "Chimbu Land and Society." *Oceania,* 30, No. 1:1–75.

Bruner, Edward M.
1973 "Kin and Non–Kin." In *Urban Anthropology: Cross-Cultural Studies of Urbanization,* edited by Aidan Southall. London: Oxford University Press.

1963 "Medan: the role of Kinship in an Indonesian City." In *Pacific Port Towns and Cities,* edited by A. Spoehr. Honolulu: Bishop Museum.

1967 "Comment" on "Urbanization and Social Change in Africa" by A. L. Epstein. *Current Anthropology* 8, No. 4: 284–85.

Burridge, Kenelm
1960 *Mambu.* London: Methuen.

Caldwell, John C.
1969 *African Rural-Urban Migration: The Movement to Ghana's Towns.* Canberra: Australian National University Press.

Caplow, Theodore, S. Stryker and Samuel E. Wallace
1964 *The Urban Ambience: A Study of San Juan, Puerto Rico.* New Jersey: Bedminster Press.

Chalmers, J. C.
1898 "Toaripi." *Journal of the Royal Anthropological Institute,* 27: 326–334.

Chapman, T.
1965 "A Need for Leadership: Problems of the Unions." *New Guinea,* 1, No. 4.

Colson, E.
1954 "The Intensive Study of Small Sample Communities." In *Method and Perspective in Anthropology.* Edited by Robert F. Spencer. Minneapolis, University of Minnesota Press. Reprinted in *The Craft of Social Anthropology,* edited by A. L. Epstein. London: Tavistock 1967.

Commons, J. R.
1924 *Legal Foundations of Capitalism.* New York: MacMillan.

Criper, C.

    1969   "The Politics of Exchange: A Study of Ceremonial Exchange Amongst the Chimbu." Ph.D. thesis, Australian National University.

Crocombe, R. G.

    1966   "Race Relations." *New Guinea,* 1, No. 6:68–71.

D'Souza, V. S.

    1962   "Social Grading of Positions in India." *The Sociological Review* n. s. 10:145–59.

Dakeyne, R. B.

    1967   "Labour Migration in New Guinea: A Case Study from Northern Papua." *Pacific Viewpoint,* 8, No. 2.

De Lauwe, P. H. C.

    1965   Social Organization in an Urban Milieu. In *UNESCO Handbook for Social Research in Urban Areas,* edited by P. Hauser. Paris: UNESCO.

Dennis, N. et al. .

    1956   *Coal is Our Life.* London: Eyre and Spottiswoode.

Deutsch, K. W.

    1953   "The Growth of Nations: Some Recurrent Patterns of Political and Social Integration." *World Politics,* January 1953: 168–195.

Durkheim, E.

    1933   *The Division of Labour in Society,* translated by George Simpson. Glencoe, Ill.: Free Press.

Dutton, T.

    1969   *The Peopling of Central Papua: Some Preliminary Observations.* Pacific Linguistics Monographs, No. 9. Canberra: Australian National University.

Elkan, W.

    1960   *Migrants and Proletarians: Urban Labour in the Economic Development of Uganda.* London: Oxford University Press.

Epstein, A. L.

1958 *Politics in an Urban African Community.* Manchester: Manchester University Press.

1961 "The Network and Urban Social Organization." Reprinted in *Social Networks in Urban Situations,* edited by J. C. Mitchell. Manchester: Manchester University Press, 1969. pp. 77–116.

1963 "The Economy of Modern Matupit: Continuity and Change on the Gazelle Peninsula." *Oceania,* XXXIII: 182–215.

1967a "Occupational Prestige on the Gazelle Peninsula, New Britain." *Australian and New Zealand Journal of Sociology,* 3:111–21.

1967b "Urbanization and Social Change in Africa." *Current Anthropology,* 8, No. 4:275–84.

Epstein, T. S.

1969 "Buyers and Prices at Indigenous Produce Markets in T.P.N.G." *The Industrial Review,* 7, No. 2, Port Moresby. pp. 18–30.

Fink, R. A.

1965 "The Esa'ala-Losuia Open Electorate." In *The Papua-New Guinea Elections 1964,* edited by D. G. Bettison, C. A. Hughes and Paul W. van der Veur. Canberra: Australian National University Press.

Fortes, M.

1945 *The Dynamics of Clanship Among the Tallensi.* London: Oxford University Press.

1969 *Kinship and the Social Order.* Chicago: Aldine.

Foster, L. R.

1956 "Survey of Native Affairs: Port Moresby Area." Typescript, Port Moresby.

Frankenberg, R. J.

1966 *British Communities.* Harmondsworth: Penguin.

Friedl, Ernestine

1962 *Vasilika: A Village in Modern Greece.* New York: Holt, Rinehart, Winston.

Gans, H.

1962 *The Urban Villagers.* Glencoe: The Free Press.

Geertz, C.

    1962 "The Rotating Credit Association: A 'Middle Rung' in Development." *Economic Development and Cultural Change,* 1, No. 3:241–63.

    1965 *The Social History of an Indonesian Town.* Cambridge: MIT Press.

Glick, Paula Brown

    1970 "Melanesian Mosaic: the plural community of Vila." In *Essays in Comparative Social Stratification,* edited by L. Plotnicov and A. Tuden, Pittsburgh: University of Pittsburgh Press.

Gluckman, M.

    1940 "Analysis of a Social Situation in Modern Zululand." *Bantu Studies,* 14:1–30; 147–174.

    1955 *The Judicial Process among the Barotse of Northern Rhodesia.* Manchester: Manchester University Press.

    1960 "Tribalism in Modern British Central Africa." *Cahier d' Etudes Africaines,* 1, No. 1:55–70.

Goffman, E.

    1961 *Encounters.* Indianapolis: Bobbs-Merrill.

Grosart, I.

    1964 "Industrial Relations in Papua and New Guinea, 1960–64." *Journal of Industrial Relations,* 6, No. 3, Sydney.

Groves, M.

    1963 "Western Motu Descent Groups." *Ethnology,* II:15–30.

    1964 "Return to New Guinea." Part 5, *Nation,* April 3, 1964, Sydney.

Groves, M., R. M. S. Hamilton and Margaret McArthur

    1971 "A Town and its Hinterland." In *The Politics of Dependence,* edited by A. L. Epstein, R. S. Parker, Marie Reay. Canberra: Australian National University Press.

Gutkind, P. C. W.

    1967 Comment on "Urbanization and Social Change in Africa", by A. L. Epstein, *Current Anthropology,* 8, No. 4:285–86.

Harrison, S.

    1960 *India, the Most Dangerous Decades.* Princeton, New Jersey: Princeton University Press.

Hastings, P.

    1969 *New Guinea: Problems and Prospects.* Melbourne: Cheshire.

Hellmann, E.

    1948 *Rooiyard: A Sociological Survey of an Urban Native Slum Yard.* London: Oxford University Press.

Hennessy, L. F.

    1964a "Indigenous Industrial Organization in Papua and New Guinea." *Australian Territories,* 4, No. 1.

    1964b "A Framework of Industrial Relations for Papua and New Guinea." *Australian Territories,* 4, No. 3.

Herskovits, Melville J.

    1948 *Man and His Works: The Science of Cultural Anthropology.* New York: Knopf.

Hogbin, H. I., and C. H. Wedgwood.

    1953 "Local Grouping in Melanesia." *Oceania,* 23, No. 4:241–276.

Hughes, C. A.

    1965 "The Moresby Open and Central Special Electorates." In *The Papuan–New Guinea Elections 1964,* edited by D. G. Bettison et al., 1965.

Kiki, A. M.

    1968 *Kiki: Ten Thousand Years in a Lifetime.* Melbourne: Cheshire; London: Pall Mall.

Kuper, H. (ed.)

    1965 *Urbanization and Migration in West Africa.* Berkeley and Los Angeles: University of California Press.

Langmore, J. V.

    1967 "Subcontractors in Port Moresby." In New Guinea Research Bulletin, No. 17. Canberra: Australian National University.

    1970 "Economic and demographic forecasts." In *Port Moresby Urban Development,* J. V. Langmore and N. D. Oram, New Guinea Research Bulletin No. 37. Canberra: Australian National University.

Lett, L.

    1944 *The Papuan Achievement.* Melbourne: Cheshire.

Lévi-Strauss, C.

    1963 *Structural Anthropology,* translated by Claire Jacobson and Brooke Grundfest Schoepf, New York, Basic Books.

    1969 *The Elementary Structures of Kinship,* edited by J. R. von Sturmer and R. Needham, translated by J. H. Bell. London: Eyre and Spottiswoode.

Lewis, Oscar

 1952 "Urbanization without breakdown: a case study" *Scientific Monthly* 75:31–41.

Lind, A. W.

 1969 *Inter-Ethnic Marriage in New Guinea.* New Guinea Research Bulletin, No. 31. Canberra: Australian National University.

Little, K.

 1965 *West African Urbanization: A Study of Voluntary Associations in Social Change.* Cambridge: Cambridge University Press.

Maher, R. F.

 1967 "From Cannibal Raid to Copra Kompani: Changing Patterns of Koriki Politics." *Ethnology,* 6, No. 3:309–31.

Malinowski, B.

 1929 *The Sexual Life of Savages.* New York: Harcourt, Brace and World.

Mann, P.

 1965 *An Approach to Urban Sociology.* London: Routledge and K. Paul.

Martin, R. M.

 1969 "Tribesmen into Trade Unionists: The African Experience and the Papua–New Guinea Prospect." *The Journal of Industrial Relations,* II, No. 2:125–72. Sydney.

Marwick, M.

 1964 "Witchcraft as a Social Strain-Gauge." *Australian Journal of Science,* 26.

Mayer, A. C.

 1966 The Significance of Quasi-Groups in the Study of Complex Societies. In *The Social Anthropology of Complex Societies,* edited by M. Banton. London: Tavistock. pp. 67–122.

Mayer, P.

 1961 *Townsmen or Tribesmen.* Cape Town: Oxford University Press.

 1962 "Migrancy and the Study of Africans in Towns." *American Anthropologist,* 64:576–92.

Mead, M.
  1956 *New Lives for Old*. New York: Morrow.
  1967 "Introduction". In *New People in Business and Industry*. New Guinea Research Bulletin, No. 20. Canberra: Australian National University Press.

Meillassoux, C.
  1968 *Urbanization of an African Community: Voluntary Associations in Bamako*. American Ethnological Society Monographs, No. 45. Seattle: University of Washington Press.

Merton, R. F.
  1957 *Social Theory and Social Structure*. Glencoe, Illinois: Free Press.

Metcalfe, P.
  1969 "The Port Moresby Workers' Association." M.A. thesis, University of Auckland.

Mihalic, F.
  1957 *Grammar and Dictionary of Neo-Melanesian*. Techny, Ill.: Mission Press.

Mitchell, J. C.
  1956 *The Kalela Dance*. Manchester: Manchester University Press.
  1960 "The Anthropological Study of Urban Communities." *African Studies,* 19:169–72.
  1964 "Occupational Prestige and the Social System: A Problem in Comparative Sociology." *International Journal of Comparative Sociology,* 5:78–90.
  1966 "Theoretical Orientations in African Urban Studies." In *The Social Anthropology of Complex Societies,* edited by M. Banton. London: Tavistock, 1966. pp. 37–68.
  1967 "On Quantification in Social Anthropology." In *The Craft of Social Anthropology,* edited by A. L. Epstein. London: Tavistock, 1967.

Mitchell, J. C., ed.
  1969 *Social Networks in Urban Situations*. Manchester: Manchester University Press.

Mitchell, J. C., and A. L. Epstein.
  1959 "Occupational Prestige and Social Status Among Urban Africans in Northern Rhodesia." *Africa,* 29:22–39.

Monckton, C. A. W.

  1934 *New Guinea Recollections.* London: John Lane, The Bodley
        Head.

Nayacakalou, R., and Aidan Southall

  1973 "Urbanization and Fijian Cultural Traditions in the Context
        of Pacific Port Cities." In *Urban Anthropology: Cross-Cul-
        tural Studies in Urbanization,* edited by Aidan Southall. Lon-
        don: Oxford University Press, 1973.

Oeser, L.

  1969 *Hohola: The Significance of Social Networks in Urban
        Adaptation of Women in Papua–New Guinea's First Low-Cost
        Housing Estate.* New Guinea Research Bulletin, No. 29. Can-
        berra: Australian National University.

Ogan, Eugene

  1973 "Dependence, Inferiority, Autonomy: A Bougainville Case
        Study in Colonialism." Paper presented at the annual meet-
        ing of the Association for Social Anthropology in Oceania,
        March 1973.

O'Neill, J.

  1940 "Port Moresby: Capital of Papua." *Walkabout,* 1 May 1940.
        pp. 3–4.

Oram, N. D.

  1964 "Urbanization: Port Moresby." *South Pacific Bulletin,* Octo-
        ber 1964:37–43.

  1967a "Rabia Camp and the Tommy Kabu Movement." In Nancy E.
        Hitchcock and N. D. Oram, *Rabia Camp.* New Guinea Re-
        search Bulletin, No. 14. Canberra: Australian National Uni-
        versity. pp. 3–43.

  1967b *Social and Economic Relationships in a Port Moresby Canoe
        Settlement.* New Guinea Research Bulletin, No. 18. Canberra:
        Australian National University.

  1968a "Culture Change, Economic Development and Migration among
        the Hula." *Oceania,* XXXVIII, No. 4:243–75.

  1968b "The Hula in Port Moresby." *Oceania,* XXXIX, No. 1:1–35.

P.A.R. Papua-Annual Report 1906–7 onward. Canberra: Government
        Printer.

Park, R. E.

1926 "A Spatial Pattern and a Moral Order." In *The Urban Community,* edited by E. W. Burgess. Chicago: University of Chicago Press.

1929 "Introduction." In H. W. Zorbaugh, *The Gold Coast and the Slum.* Chicago: University of Chicago Press.

1939 "Symbiosis and Socialization: A Frame of Reference for the Study of Society." *American Journal of Sociology,* 45, No. 1 :1–25.

Pitcairn, W. D.

1891 *Two Years among the Savages of New Guinea.* London.

Pitt-Rivers, Julian

1971 "On the Word 'Caste' ". In *The Translation of Culture,* edited by T. O. Beidelman. London: Tavistock. pp. 231–256.

Plotnicov, L.

1967 *Strangers to the City: Urban Man in Jos, Nigeria.* Pittsburgh: University of Pittsburgh Press.

Pocock, D. F.

1960 "Sociologies—Rural and Urban." *Contributions to Indian Sociology,* 4 :63–81.

Polansky, E.

1966 "Rabaul." *South Pacific Bulletin,* 2nd Quarter.

Pons, V.

1969 *Stanleyville: An African Urban Community Under Belgian Administration.* London: Oxford University Press.

Rowley, C. D.

1965 *The New Guinea Villager: A Retrospect from 1964.* Melbourne: Cheshire.

Ryan, D.

1968 "The Migrants: $10 Weekly in a Moresby Shanty Town." *New Guinea,* 2, No. 4 :60–66.

Sahlins, M. D.

1966 "On the Sociology of Primitive Exchange." *The Relevance of Models for Social Anthropology,* edited by M. Banton. London: Tavistock.

Salisbury, Richard F., and Mary E. Salisbury

    1972 "The rural oriented strategy of urban adaption: Siane migrants in Port Moresby". In *The Anthropology of Urban Environments,* edited by Thomas Weaver and Douglas White, Monograph 11 of the Society for Applied Anthropology. Washington, D. C. pp. 49–68.

Seligman, C. S.

    1910 *The Melanesians of British New Guinea.* Cambridge: Cambridge University Press.

Shih, Kuo-Heng

    1944 *China Enters the Machine Age.* Cambridge: Harvard University Press.

Sinclair, A.

    1957 *Field and Clinical Survey Report of the Mental Health of the Indigenes of the Territory of Papua and New Guinea.* Port Moresby.

South Pacific Post. Port Moresby: South Pacific Post Ltd.

Southall, Aidan, ed.

    1973 *Urban Anthropology: Cross-Cultural Studies of Urbanization.* London: Oxford University Press. See especially "The Density of Role-Relationships as a Universal Index of Urbanization," pp. 71–106.

Stuart, Ian

    1970 *Port Moresby: Yesterday and Today.* Sydney: Pacific Publications.

Sundkler, B.

    1962 *Bantu Prophets in South Africa.* London: Oxford University Press. (first published 1948)

Teeling, W.

    1936 *Gods of Tomorrow: The Story of a Journey in Asia and Australasia.* London: Lovat Dickson.

Thomas, R. M.

    1962 "Reinspecting a Structural Position on Occupational Prestige." *American Journal of Sociology,* 67:561–565.

Tiryakian, E. A.

    1958   "The Prestige Evaluation of Occupations in an Underdeveloped Country: The Philippines." *American Journal of Sociology,* 63:390–399.

Turner, V. W.

    1957   *Schism and Continuity in an African Society.* Manchester: Manchester University Press.

UNESCO

    1956   *Social Implications of Industrialization and Urbanization in Africa South of the Sahara.* Paris: UNESCO.

Van der Veur, K., and P. Richardson.

    1968   *Teachers in the Urban Community.* New Guinea Research Bulletin, No. 21. Canberra: Australian National University.

Van der Veur, P. W.

    1964   "Questionnaire Survey among the Potential Papuan Elite in 1962, West New Guinea." *Bijdragen,* 120, No. 4:424–60.

    1966   "Occupational Prestige among Secondary School Students in West New Guinea (West Irian)." *Australian and New Zealand Journal of Sociology,* 2, No. 2.

Van Velsen, J.

    1961   "Labour Migration as a Positive Factor in the Continuity of Tonga Tribal Society." *Economic Development and Cultural Change,* 10:265–78.

Watson, W.

    1958   *Tribal Cohesion in a Money Economy.* Manchester: Manchester University Press.

Williams, F. E.

    1924   *The Natives of the Purari Delta.* Papua Anthropology Report No. 5. Port Moresby: Government Printer.

    1930   *Orokaiva Society.* London: Oxford University Press.

    1940   *Drama of Orokolo.* Oxford: Clarendon Press.

Williams, R. M.

    1964   *Strangers Next Door.* New Jersey: Prentice-Hall.

Wilson, M., and A. Mafeje.

    1963   *Langa: A Study of Social Groups in an African Township.* Cape Town: Oxford University Press.

Wirth, L.

    1938 "Urbanism as a Way of Life." *American Journal of Sociology,*
       44:1–24.

    1966–67 "Papua–New Guinea Nationhood: The Problem of a Na-
       tional Language." *Journal of the Papua and New Guinea So-*
       ciety, 1, No. 1:7–19.

Xydias, N.

    1956 "Prestige of Occupations." In UNESCO, 1956.

INDEX

Ambience, personal, 106
Ardener, S., 121, 160
Babalau, 137f
Baldamus, W., 198
Banton, M., 81, 169, 214, 223
Barnes, J., 92, 116
Barth, F., 23, 30, 210, 216
Bava: labor history, 48, 125
Brown Glick, P., 26
Brown, H., 171
Bruner, E. M., 21, 26, 227
Burridge, K., 220
Business, attitudes towards, 180, 182, see also James, John, Paul (nD)

"Cargo-vessel", image of town, v., 25, 230
Chapman, T., 203, 209
Civil disturbance, see Riots
Colonial structure, 225
Commitment, 173
Common employment, basis of relations, 114–115, 118
Commons, J., 196
Compatriot groupings, see *Wantok* groupings
Compatriotism: see also *Wantok* groupings, 9, 26, 132, 169, 220, 222, 228f; and differential colonial incorporation, 26, 27; and language, 222; and locality, 222; and race and kinship, 227; and trading networks, 28; and urban scale, 228; and village involvement, 185f; as basis for P.M.D. strike, 201, 211; as basis of barracks' life, 133, 169; cultural distance, 80, 131–132, 166, 168–169; ethnic distinctiveness and heterogeneity, 132; ethnic labels as source of self-esteem, 131; ethnic stereotyping, 80, 125, 130, 221, 228; ethnocentrism, 80, 131; fighting between compatriot groups, 9; fragility of ethnic ties, 144, 228; "localism" and local groups, 170; peripheral to village society, 221; regional labels, 26, 98, 147, 221; sociogeographic sets, 98; volatility of ethnic ties, 144, 228

Consumption, 182
Cultural distance, defined, 80, see Compatriotism
Culture, urban, see Urban culture

Dakeyne, R., 182
David: in Old Office, 49
Dennis, N., 208, 209
Deutsch, K., 80
Durkheim, E., 46

Ecology, defined, 24
Economy: administration, 13; building and construction, 13; entrepreneurs, 216; manufacturing, 13; wage workers, 216
Egocentric analysis, 21, 28
Elkan, W., 182, 194
Epstein, A. L., viii, 155, 169, 176, 202, 214, 220, 225
Epstein, T. S., 94n
Ethnic groups, see *Wantok* groupings
Extended case method, viii, 23, 28, 44

Fortes, M., 98n
Frankenberg, R., 85, 98n
Friedl, E., 163

Gabriel: and Mekeo Sports Club, 67; clash with Lucian, 53, 58; "cowboy" style, 75; financial position, 67; kindred at Hanuabada, 68; labor history, 48, 59–60; urban schooling, 67
Geertz, C., vii, 121, 137, 160, 230
Gluckman, M., 169
Grosart, I., 198
Groves, M., vi, 3, 27, 226

Harrison, S., 222
Hastings, P., vi
Health, ideas, 159
Hellmann, E., 155
Hennessy, L., 198
Hereva: and Mailala, 141, 149, 150, 157–158; and Township, 156
Herskovits, M., 80
Hete (nE): acceptance by "Mbawe" set, 109, 125; labor history, 104, 105; savings, 181
Heterogeneity, 17, 24, 25, 35

Hogbin, I., 188
Hogbin, I. and C. Wedgewood 171, 221
Horae: and "Mbawe" set, 110; perceived as "Popondetta", 124
Housing: see also P.M.D. housing; an urban resource, 161; households as centres of social gravity, 163; provision by administration, 8
Humphrey (nB): and Mailala, 151, 205; and "Popondetta" migrants, 103; and soccer team, 106; experience as a newcomer, 132; Konemase and daughter's party, 154; labor history, 47, 105; marriage, 108

Institutionalization, defined, 23
Involvement, 173

James: and leadership, 85, 192; and Mekeo Sports Club, 61; and Transport Group, 64–66, 192–194; and young Mekeo town dwellers, 63, 64; "business", 193; labor history, 49, 59, 168; marriage, 193; married accommodation, 193–194; relation to Europeans, 72–73, 76; relationship to management, 85; studies and education, 74; web of urban ties, 76
John: and leadership, 86, 87, 192; and Phillip (nN), 111; attitudes towards occupational prestige, 180; attitudes towards racial relations, 84; business activities, 86; labor history, 47, 48; notices in Old Office, 55

Kerema exclusiveness, 164–165, see Wantok groupings
Kiki, A. M., 8, 61n, 167, 199
Kinship: as base for relations, 114, 144; role system, 215; statuses, 217
Kompani, see Voluntary associations
Langmore, J., v, 216
Leadership, 192
Lévi-Strauss, C., 22, 45, 87–88
Lind, A., 188
Locality, 28, 222
Locality groups, 27–28

Lucian: irritation with Gabriel, 53, 58; labor history, 48, 49

Mailala: and Hereva, 141, 149f; and Humphrey (nB), 151, 205; and Vake, 141, 150; labor history, 137f; "shame" at housing, 205
Mann, P., 219
Martin, R., 208, 209
Marwick, M., 142
Mayer, A., 98n
Mayer, P., 24, 168, 220
Mead, M., 28, 221
Mero, young man from Dabunari, 157
Merton, R., 85, 150
Metcalfe, P., 199, 208
Micro-history, urban, 28
Minimum Urban Wage Agreement, 8
Mitchell, J. C., 132, 149, 168, 169, 173, 175, 225
Money, a key cultural theme, 160–161
Motuan hospitality, 165, see Wantok groupings
Multiplex ties, 106

"Natural areas", 15
Nayacakalou, R. and A. Southall, 225

Occupational prestige, visual test, 174, 231
Oram, N., vi, 117, 165, 168, 179

Papua and New Guinea Workers' Association, see Port Moresby Workers' Association
Papua vs. New Guinea, 79, 118, 131, see Wantok groupings
Park, R., 24, 25, 29, 46, 91, 213
"Passenger-ship", image of town, v, 3, 25, 230
Patrick: labor history, 48
Paul (nD): and rural "business", 107; attitudes towards occupational prestige, 180; labor history, 104f; returns to village, 191
Phillip (nN): accommodation, 111; and Baki, 112; and John, 111f; labor history, 104, 105; savings, 181
Phylai, 27
Pidgin, 10, 79, 81–82, 140, 148–149
Pitt-Rivers, J., 216
Ples, see Locality
Plotnicov, L., 173
Pluralism, 26

P.M.D.: adaptations to workplace, 24; as system of authority, 196–198; barracks, general features, 92–94; barracks' population, 95–98; duration of employment, 35; housing, 23, 40, 146; labor contract, 24, 196, 198; labor supply, 34; management selection and education, 30, 37, 38; management selection and social context, 38; managerial control and allocations, 23, 24, 34; productive system, 23; skill and region of origin, 36; skills and housing, 43; spatial arrangements, 24; strike, 199f; technical roles, 24; technological constraints, 23, 24, 33; wages, 23; work force and work situation, work sections and ethnic "lines", 39; workers' self-selection, 30; Works Committee, 210n

Police Motu, 10, 79, 81–82, 140, 148–149

Pons, V., 214, 217

Population, 5, 6, 7, 10: age structure, 12, 13; labor compounds, 6; marital structure, 12; native villages, 6; settlements, 6; sex ratio, 12

Port Moresby Workers' Association, 8

Process, 23, 214

Race relations, 13, 220; attitudes of Europeans, 4; discrimination, 5; dual standards in housing, 41; dual standards in industry, 41; dual wages and privileges, 9; indigenous attitudes, 10; pervading political and economic roles, 226; racial role system, 215; racial statuses, 216; relaxation of legal discriminations, 9; work roles system, 215, 216

Reciprocity, 106

Research techniques, 20f

Riots, 8

Role: and role-relationships, 214; and status, 24, 216; differentiation, 223f; domains, 223; work roles, 215

Rowley, C., vi

Rural-urban continuity, 25, 26

Ryan, D., 122

Salisbury, R. and M., 21

Sampling, 17, 174

Samuel (nK): "civilization", 129; description of fighting and drinking, 127, 128; labor history, 107; pride in "Popondetta", 131; tie with other widower, 123

Savings, 182

Sidney: labor history, 49; social isolation, 69

Sinclair, A., 208

Social networks, 23, 106

Sociocentric analysis, 21, 124, 125

Sociogeographic labels, see *Wantok* groupings

Southall, A., 214, 215, 219, 220, 223, 227

Spencer, H., 46

Status and role, 24, 216

Strangeness, experience of, 80

Strikes: 1929, in Rabaul, 8; 1957, first in Papuan Public Service, 8; 1961, soldiers in P.I.R., 8; 1965, in Port Moresby, 19, 199f

Structure, 21, 22, see Colonial structure; Urban structure

Style: "cowboy", 75, 83; "educated", 83

Symbiosis, defined, 24

"Target" workers, 182

Tau, young man from Barakau, 157

Taxi-service employees: links with Barakau, 156–157; Mailala, 142; Township, 156

Theft in compounds, 125, 126, 130

Township, from Barakau: and Hereva, 156; and taxi-service, 156, 157; floods Vake's quarters, 156

Trading networks, 28

Tribes, absence of, 27

Urban anonymity, 25

Urban and peri-urban localities: Boroko, 6, 15; commercial centre, 11; Ela and original township, 15; Gabutu, 15; Hanuabada, 4, 5, 68, 137f; Hohola, 8, 15; Kaugere, 8; Kogeva, 11; Koke-Badili, 6, 9, 15, 16, 17, 20, 94; Konedobu, 5, 6; Pari, 154; Six Mile, 13; Sogeri, 4; Vabukori, 15; Waigani, 15

Urban culture, 21, 22, 153f: as structural discontinuity, 21, 22; "knowledge about", 155–158

Urban residential relationships, 217

Urban structure, 23, 214

Vake: and Mailala, 141, 150; and Township, 156
Van der Veur, P., 176
van Velsen, J., 173
Vincent, (nC): labor history, 47, 104; photo of college mate, 105; remains in town, 191
Voluntary associations: and compatriotism, 229; Kerema Welfare Association, 8; kompani, 121, 160; Lord of the Isles Society, 9; Methodist Welfare Association, 8; Rugby, 166

Wanpis, 100
Wantok, 28, 147, 223, 227: and Wanwok, 229
Wantok groupings: Baimuru, see Purari; Bogia, 140, 149; Bush Mekeo, 140; Chimbu, 119f, 124n, 129, 130; Elema, see Keremas; Goilala, 9, 129, 130, 131n, 221; Gulf, see Keremas; Highlands (New Guinea), 10, 119; Islands, 222; Kairuku, 40; "K.A.K.", 124; Keremas, 6, 8, 10, 39, 40, 103, 117, 122f, 127, 129, 164f, 210; Kikori, see Purari; Koko-
da, see Popondetta; "Koro", 103; Managalese, see Popondetta; Manus, 221, 222; Marshall Lagoon, 124; "Mbawe", and civilization, 191; "Mbawe", and denominationalism, 191; Mekeo, 59f, 131n, 222; Mekeo, Bush, see Bush Mekeo; Mendi, see Southern Highlands; Milne Bay, 9; Morobe, 9; Northern District, see Popondetta; Orokaiva, see Popondetta; Popondetta, 101f, 129f, 221; Purari, 117f; Sepik, 137, 156, 221; Southern Highlands, 117f; Tari, see Southern Highlands; Tolai, 220, 222; Tufi, see Popondetta
Watson, Lepani, 9
Watson, W., 195
William (nA): and "Mbawe" migrants, 108, 110, 125; Bava's shirt, 125; labor history, 103, 105; remains in town, 191
Williams, F. E., 117, 221
Wilson, M. and A. Mafeje, 91
Wirth, L., 25

Xydias, N., 174

END OF VOLUME